THE NEW
HEALTHY BREAD
in Five Minutes a Day

ALSO BY JEFF HERTZBERG, M.D., AND ZOË FRANÇOIS

The New Artisan Bread in Five Minutes a Day:
Revised and Updated with New Recipes

Artisan Bread in Five Minutes a Day:
The Discovery That Revolutionizes Home Baking

Healthy Bread in Five Minutes a Day:
100 New Recipes Featuring Whole Grains, Fruits,
Vegetables, and Gluten-Free Ingredients

Artisan Pizza and Flatbread in Five Minutes a Day

Gluten-Free Artisan Bread in Five Minutes a Day:
The Baking Revolution Continues with 90 New, Delicious, and
Easy Recipes Made with Gluten-Free Flours

THE NEW
HEALTHY BREAD
in Five Minutes a Day

Revised and Updated with New Recipes

JEFF HERTZBERG, M.D., and ZOË FRANÇOIS
Photography by STEPHEN SCOTT GROSS

THOMAS DUNNE BOOKS
ST. MARTIN'S PRESS ☙ NEW YORK

THOMAS DUNNE BOOKS.
An imprint of St. Martin's Press.

THE NEW HEALTHY BREAD IN FIVE MINUTES A DAY: REVISED AND UPDATED WITH NEW RECIPES. Copyright © 2016 by Jeff Hertzberg, M.D., and Zoë François. All rights reserved. Printed in the United States of America. For information, address St. Martin's Press, 175 Fifth Avenue, New York, N.Y. 10010.

www.thomasdunnebooks.com
www.stmartins.com

Designed by Phil Mazzone

Photographs copyright © 2016 by Stephen Scott Gross

Library of Congress Cataloging-in-Publication Data

Names: Hertzberg, Jeff, author. | François, Zoë, author.
Title: The new Healthy bread in five minutes a day / Jeff Hertzberg, M.D. and Zoë François ; photography by Stephen Scott Gross.
Other titles: Healthy bread in five minutes a day | New healthy bread in 5 minutes a day
Description: Revised and updated with new recipes. First edition. | New York : St. Martin's Press, [2016] | Includes bibliographical references and index.
Identifiers: LCCN 2016032269| ISBN 9781250077554 (hardcover) | ISBN 9781466889767 (E-book)
Subjects: LCSH: Bread. | Cooking (Bread) | LCGFT: Cookbooks.
Classification: LCC TX769 .H476 2016 | DDC 641.81/5—dc23
LC record available at https://lccn.loc.gov/2016032269

Our books may be purchased in bulk for promotional, educational, or business use. Please contact your local bookseller or the Macmillan Corporate and Premium Sales Department at 1-800-221-7945, extension 5442, or by e-mail at MacmillanSpecialMarkets@macmillan.com.

First Edition: November 2016

10 9 8 7 6 5 4 3 2 1

To my grandparents Esther and Abe Weissman, who taught me that bread is better than cake.

—Jeff

To my mom for a lifetime of love, grace, generosity, and humor—the most important ingredients of all.

—Zoë

ACKNOWLEDGMENTS

We're six books into our project, and our spouses, Laura Silver and Graham François, continue to put up with crazy hours, interrupted dinners, and houses coated with flour dust. We're not trained as writers or editors, but Laura is, and she made sure our editors got manuscript versions that had already been vetted. And Graham created our incredible website, where we still answer reader questions ourselves.

Friends and family once again generously agreed to test our recipes and provide all kinds of help when we needed it. Thanks to Leslie Bazzett, Jay, Tracey, Gavin, and Megan Berkowitz, Sarah Berkowitz, Nathan Burton, Betsy Carey, Marion and John Callahan, Allison Campbell Jensen, Alex Cohn, Barb Davis and Fran Davis, Anna and Ewart François, Leslie Held, Jaden Hair, Judy and Larry Hicks, Kathy Kosnoff and Lyonel Norris, Jeff Lin of BustOutSolutions.com (for Web support), Kristin Neal and Bill, Carey, and Heather Neal, Craig and Patricia Neal, Lorraine Neal, Danny Sager and Brian McCarthy, Sally Simmons and David Van De Sande, the Sommerness family, and Debora Villa and Ralph Gualtieri. Riv-Ellen Prell and Steve Foldes were good sports about taste-testing early versions of some very nontraditional 100% whole wheat challahs, and our friend Flo Makanai of MakanaiBio.com e-mailed from Paris with help on an obscure French translation.

From the publishing world, writers Beth Fouhy and Peggy Orenstein helped us navigate the murky waters of book publicity. The great team at Craftsy.com produced Zoë's fabulous instructional video, **Artisan Bread in Minutes.** As always, we relied on the wisdom of our literary agents, Jane Dystel, Miriam Goderich, and Lauren Abramo. Rebekah Denn of *The Seattle Times* connected us with sources for artisan flours we hadn't tried before. At Thomas Dunne Books, thanks go to our editor, Peter Wolverton, for encouraging us to update this work (and then helping us do it); plus the rest of the Thomas Dunne team: Amelie Littell, Amy Goppert, Olga Grlic, Elizabeth Curione, Leah Stewart, Emma Stein, and Judy Hunt (who created another great index). Lynne Rossetto Kasper, Sally Swift, Jennifer Luebke, and Jen Russell of *The Splendid Table* radio program gave us our first (and subsequent) national exposure on National Public Radio.

Gratitude to colleagues in our baking and culinary adventures past and present: Robin Asbell; Steven Brown of Tilia; Stephen Durfee of the Culinary Institute of America; Barbara Fenzl of Les Gourmettes Cooking School; Michelle Gayer of The Salty Tart; Dorie Greenspan; Thomas Gumpel of Panera Bread; P.J. Hamel and Jeffrey Hamelman of King Arthur Flour; Bill Hanes and Kelly Olson of Red Star Yeast; Kim Harbinson of General Mills, Molly Herrmann of Kitchen in the Market; Raghavan Iyer; Dusti Kugler, Kelly Lainsbury, Madeline Hill, and Molly Mogren of Food Works; Brenda Langton of Spoonriver restaurant and the Minneapolis Bread Festival; Silvana Nardone; Stephanie Meyer of FreshTart.com; Riad Nasr, Karl Benson, and the team at Cooks of Crocus Hill; Peter Reinhart; Suvir Saran and Charlie Burd of American Masala; Tara Steffen of Emile Henry; Maria Speck; and Andrew Zimmern. Neither of us are

celiacs nor eat a gluten-free diet, so we are particularly grateful to Danny and Shauna James Ahern of the Gluten-Free Girl website, who advised us on the gluten-free chapter. And thanks to Gold Medal Flour for putting our recipe on their flour bag.

This is our third book with Stephen Scott Gross— shooting gorgeous color photography yet again. In some ways, this whole grain book has been the toughest to update: how much more is there to say—visually—about round brown things? Thanks for the eloquence, Stephen. And we couldn't have done it without Sarah Kieffer of

TheVanillaBeanBlog.com, who styled our photo shoots and contributes mightily to our blog as well. Sarah's coming out with her own gorgeous cookbook, *The Vanilla Bean Baking Book*, in the fall of 2016. Veronica Smith was prop mistress extraordinaire, and Joel Larson saved the day by making his superlative studio space, Minneapolis's Cargo Studios, available for our photo shoot.

Most of all we are thankful for the love and support of our families: Zoë's husband, Graham, and her two boys, Henri and Charlie, and Jeff's wife, Laura, and his girls, Rachel and Julia. They're our best taste testers and most honest critics.

It does not cost much. . . . It leaves you filled with peace, and the house filled with one of the world's sweetest smells . . . probably there is no chiropractic treatment, no Yoga exercise, no hour of meditation . . . that will leave you emptier of bad thoughts than this homely ceremony of making bread.

—M. F. K. Fisher in *How to Cook a Wolf,* 1942

THE SECRET

The "Secret" works with super-healthy ingredients: Mix enough dough for many loaves and store it in the refrigerator.

It's easy to have freshly baked healthy breads whenever you want them, with only five minutes a day of active effort. First, mix the ingredients in a container all at once, and let them sit for two hours. Now you are ready to shape and bake the bread, or you can refrigerate the dough and use it over the next five to fourteen days (depending on the recipe). You've prepared enough dough for many loaves. When you want fresh-baked whole grain or gluten-free bread, take a piece of the dough from the container and shape it into a loaf. Let it rest for a while and then bake. Your house will smell like a bakery and your family and friends will love you for it.

INTRODUCTION: HEALTHY BREADS CAN BE MADE IN FIVE MINUTES A DAY, TOO

My wife, Laura, taught me to bake bread—it was something she brought to the marriage, along with a 1982 Honda Civic and her mother's 1951 Sunbeam mixer (whose ball-bearings skittered across the floor the first time we tried to start it up). She'd learned to bake in the 1980s, during a stint as bread baker in her college food co-op. It seemed like a lot of effort, but I naively thought it'd be a nice stress-reducing hobby to take up during an exhausting medical residency, and Laura was happy to relinquish the task to me. But with my 80-hour workweeks, I gradually realized that I could save time by making bigger and bigger batches of wet dough, which could be stored in the refrigerator. We're happy to say that same lazy method works with whole wheat and with sourdough. Enjoy!—Jeff

No one is more excited than we are that we're still writing bread cookbooks, nine years after ***Artisan Bread in Five Minutes a Day,*** first published in 2007 (with a second edition in 2013). ***Healthy Bread in Five Minutes a Day*** came in 2009, and we got our chance to replace much of the white flour in the traditional European and American baker's pantry with whole grains, and added healthier oils, fats, nuts, fruits, and vegetables. And we included our first-ever gluten-free chapter.

We'd always had a feeling that we'd someday be updating ***Healthy Bread in Five Minutes a Day*** as well. Why? The healthy-baking community searches out

Vermont commune where she was raised. In her twenties Zoë was a vegetarian; she didn't eat refined sugar and headed off to the Culinary Institute of America (CIA) to follow her passion, pastry. Her goal: bake without refined sugar, but create ethereal pastries that didn't weigh a ton and taste like sweetened tree bark. But while studying at the CIA, Zoë was tempted by the miracles of sugar, bleached flour, heavenly butter, and all of the other ingredients she had once shunned. Years later Zoë would figure out a way to have it all: great-tasting but healthy pastries, desserts, and, of course, breads—and that journey to a healthier diet is reflected in this book.

If you've gotten this far, you're probably ready for **a wee bit of science** (not too much). It starts with a simple observation: Being alive takes energy, and that energy comes from "burning" carbohydrates and other food-fuels with oxygen in our bodies (that's called *oxidation*). Even though oxidation is perfectly natural and healthy, it releases some nasty chemicals. So does exposure to sunlight, chemicals, pollutants, and radiation. All that oxidation and energy can create what biochemists call "superoxide radicals," which we've heard of as "free radicals," high-energy chemicals that can do damage to our cells. Free-radical damage has a role in a host of chronic diseases, including cancer, hardening of the arteries, heart disease, stroke, and arthritis. **The good news:** Our bodies get help in getting rid of free radicals from phytochemicals (beneficial plant chemicals) and vitamins in our food, both natural substances with powerful health benefits—and they're found in whole grains, vegetables, and fruit. They act as potent antioxidants, chemicals that absorb damaging energy from free radicals. Phytochemicals with antioxidant activity tend to be richly colored: green, yellow, blue, and red. Some of the most colorful fruits and vegetables have the largest stores of phytochemicals. As you work through chapter 7, Breads with Fruits and Vegetables, you'll feast your eyes on a stunning and colorful palette of breads. Substances like phytochemicals are the reason that the U.S. government recommends that you eat nine or more servings of fruits and vegetables per day.

Vitamins are essential helpers for the body's normal chemical functions (metabolism), allowing the chemical reactions we depend upon to take place. Lack of vitamins cause some of the world's most devastating but curable deficiency diseases, which have pretty much disappeared in the industrialized world. But deficiency diseases are the tip of the iceberg—many vitamins don't just act as metabolic catalysts, they're also antioxidants. This is especially clear for vitamin E. There is strong evidence that normal levels of vitamin E prevent heart, blood, muscle, and eye problems. Vitamin E is found in wheat germ (from whole grain wheat), vegetable oils, seeds, and nuts. Vitamin C, another powerful antioxidant, works in concert with vitamin E. Throughout the book, we'll jump in with sidebars about vitamins—vitamin A, the eight B vitamins (see Appendix, page 395), plus vitamins C, D, E, and K (please do not ask us why there is no vitamin F, G, H, or I). Most nutritionists agree that vitamin requirements are best met through a diet rich in fruits and vegetables, rather than by taking vitamin supplements. That's not to say supplements aren't ever helpful; they certainly can be when daily requirements aren't being met through food intake. But the vitamins that occur naturally in food are better because they're more easily absorbed through digestion than supplements are, probably resulting in higher levels of vitamins and antioxidants in our bloodstream and tissues. This book will help you put more of those natural vitamins and antioxidants into your family's diet.

There are a lot of wild nutrition claims out there, and we've steered clear of them in this book—we do not believe that there is a magic bullet to promote health or cure disease with particular food sources or supplements. But there are some scientifically based statements that have stood the test of time:

1. **Whole grain flour is better for you than white flour.** Because whole grains include the germ and the bran, in addition to the starch-rich but fiber- and vitamin-poor endosperm (see chapter 2, Ingredients, page 9), whole grain flours bring a boatload of healthy substances into your diet, including phytochemicals (beneficial plant chemicals), vitamins, and fiber. Those are pretty much absent from white flour. Iron, niacin, folic acid, riboflavin, and thiamine are added back into enriched commercial white flour, but no other nutrients—so whole wheat delivers more complete nutrition than enriched white flour. But there's more—because bran and germ in whole grains dilute the effect of pure starch in the endosperm, the absorption and conversion of starches into simple sugars is slowed, so blood glucose (the simplest sugar) rises more slowly after consumption of whole grains than it does after eating refined white flour products. Complex, high-bran carbohydrates are said to have a lower

"glycemic index," a measure of how fast your blood sugar rises after eating a particular food. The evidence for better handling of blood sugar, better digestive function, and heart health convinced the American Diabetes Association (ADA) and the U.S. Department of Agriculture (USDA) to make two recommendations in their current guidelines:

- **Consume a high-fiber diet,** with at least 14 grams of dietary fiber per 1,000 calories consumed in an ideal-calorie diet each day. For a 2,000-calorie diet (appropriate for most women), that means about 28 grams of fiber a day. For a 2,500-calorie diet (appropriate for most men), that means 35 grams a day). 100% whole wheat bread contains a little less than 2 grams of fiber per slice if you cut a thin 1-ounce slice, and 3 to 4 grams if you cut a 2-ounce slice. White bread contains a quarter of that.

- **Make sure that at least half of your grain intake is *whole* grain.** The recipes in this book will help you meet that goal.

2. Monounsaturated and polyunsaturated oils are better for you than saturated and trans fats (like butter and hydrogenated oil). See page 28 in our Ingredients chapter for a more complete discussion. Switching to these oils or other heart-healthy fat sources can benefit those with high blood cholesterol.

3. Low-salt breads will benefit people with hypertension, heart failure, and kidney failure. This applies to all our breads—they all can be made with low or even zero salt, though the flavor will of course be different.

4. Nuts and seeds contain heart-healthy oils. Though they're concentrated calorie sources, nuts and seeds are rich in vitamins, minerals, and heart-healthy fats (monounsaturated and omega-3 polyunsaturated fats).

5. Fruits and vegetables are the best sources for phytochemicals and vitamins. We have a whole chapter of breads enriched by fruits or vegetables, which are fiber-rich and loaded with vitamins and antioxidants. We'll discuss the unique benefits of particular fruits or vegetables in sidebars next to recipes.

And one final word of advice about diet and health: Please don't obsess about food. This is supposed to be fun. If you can put some healthy ingredients into your bread and you like the flavor, do it. Otherwise, eat something else.* And, remember that making your own great bread saves you money. When the economy goes into a tizzy (and even when it doesn't) you have to wonder why people pay $6.00 for a loaf of bread in specialty bakeries, when they can make their own, very simply, for about 50 cents a loaf. An added benefit: The world's most heavenly source of home heating this winter will be your oven, cranking out the aroma of freshly baked bread.

As you read through the book, please visit our website (BreadIn5.com), where you'll find instructional text, photographs, videos, and a community of other five-minute-a-day bakers. Other easy ways to keep in touch: follow us on Twitter (@ArtisanBreadIn5), or on Facebook, Pinterest, or Instagram (all @BreadIn5), or YouTube (YouTube.com/BreadIn5). And you can master the techniques by taking our seven-lesson online course with Zoë—go to BreadIn5.com/Our-Artisan-Bread and follow the links to enroll. In that course, Zoe uses white-flour dough and references *The New Artisan Bread in Five Minutes a Day*, but the techniques for using whole grain dough are much the same. Over 4,000 folks are already enrolled in the class (you'll have access to it anytime, to view over and over again).

Happy baking, and enjoy all the bread!

*But we really, really like bread.

2

INGREDIENTS

The traditional European and American baker's pantry relies heavily on white flours, but this book uses them more sparingly. Our discussion here concentrates more on whole grains, plus specialty wheat varieties like sprouted grains, and what has come to be known as "ancient" grains.

Flours, Grains, and Wheat Extracts

Whole grains of wheat are seeds that have three main parts:

- The brown or reddish-brown fibrous outer *bran* layer that protects the seed's contents and imparts a slightly bitter taste. Bran is a naturally occurring fiber that absorbs water in the intestine and promotes normal digestive function.
- The brown-colored *germ*, which is the future baby wheat plant. It's highly nutritious and contains oil that's particularly rich in vitamins A, D, E, and K.
- The white *endosperm*, containing starch and protein, nourishes the new plant when it sprouts. In wheat, the protein is mostly gluten.

⁓

Adjusting water when using whole wheat flours other than Gold Medal and Pillsbury: Chapter 5 (the Master Recipe) contains two dough formulas, one that's about 70% whole wheat, and a version of the same recipe that's 100% whole wheat. The various whole wheat (or wheat variant) flours we tested required different amounts of liquid to create our usual wet (but not too wet) dough. Those liquid amounts are listed in tables right under the ingredients tables, along with how those amounts change if you omit vital wheat gluten. When you use these numbers to adjust liquids in other recipes, remember that we mean *all* liquids, including water, milk, yogurt, eggs, liquid sweeteners, and oil. For recipes that don't require an adjustment for whole wheat variants, we don't direct you back to chapter 5's tables, but we do give you the water adjustment if you want to omit vital wheat gluten.

Vital wheat gluten (sometimes called "vital wheat gluten flour"): You can boost dough "strength" (and the bread's protein level) by using this powdered extract of wheat's endosperm. We use one to two teaspoons per cup of flour or dry grain ingredient, and then add a little more water. So, why increase the gluten in whole grain bread?

In whole grain wheat flours, the nutritious bran and germ are ground into the flour and take the place of some of the gluten-rich endosperm (the white part of the wheat kernel). So, whole wheat flour has significantly less gluten than white flour, and this will mean less rising power and a less "open" airy crumb (the interior of the bread). What's worse is that whole wheat's bran particles have sharp edges that cut and disrupt developing gluten strands. So breads made with whole wheat flour tend to be denser than white breads. Extra gluten can help counter that and promote an airier whole grain result.

Storing the dough creates another challenge. In our five-minute approach, the initial rise traps enough gas to allow the dough to be used successfully for up to two weeks (depending on the recipe). With whole grain dough, you can use vital wheat gluten to strengthen the protein network and trap more gas. You don't have to do it, but some of our testers preferred the more structured, higher-rising loaf that you get with vital wheat gluten.

Two supermarket brands of vital wheat gluten are generally available in the U.S.: Bob's Red Mill and Hodgson Mill. King Arthur Flour also has one available online or through mail order. Some readers, especially those outside the U.S., have told us that their only option is a product called "Seitan Powder," and while we haven't tested with it, it's worth some experimentation. Vital wheat gluten is easy to incorporate into recipes but can form firm lumps in dough if not handled properly. To prevent that, **always whisk vital wheat gluten with the dry ingredients *before* adding liquids.** Product labeling varies by brand in terms of how much to use in recipes. We experimented to find a dose of vital wheat gluten that gave us a nice rise and an open crumb, but didn't result in a rubbery feel that comes when you've used too much. The less white flour in a recipe, the more you need. Bob's Red Mill and Hodgson Mill can be used interchangeably, but if you use something else, you may need to experiment to find a level that gives you the result you like.

Refrigerate vital wheat gluten in an airtight container after opening the package.

Added gluten can be optional: You can leave out the vital wheat gluten that we call for in most of our whole grain recipes. In our Master Recipe (page 79), we give options for altering the recipe (using less water) so that you can rely on the gluten occurring naturally in the recipe's flour—with a bit of experimentation, you can apply that logic to all the recipes in the book. In general, we found that using vital wheat gluten requires an extra half cup of water in our four-pound dough recipes. Leave out the vital wheat gluten, and you need to decrease the water by a half cup.

Vital wheat gluten helps to keep loaves light and airy with our stored-dough method, but some of our testers were happy to forgo a little airiness in exchange for decreasing the gluten level.

White whole wheat: White whole wheat flour is made from wheat varieties that have pale-colored, mild-tasting bran layers, but it packs the same nutrition as regular whole wheat. It measures like traditional whole wheat and can be substituted for it. Use it in recipes when you don't want the assertive taste of whole wheat to come through other, more delicate, flavors. But don't expect it to taste or mix like white flours, and don't try to substitute it 1:1 for them. It absorbs water like traditional whole wheat, so if you substitute 1:1 for white all-purpose flour in recipes, you'll get a dry, tight dough that won't store well at all.

If you really want to get closer to the flavor and appearance of white flour in a whole grain product, we've found that Kamut (khorasan) is closer to white flour than white whole wheat (see page 11).

All-purpose white flour is a medium-protein white flour, and many of the breads in this book use at least a little white flour. Why? Well, white flour lightens the loaf. If you're weaning your family off all-white flour breads, our basic recipe in chapter 5 (page 79), made with about 70% whole grains, is a great place to start, though you can also make that recipe with 100% whole wheat (page 91).

All-purpose flour has a protein content of about 10%, and that protein is mostly gluten. We prefer **unbleached** all-purpose flour for its natural creamy color, not to mention our preference for avoiding unnecessary chemicals (whole wheat flour is always unbleached, and in Europe, flour is never bleached, by law). That said, bleached flour works fine in our recipes that call for white flour. But beware—cake or pastry flours are too low in protein (around 8%) to make successful bread. And if you swap in bread flour as your white flour, you'll need a little more water.

Canadian flours: These can be higher in protein, so if dough looks too dry, or if the loaf doesn't expand well and the crumb is tight, add about an extra quarter cup of water to the recipe.

Rye flour: Even though there is a wide variety of rye flours available in the U.S., most of them are very high in rye bran and could be labeled as whole grain flour. Exceptions are "light" and "medium" rye, which are lower in bran than the alternatives. Since those are hard to find and we wanted a healthier result, we tested our recipes with the high-bran products that are readily available in the supermarket, such as Bob's Red Mill and Hodgson Mill. See the Appendix on page 395 for protein and fiber content in nationally available rye flours. Rye flours always need to be paired with wheat flours because they have lower levels of gluten than wheat.

Oats add a wonderful hearty flavor and contribute to a toothsome texture, but they don't have gluten. So, like rye flour, oat products need to be paired with wheat flour to produce a loaf that rises, and vital wheat gluten definitely helps. Rolled oat varieties sold as "old-fashioned" (not pre-cooked) are best—the milling process actually rolls the whole kernel flat. Steel-cut oats are more coarsely ground and will yield a coarser result—the kernel is not flattened but rather broken into fragments. Steel-cut oats are often sold as "Scottish" or "Irish" oats. With about 16 grams of fiber per cup, rolled oats have more fiber than whole wheat flour.

Bulgur is made from wheat kernels that are boiled, dried, husked, and cracked. It is sometimes called "Middle Eastern pasta," because it is so versatile, takes on many flavors, and cooks quickly. It is even higher in fiber than oats (26 grams per cup).

Barley: Barley is one of our oldest grains; it has been found worn as necklaces by mummies in Egyptian tombs. Now mostly associated with beer making, the grain has a pleasant taste and is high in fiber (20 grams per cup). Barley is low in gluten, so it needs to be mixed with wheat flours to get a decent rise.

Wheat germ: Wheat germ has a wonderful flavor and is very high in omega-3 fatty acids, one of the healthiest fats of all, not to mention vitamins A, D, E, and K. We add wheat germ to some recipes to boost flavor and nutrition.

Organic flours: Many of our readers told us that they started baking their own bread so that they could eat organic bread and not go broke doing it—store-bought organic bread is expensive, and even worse, it's often not very good. If you like organic products, by all means use them. There are now a number of organic flour brands available in the supermarket, but the best selection remains at your local organic food co-op.

"ANCIENT" GRAINS AND OTHER ALTERNATIVE WHEAT VARIETIES

In chapter 5, we explore swaps for ordinary whole wheat with spelt, khorasan (Kamut), and sprouted whole wheat flours. Why the quotation marks around the word "ancient"? Well, it turns out that there's not much evidence in science, botany, or history to suggest that what are being called ancient grains have actually been cultivated for longer than ordinary wheat. The first known cultivation of wheat coincides with the start of recorded history—which is as far back as you can go. All wheat varieties have ancient origins, but some of them didn't have a high yield or didn't store or travel well, so they haven't been widely cultivated for a long time. They're delicious and subtly different from standard wheat. All of these wheat varieties have gluten (though often they have less), so they're *not* for people with celiac disease (gluten-free recipes in this book are found in chapter 9 on page 297).

If these flours appeal to you, try them in chapter 5's Master Recipe, with the water adjustment as we specify. Once you're comfortable with the guidelines we give for water adjustment, you can apply them to flour swaps in any of the recipes in the book. One strong recommendation: If you swap in one of these flours, measure by weight, not by volume. These flours don't have the same density as regular whole wheat, and we had much more consistent results when we weighed (see page 53).

Spelt flour: A variety of wheat that is high in protein, but slightly lower in gluten than standard wheat. It has a delicious flavor, and is noticeably less bitter than regular whole wheat. Look for whole grain varieties.

Emmer flour: Closely related to spelt, emmer is another lesser-known wheat variant. Confusing the picture is that both grains are sometimes called *farro*, especially when left in whole-kernel form and served as a side dish like rice. But emmer is higher in protein than spelt, and some of our diabetic readers are using it in the hope that it might be slower to raise blood sugar than other wheats (the jury is still out on that one). The germ and bran make up a larger portion of the emmer grain than they do in spelt, and while this is a very nutritious package, it can create a dense bread if used in high proportion in recipes. We've found a whole grain version in the U.S., grown by Bluebird Grain Farms (see Sources for Bread-Baking Products page 398).

Kamut (khorasan) flour: Strictly speaking, this wheat variety should be called by its generic name, khorasan, but most bakers have heard of it by its registered trademark, Kamut, which is the name owned by the company that has successfully marketed it. We tested with an organic version from Bob's Red Mill. It's less bitter than ordinary whole wheat, and it bakes up with a lighter color. Of all the whole wheat flours we've tested, this makes the closest approximation of white bread that we've experienced.

Sprouted wheat flour: You'll hear health claims about sprouted wheat flour, made from wheat kernels that are allowed to sprout before being kiln-dried and ground. The newly formed wheat plant begins to digest some of the starch and gluten in the wheat kernel, and that has prompted the health claims—in theory, this means a lower-carbohydrate and lower-gluten flour. While we don't think there's convincing medical evidence to support any health claims here, and we don't know whether the decreases in carbs or gluten have health significance, what we can tell you is that this flour makes a delicious and very moist whole wheat bread—in fact, the moistest we've ever baked. If whole grains have turned you off because the results seem dry, this is the flour for you. We tested with an organic version from Arrowhead Mills, and natural food co-ops are your best bet to find it in a store rather than online. Be sure to fully bake bread made with this flour, or you may find it gummy.

FRESH-GROUND FLOURS

Many readers have asked about grinding their own wheat berries (kernels) to make whole grain flour, using the electric grinders that have become available for home use. We decided to try fresh-ground flour, but truth be told, we didn't grind it ourselves—we bought it at a farmers' market. We know the folks who ground it, so it's as close to fresh-ground flour as possible. The big surprise was that this particular flour had almost exactly the same density as supermarket whole wheat flour (a little more than 4½ ounces per cup), so we simply swapped it in for commercial whole wheat flour in the basic Master Recipe (page 81). The dough was a touch wetter than usual, but we just ignored that (as we like to say, "if you worry about the bread, it won't taste good").

We loved the gorgeous whole wheat loaf that came out of this experiment. It developed a very firm and crisp crust (oftentimes, the oil in the wheat germ makes it difficult to get a crisp crust). The flavor was terrific—the improvement over commercial flour was subtle but delightful. The bread had a certain brightness and sweetness, which was a neat trick since we tested with no added sweetener. The flavor was, well, very fresh—with less of the bitterness we're accustomed to in whole grain breads.

But be careful: If you grind your own fresh flour, it will likely have a different density, moisture content, bran content, and fineness of grind compared to commercial whole wheat. Because of that, you'll probably need to adjust the liquids up or down to achieve the same result you get with commercial flours. Be prepared to experiment. Once you start grinding your own, you'll see why commercial millers earn their money—a particular miller's brand will always turn out the same way in a given recipe. Not so with flours you grind yourself—this has been confirmed by the many readers who've posted to our website about difficulties they've had with hydration—it's very difficult to predict how much water you'll need with home-ground flour. It's almost always coarser than commercial, and that also affects how much water it absorbs. And you can't be certain how long the kernels were stored before being sold to you, which means you don't know how long the kernels have been drying out. Still—if you're feeling adventurous, or if you can buy wheat berries or fresh-ground flour from a local miller you trust, give fresh-ground a try.

GLUTEN-FREE GRAINS

Double-check with your doctor before consuming any new grain if you are allergic or intolerant of wheat or wheat gluten—all wheats and wheat variants contain gluten. Our only completely gluten-free recipes in this book appear in chapter 9. We use some gluten-free ingredients listed below in wheat-based breads throughout the book, but those recipes are not gluten-free overall and can't be eaten by celiacs. We tested our gluten-free recipes using Bob's Red Mill products, because they're the only widely distributed gluten-free baking ingredients in U.S. supermarkets. If you swap for a different brand, you'll probably have to make significant water adjustments. **Measuring gluten-free flours: If you measure gluten-free flours by volume, be sure to pack them firmly into the measuring cup (as if you were measuring brown sugar). Otherwise, you'll get inconsistent results.**

Buckwheat: Buckwheat is actually a cousin to the rhubarb plant, and not wheat at all, but its seeds behave and taste like a grain when ground into flour. The unground kernels are called groats. It is high in antioxidants and protein.

Cornmeal and corn masa: Look for whole grain varieties and avoid cornmeal products labeled as "degerminated"; this process strips away the germ, which contains most of the nutrients (though degerminated cornmeal has a longer shelf life). Yellow cornmeal is higher in vitamin A than the white variety. In Latin American cultures, corn is treated with alkali to create *masa* (also known as *masa harina*); this releases niacin, an essential B vitamin. Untreated corn is a poor source of niacin because it remains bound to indigestible parts of the kernel.

Cornstarch: Cornstarch is often found in gluten-free recipes. It has very little nutritional value, but helps to create a nice smooth texture and acts as a binder in the dough.

Mesquite flour: Mesquite is a woody plant native to northern Mexico and the southwestern United States. Many people have had Southwestern specialties grilled over the plant's fragrant branches, but less well-known are the edible pod and seed, which can be ground into a high-protein and nutritious flour. It makes a fabulous and unusual bread or focaccia (see pages 232 and 275). It has a naturally sweet flavor that goes well with agave syrup. It's not easy to find; we got ours by mail order from Native Seeds/SEARCH (see Sources, page 398), where it's sold as "mesquite bean flour." Note that our mequite bread recipe has wheat flour in it, so it's not for celiacs.

Millet: This tiny grain is high in protein and vitamin B. Unground, it has a mild flavor that becomes nutty when toasted, and it creates a terrific texture in our Toasted Millet and Fruit Bread. That loaf, on page 195, is not gluten-free, but we do have a gluten-free millet loaf in *Gluten-Free Artisan Bread in Five Minutes a Day* (2014).

Quinoa (*keen-wah*): Quinoa is a relative of Swiss chard and beets. It has a lovely flavor, cooks quickly, and has lots of high-quality protein, which means it contains all the essential amino acids. It is also high in calcium, iron, and B vitamins. Like the millet bread, the quinoa loaf we included on page 192 is *not* gluten-free.

Rice and rice flours: Rice is one of the world's great food staples—all the cultures of the Far East depended on it to develop their civilizations. Brown rice flour has its external bran left in place, and it's higher in nutrients than white rice flour. It's much higher in fiber than white rice flour, but has half the fiber content of whole wheat. In our gluten-free chapter, we only used brown rice flour where we call for rice, and tested with the Bob's Red Mill product. Avoid "glutinous" rice flour, Asian market flours, "superfine rice flour," or "sweet" rice flour, all of which will give you completely different results.

Sorghum: Sorghum is a very popular cooking grain related to sugarcane. It is used around the world, but has just recently found its way into American kitchens.

Soy flour: This flour is milled from soy beans, which are very high in protein. They are also one of the few foods that contain all of the essential amino acids.

Soy flour is an excellent way to boost the protein in gluten-free bread, and it can also be used in wheat breads the same way.

Tapioca flour/Tapioca starch: Tapioca is made from a root that's known by many names: cassava, manioc, or yuca. It is extracted and ground into a flour that is high in calcium and vitamin C, but low in protein. It has traditionally been used for its starchy thickening properties, but it is now frequently used in gluten-free baking. It is sold as both tapioca flour and tapioca starch, and the most popular product has both of those names on the label.

Teff: An indispensable grain in Ethiopia, teff has been virtually unheard of in the rest of the world until recently. It is a type of millet that is very small but packed with iron and calcium. It is a wonderful sweet grain that is gluten-free and therefore gaining in popularity. When combined with caraway seeds in a bread, it's a dead ringer for a traditional German or Eastern European caraway rye loaf.

Wild rice: Although technically an aquatic grass like plain rice, wild rice from North America distinguishes itself from its Asian counterpart by its distinct flavor and texture. It has long been prized in traditional Native American cultures, and more recently its nutritional profile and flavor have attracted interest from health-conscious eaters. Our Wild Rice Pilaf Bread on page 201 is not gluten-free.

Xanthan gum: This powdered additive, a naturally derived gum that creates gas-trapping structure in gluten-free dough, is used in gluten-free baking to replace the stretchiness and chew that breads would otherwise get from gluten in wheat. It's a tried-and-true ingredient that's been around for years.

Ground psyllium husk: When some of our readers reported sensitivities to xanthan gum, we began testing ground psyllium husk as a substitute, and it works well. This product, milled from the outer coating of an edible seed, has been used as a natural fiber supplement for years. It's available at your local pharmacy, food co-op, or online, and is sometimes labeled "powdered" psyllium husk.

Water

Throughout the book, we call for lukewarm water. This means water that feels just a little warm to the touch; if you measured it with a thermometer it would be no higher than 100°F (38°C). The truth is, we never use a thermometer and we've never had a yeast failure due to excessive temperature—but it can happen, so be careful. Cold water from the tap will work (and you cannot kill yeast with cold water), but the initial rise will take much, much longer (the bread will be just as good, and some of our taste testers preferred the taste of cold-risen dough). Typically, in our homes, we're not in a hurry, so we often use cold water and let it sit for as long as necessary. Egg or dairy-enriched doughs are different—they can sit at room temperature for two hours and then be allowed to complete their rising in the fridge (for food safety's sake).

About water sources: We find that the flavors of wheat and fermentation overwhelm the contribution of water to bread's flavor, so we use ordinary tap water run through a home water filter (what we drink at home). Assuming your own tap water tastes good enough to drink, use it filtered or unfiltered; we can't tell the difference in finished bread.

Yeast: Adjust It to Your Taste

Use whatever yeast is readily available; with our approach you'll get great results with any type of granulated packaged yeast (we tested with the Red Star brand). Packages labeled "active dry," "instant," "quick-rise," or "bread-machine" will all work well.

Fresh cake yeast works fine as well (though you will have to increase yeast volume by 50 percent to achieve the same rising speed). The long storage time of our doughs acts as an equalizer between all available yeast products. If you're in a hurry and want to use the dough immediately after its initial rise, you may appreciate the quicker start-up of "instant" or "quick-rise" yeast. And gluten-free bakers should note that Red Star's Platinum yeast is an instant yeast that

Yeast love to keep cool: Jefferson University yeast biochemist Hannah Silver, Ph.D., loves great bread, and bakes her own with our method. We asked her why aged dough develops such great flavor: "Yeast extracts are sometimes used to enhance flavor in commercial food, because they intro-duce a savory complexity, sometimes called *umami,* the so-called fifth basic taste recognized by the human tongue (in addition to sweet, salty, bitter, and sour). The flavor you get with stored dough comes from chemicals produced by yeast as they use sugars and starches to make carbon dioxide gas (which forms bubbles to leaven the bread) and alcohol (which boils off in baking)."

We asked Dr. Silver why the yeast stay active enough for leavening even after two weeks. "It's the refrigeration. In the lab, we store ours at 176 degrees below zero, and the yeast pretty much go to sleep. But if you leave them out on the counter with a starch or sugar source, they get overactive and eventually stinky. You'd never get away with two-week dough storage without refrigeration—the yeast would soon use up all the nutrients and become inactive."

Someone once asked us why, in five thousand years of bread baking, had no one come up with our approach. Well, it's really just one hundred years or so—that's about how long refrigeration has been around, according to Tom Jackson in *Chilled: How Refrigeration Changed the World and Might Do So Again.*

contains dough conditioners derived from wheat protein, so it's *not* gluten-free and shouldn't be used for gluten-free baking. **One strong recommendation: If you bake frequently, buy yeast in bulk or in 4-ounce jars, rather than in packets (which are much less economical).**

Food co-ops often sell yeast by the pound, in bulk (usually the Red Star brand). Make sure that bulk-purchased yeast is fresh by chatting with your co-op manager. Freeze yeast after opening to extend its shelf life, and use it straight from the freezer, or store smaller containers in the refrigerator and use within a few months. Between the two of us, we've had only one yeast failure in many years of baking, and it was with an outdated envelope stored at room temperature. **The real key to avoiding yeast failure is to use water that is no warmer than lukewarm (about 100°F). Even cold water will work (though the initial rise will take much, much longer). Hot water kills yeast.**

Will the recipes work with small amounts of yeast? Some readers prefer less yeast in their dough—finding that a long, slow rise produces a better flavor—but it's really a matter of taste. Less yeast works well for all of our recipes (ex-

---

〰️

Using yeast packets instead of jarred or bulk yeast: Throughout the book, we call for 1 tablespoon of granulated yeast for about 4 pounds of dough. **You can substitute one packet of granulated yeast for a tablespoon, even though, technically speaking, those amounts aren't perfectly equivalent (a tablespoon is a little more than the 2¼ teaspoons found in one packet).** When you start with lukewarm water (not cold), we've found that it makes little difference in the initial rise time or in the performance of the finished dough. If you're finding the initial rise isn't finished in two hours, just let the dough rest at room temperature for a little longer.

cept for this book's gluten-free dough)—but the initial rise will be slower. The recipes in this book use less yeast than those in our very first edition of *Artisan Bread in Five Minutes a Day* from 2007—but you can use even less if you have time to spare. We've had great results using as little as one-quarter of our standard amount of yeast. If you significantly decrease the yeast, the initial rising time may increase to eight hours, or even longer, depending on how much you decreased it and the temperature in your kitchen. Just a bit of yeast is great when you're using naturally fermented sourdough as a leavener, and want extra assurance that you'll get a good rise. You'll still have most of the flavor benefit of natural sourdough (see chapter 11).

After several days of high-moisture storage, yeasted dough begins to take on a flavor and aroma that's close to the flavor of natural sourdough starters used in many artisan breads. This will deepen the flavor and character of all your doughs. The traditional way to achieve these flavors—pre-ferments, sours, and starters like *biga*, *levain*, and *poolish*—all require significant time and attention. If you're interested, we've developed a recipe for a simplified but traditional levain in chapter 11, starting on page 385. But, if you've never made bread before, start with our doughs made with packaged yeast.

Another way to coax extra flavor out of a dough risen with packaged yeast is to use cool or even cold water

> ❧
>
> **Modern Yeast . . .**
>
> . . . almost never fails if used before its expiration date, so you *do not* need to "proof" the yeast (i.e., test it for freshness by demonstrating that it bubbles in sweetened warm water), and you don't need to add any sugar. Skip it. It wastes five precious minutes when you could be fishing around for compliments from your family about the fresh bread you've baked.

to mix the dough. If you try this, the initial rise time increases dramatically, even more so if you also decreased the yeast, so you'll need more advance planning. **Because of food-safety concerns, if your dough has eggs and you're considering a long, slow rise, do only the first two hours at room temperature,** then complete the rising in the refrigerator (and expect a long wait). According to the U.S. Department of Agriculture, raw eggs shouldn't be kept at room temperature for longer than two hours.[1]

Salt: Adjust It to Your Taste

In traditional bread recipes, salt is used not only for flavor but also to help tighten and strengthen the gluten. Because our dough is slack in the first place, and is stored for so long, we don't detect differences in dough strength between high- and low-salt versions of our breads, so adjust it to suit your palate and any dietary restrictions you might have. So, how much? We love the taste of salt, but for this health-oriented book, we decided to go easy on salt. If you're missing the salt and your diet allows it, feel free to increase it to taste—where we call for 1 tablespoon of Morton kosher salt, you can use up to 1½. On the other hand, if health conditions require it, you can decrease the salt and the recipes will still work well. Cutting the salt in half can be a good option for people who want to restrict sodium in their diet. In fact, you can bring the salt all the way down to zero, if you like, but the flavor will be very different—our taste testers found no-salt bread to be very bland.

Salt-free breads can help people with certain health problems like heart failure, kidney disease, high blood pressure, Meniere's disease, or fluid retention: In Italy, the Tuscans have a long tradition of a salt-free bread, apparently arising during a time of high taxation on salt from papal authorities, and many older baking books include recipes for it. It's particularly nice for dipping into salted soups and in other situations where it's not eaten alone. Be aware that salt-free yeast dough might behave badly at high altitude (see page 75).

All of our recipes were tested with Morton brand kosher salt, which is coarser than table salt. If you're using something finer or coarser and you're measuring salt with tablespoons, you need to change the amount, because finer salt

---

[1] U.S. Department of Agriculture Fact Sheet. *Egg Products Preparation: Shell Eggs from Farm to Table.* http://www.fsis.usda.gov/wps/portal/fsis/topics/food-safety-education/get-answers/food-safety-fact-sheets/egg-products-preparation/shell-eggs-from-farm-to-table, accessed Feburary 1, 2016.

packs denser into the spoon. You'll get the same saltiness from these tablespoon amounts:

Table salt (finer): ⅔ tablespoon
Morton Kosher Salt (coarse): 1 tablespoon
Diamond Kosher Salt (coarsest): 1⅓ tablespoons

SALT SUBSTITUTE

Salt substitutes are made from potassium chloride, which, like regular salt (sodium chloride), is a naturally occurring mineral that's required by all living things. Unlike sodium chloride, potassium-based salt *does not* raise blood pressure and promote fluid retention, so it's sometimes recommended for people with hypertension, and others on a sodium-restricted diet. In fact, potassium may help control blood pressure in some people. When added to bread dough, it can replace some of the salty flavor that you lose when you omit sodium salt from our recipes. Some readers have substituted it volume for volume for kosher salt in our recipes, but we recommend that you start with a partial substitution, half or less—to our taste, the full substitution left a metallic aftertaste. *And most important—consult your doctor before using a salt substitute, because some medications and medical conditions can cause retention of potassium, with dangerous buildup of the mineral in your bloodstream.*

> **Weighing yeast and salt:** In the recipes, we provide weight equivalents for yeast and salt, which is a more professional technique—but professional bakers measure out enormous batches. Be sure your home scale weighs accurately in the lower ranges; otherwise spoon-measure yeast and salt.

Oils and Fats

When people first taste homemade artisan bread, they're sure that the moisture and flavor must be coming from butter or other fats in the dough. For our basic breads, they're wrong—the moisture comes from—you guessed it—moisture, the high level of water in our dough. But for some of our breads, like the challahs and brioches in chapter 10, fats and oils are important components of the flavor and texture. Much has been written about the health effects of fats and oils, and much of it is confusing, unsettled, and controversial. Frankly, there's been a lot of quackery in the popular media. We've greatly expanded our list of oils since the first edition and, if you want to try a new oil, it will probably work in our recipes.

UNSATURATED OILS (MONOUNSATURATED AND POLYUNSATURATED)

Vegetable oils (except for coconut oil, which is mostly saturated fat) are liquid at room temperature, and are among the healthiest options for enriching breads. They tend to raise "good" cholesterol (HDL) and lower "bad" cholesterol (LDL)—saturated and trans fats can do the opposite. All edible fats contain about 14 grams of fat per tablespoon (120 calories), so if your goal is weight loss, it doesn't make much difference which fat you use. But, the choice of fats in your diet can make a difference in your cholesterol profile and heart health. That said, it's difficult to come up with hard-and-fast health recommendations for which oil or fat is best. They vary in their ratio of polyunsaturated and monounsaturated fat, and exactly what's best is an area of some controversy. None of the oils *except for flaxseed oil* is particularly high in the healthiest unsaturated fat, omega-3 polyunsaturated fat. In general, liquid oils made from plant sources can be swapped into any recipes calling for vegetable oil.

Olive oil is rich in monounsaturated fat and has one of the most delightful flavors in Western cooking—there's nothing like it (except maybe olives). It's a cornerstone of the so-called Mediterranean diet, which relies on olive oil's monounsaturates as a major fat source, plus abundant vegetables and grains, and limited meat. **Olive oil isn't a completely neutral flavor, but if you like its flavor as much as we do, you can use it in any of our recipes calling for oil—it doesn't change the flavor all that much—even in challah.** It's central to the flavors in many of our Mediterranean-inspired pizzas, flatbreads, and bread sticks. While ordinary olive oil has a relatively low smoke point and shouldn't be used for deep-frying, *extra-virgin* olive oil is different—so long as you're keeping to the temperature we recommend for deep-frying doughnuts (see page 359), extra-virgin oil can be heated to deep-fry temperature (regular olive oil may smoke). You can use either regular or extra-virgin olive oil in the dough recipes.

Vegetable oil, either blends, or pure products made from **soybean, safflower, sunflower, peanut, canola, or corn** are rich in polyunsaturated fat. All work well in our recipes and they're nice, reasonably priced options. They don't impart any particular flavor to baked breads. Here are some others that worked well in the recipes:

- **Avocado oil:** imparts a hint of avocado flavor; it's delicious.
- **Grapeseed oil:** completely neutral in flavor.
- **Flaxseed oil:** We were pleasantly surprised to find that flaxseed oil has a neutral flavor when used in challah and other recipes calling for up to a half cup in a four-pound batch of dough. This is a super-healthy oil, and according to the Flax Council of Canada, it's stable at baking temperatures. The only drawback? The price—it's much more expensive than ordinary vegetable oils, but if you're trying to boost your omega-3 fatty acids, it may be worth it to you. We tested with the clear lignan-free oils, which have the mildest flavor. Flaxseed oils must be refrigerated as they are prone to go rancid.

SATURATED FATS AND OILS

Saturated fats are solid at room temperature and tend to raise "bad" cholesterol (LDL) and lower "good" cholesterol (HDL)—so in general, a healthy diet should limit their intake. See the Appendix (page 395) for more about saturated versus unsaturated fats in various ingredients. The saturated fats include trans fats, which are the unhealthiest fats of all. The worst trans-fat offenders are artificially produced—partially hydrogenated oils that are solid at room temperature, usually labeled as "vegetable shortening." **Don't use it,** and don't be fooled by the words "vegetable"—this is not a healthy food. One area of confusion is product labeling touting a "cholesterol-free" product. Only animals produce cholesterol, and *all* vegetable oils and fats, whether liquid or solid, are cholesterol-free. So be wary of ads that promote cholesterol-free vegetable products—this is a marketing come-on. Pre-formed cholesterol in food is much less important to our blood cholesterol than the types of fats we eat (saturated, trans, polyunsaturated, or monounsaturated), and whether our weight is under control. See our table in the Appendix (page 395) for more information on fats, oils, and spreads that you can use in our breads.

Butter: Butter is delicious, but because it's high in saturated fat, it increases "bad" cholesterol (LDL). In this book, we use it sparingly, and give you some zero saturated and zero trans-fat swap options. But if truth be told, life's too short to miss out on a little butter with fresh bread. If you need some justification, butter is high in vitamins A and E, both essential nutrients. If you're going to eat butter once in a while, spread some European-style artisan salted butter on the freshest and most delicious bread you make. Just use it in moderation, as a treat.

Ghee is butter that has been clarified and slightly toasted. It is a staple in Indian kitchens because of its wonderful flavor. Since the heat-sensitive milk solids are toasted and then strained off, *ghee* can be heated to a much higher temperature than regular butter. It can be found in many South Asian markets, but we prefer to make our own. The following recipe will yield ¾ of a pound (about 1⅔ cups). Melt 1 pound of unsalted butter in a medium saucepan over low heat. When it has completely melted, bring it to a boil and continue until it is frothy. Reduce the heat to low and cook gently until the milk solids have settled to the bottom of the pot and are golden brown. Strain the ghee through a fine-mesh sieve. Allow it to cool completely, cover, and refrigerate. The ghee will last in the refrigerator for a month.

Coconut oil: Though vegetable-based, coconut oil is high in saturated fat, and is solid at room temperature, so melt it in a microwave or double-boiler before using. It works well as a substitute for other vegetable oils in our recipes, and like other vegetable oils, it's completely vegan. Enriched dough made with coconut oil will have a drier feel than doughs made with vegetable oil or butter. It lends a mild coconut flavor to enriched breads; our taste testers loved it. Based on current standard recommendations, use this saturated fat source in moderation (like butter).

Margarine: Old-style hard stick margarine is made with unhealthy hydrogenated oils, and it has trans fat, which is the worst kind of all (just like vegetable shortening). **Don't use it.** Check the label, and if you want to use a margarine product, seek out one of the soft "tub" products: look for a zero trans fat, zero hydrogenated oil brand. It can be difficult to find salt-free versions, so decrease the salt in your recipe a bit if you end up using a salted brand.

Butter substitutes: Butter substitute spreads are made by blending unsaturated oils with by-products of butter in patented manufacturing processes. They're designed to deliver buttery flavor with little or no saturated and trans fats. Based on today's understanding of fats, nutrition, and health, many of the products may be on the right track. Despite being unsaturated, they're solid at room temperature and perform well in brioche.

Seeds and Nuts

We love to boost the nutrition of whole grain bread by topping it with a mixture of healthy seeds like sesame, flax, caraway, raw sunflower, poppy, and anise. They'll stick to the bread if you first paint the surface with water before sprinkling the seeds on top. All seeds can go rancid if you keep them too long, so taste a few if your jar is older than a year. Freeze them if you are storing for longer than three months.

Anise seeds: Anise seeds have the flavor of licorice, which works beautifully on top of full-flavored breads.

Caraway seeds: These are so central to the flavor of many rye breads that a lot of people think that caraway is actually the flavor of the rye grain. It's not, but for us, something does seem to be missing in unseeded rye bread. If you put them on plain whole wheat breads, you may think you are eating whole grain rye bread.

Flaxseeds: These little brown beauties are slightly larger than a sesame seed and pack lots of omega-3 fatty acids, lignans (which may have anticancer properties), manganese, fiber, protein, and other nutrients our bodies need. They may help protect against heart disease, cancer, diabetes, high blood pressure, and even hot flashes. We use them whole to top loaves, but the nutrients are more readily absorbed by the body when they are ground into a powder, so that's how they're used in the dough mixtures. Buy ground flaxseed in small amounts—because of its high oil content it tends to become rancid more quickly than other flours. If your flaxseed breads have an unpleasant fishy taste, you know you used rancid flax. You can also buy whole seeds and grind them in a spice or coffee grinder. As in the discussion of oils above, flaxseed oil is a great heart-healthy option in our challah doughs.

Two other points: the Flax Council of Canada (Canada is the world's largest producer of flax) says that ground flaxseed can be stored for 30 days in a cool place in an airtight, opaque container, while whole seeds can be kept at room temperature for up to a year. To be on the safe side, we like to freeze them if we're storing them for longer than 3 months. And furthermore, despite older references that suggest high heat can break down flax's nutrients, more recent studies have shown that it can be heated to high temperatures without damage.

Nuts: Store nuts in the freezer so that their oils will not go rancid. Buy them either natural or blanched.

Poppy seeds: Poppy seeds are used in Western, Middle Eastern, and Asian cuisines. They're central to the flavor of challah and many Eastern European breads and pastries.

Pumpkin seeds (*pepitas*): Buy the dark green husked seeds, which are the most nutritious part of the pumpkin. They are rich in minerals, protein, and mono-unsaturated fat. The husk isn't edible, so don't try to use seeds straight out of a pie pumpkin.

Sesame seeds: Not only do they have a wonderful nutty flavor, but these tiny seeds are full of nutrients. They are a good source of calcium, iron, vitamin B_1, zinc, and fiber. Black sesame seeds, which are traditional in Turkey and the Middle East, have a stronger flavor than white ones. Try both and see what you think.

Sunflower seeds: These seeds are a great source of vitamins E and B_1, along with a host of minerals. You can use roasted or raw sunflower seeds in a dough, but if you're using them on a top crust, use the unroasted ones or they might overbrown or even burn.

Other Flavorings

Caramel coloring: Caramel color powder is actually a natural ingredient made by overheating sugar until it almost burns. It's crucial for pumpernickel breads (pages 170 and 174), in which it provides more than just color—it imparts a bitterness that really complements the wheat and rye flavors in pumpernickel bread. The easiest way to use it is to buy the powder from a baking specialty store or from King Arthur Flour (see Sources for Bread-Baking Products, page 398), but if you can't easily get it, you can make your own. What you make will be a liquid that is added to recipes; you should decrease liquid ingredients in the recipe to account for the extra you are adding in the form of caramel. Put 3 tablespoons of sugar and 1 tablespoon of water into a small saucepan over low heat. Melt the sugar, then increase the heat to medium-high, cover, and bring it to a boil for 2 minutes. Continue to boil, uncovered, until the mixture becomes very dark and just begins to smoke, Immediately add ¼ cup of boiling water to the pan (it may sputter and water may jump out of the pan, so wear gloves and keep your face away from it). Dissolve the caramelized sugar and cool it to room temperature. Use about ¼ cup of this mixture in place of commercial caramel color powder in our Bavarian-Style Whole Grain Pumpernickel Bread recipe (page 170); decrease the water in the recipe by ¼ cup to account for the difference between liquid caramel and powdered caramel color.

Chocolate: Some of our enriched breads call for chocolate, either cocoa powder, bar chocolate, or chunks. You will notice an improvement in flavor and recipe performance if you use the highest-quality chocolate available. For bittersweet bar chocolate, Valrhona is our favorite, but Callebaut, Scharffen Berger, Lindt, Perugina, Ghirardelli, and other premium brands also work quite well. Our favorite unsweetened cocoa powder is Valrhona, but Droste's, Ghirardelli, and other premium brands also give good results. In our recipes, it doesn't matter if the cocoa powder is Dutch-processed (alkali-treated) or not: The question of Dutch-process is only important for baked goods risen with baking soda or baking powder—yeast doesn't seem to care. If premium chocolate is unavailable, try the recipes with your favorite value-priced supermarket brands of solid chocolate or cocoa. Hershey's Special Dark Cocoa powder (unsweetened) is a terrific product for the money. The premium stuff is not an absolute requirement by any means.

Beer: The addition of beer to bread dough adds complex yeasty flavors that won't otherwise develop until the dough has been stored for at least twenty-four hours. By swapping a cup of beer for water in a recipe you can achieve complex flavors much faster. Use any beer except strongly flavored stouts and porters.

Natural Sweeteners

These sweeteners have trace amounts of plant nutrients (refined white sugar has virtually none). But they still spike blood sugar levels and contain lots of calories, so for diabetics or anyone on a weight-loss program, these should be used in moderation. Like salt, sugars help to hold moisture in the bread and keep bread from going stale—salt and sugar are hygroscopic (water-attracting).

Agave syrup: Agave syrup (sometimes labeled "agave nectar") tastes the tiniest bit like tequila, and no wonder. The agave plant is the source of the fermentable juice that makes the world's best tequila, and agave syrup is the concentrated sweetener made from that juice. It provides a smooth and distinct flavor in Mesquite Bread (page 232), and is available from natural food co-ops and online or by mail order. You can substitute it for honey or maple syrup if you prefer the flavor in recipes calling for those natural sweeteners.

Barley malt: Made from sprouted barley, it is very dark, sweet with malt sugar, and quite thick. It adds a beery, yeasty flavor to bread. Barley malt is the main ingredient in beer, and malt sugar is a great sugar for feeding yeast.

Brown sugar and raw sugar: Like white sugar, these less refined sugars are made from sugarcane or sugar beets, but they retain trace amounts of the nutrients found in molasses. They impart a caramel flavor as well. Raw sugars are most commonly found as demerara, muscovado, and turbinado and have a larger grain than regular brown sugar.

Honey: This is the sweetener we call for most frequently in the book, produced by busy bees the world over from naturally occurring sugars in the nectar of flowers that they visit. Honey's flavor is determined by the type of plant nectar the honeybee collects. Some honeys have very intense flavor, such as buckwheat honey, while others are quite mild, such as clover honey. We've had nice results with all kinds of honey, so experiment with different types and see which you prefer.

Maple syrup: The most commonly found maple syrup is Grade A, which is lightest in color and mildest in flavor. Many consider it the more desirable grade, but we actually prefer to use Grade B, which is made later in the production season and has a darker color, stronger flavor, and more of the minerals magnesium and zinc. It is great for baking because the flavor stands up to the other ingredients, but either Grade A or B will work nicely.

Molasses: Molasses is an unrefined sweetener derived from sugarcane. Blackstrap molasses is the product of three boilings of the sugarcane, and so it concentrates the nutrients. Its iron, magnesium, calcium, copper, potassium, and vitamin B_6

content makes it one of the most nutrient-rich sweeteners, more so than molasses that isn't labeled as blackstrap. It is used in the recipes to add color and a deep, rich flavor. Unsulphured molasses has the best flavor.

Stevia: Our readers, especially diabetics who must avoid sugar, have asked us about this herbal sweetener—stevia sweetens without sugar. But it's not an artificial sweetener, it's an extract of a South American herb whose leaves contain a naturally occurring, zero-calorie substance that is much sweeter than sugar. There are two kinds of stevia products, pure ones (liquid or powder), and those combined with other substances—starch or sugar-derived additives like erythritol or maltodextrin—so that the resulting product measures and looks like sugar. If you use the pure stevia products, you only use a small amount—it has much more concentrated sweetening power. The labeling will tell you the volume equivalency to sugar. There's some controversy about the additives in the mixed commercial stevia products designed to measure like sugar. The question is whether these substances are prone to raise blood sugar. Most experts suggest that diabetics can consume these additives in modest quantity. Read the label, check with your health provider, and use your best judgment. If you want to be extra careful, avoid the products that include any additives and stick with pure stevia powders or liquids. Our favorite-tasting product is a pure liquid extract, and it works well as a swap for honey in the whole wheat challah recipe, but it only required 20 drops of the liquid—that's how concentrated this stuff is. Water had to be increased by a couple of tablespoons. You can experiment with stevia in place of sugar, honey, or other sweeteners in any of our recipes, or at least as a way to decrease the sugar in a recipe. It doesn't taste exactly the same, but many people find it to be a natural product that makes a nice substitute.

Dairy Products

Cheese: We add a number of different cheeses to our doughs. They're not only a great source of flavor, but also add protein and calcium to the bread.

Milk: The addition of milk to bread dough tenderizes the bread, and also adds sweetness and protein. Lactose (milk sugar) helps to keep the loaf fresher longer. Too much milk in dough, however, can have an adverse effect on the rising power of your loaf. With our whole grain breads we can't afford to lose any rise. In *CookWise*, food scientist Shirley O. Corriher suggests scalding the milk first, which helps to eliminate the problem. We don't call for it in the recipes, but if your dough is dense it is worth a try.

Yogurt: Plain yogurt, either whole milk, lowfat, or nonfat, contains lactic acid, which helps to promote strong gluten development. It also acts as a preservative to prevent baked bread from going stale so quickly. It adds a lovely tangy flavor to the bread and is a great source of protein, calcium, and zinc.

Dairy substitutes: We've had many readers substitute soy, rice, and almond milk for dairy with good results.

3

EQUIPMENT

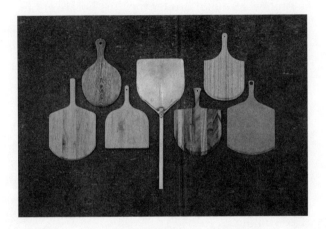

I n the spirit of our simple approach, we've kept our list spare, and present items in order of importance. The most helpful items are:

- Equipment for baking with steam: we'll give you four options
- Oven thermometer
- Baking stone, cast-iron pizza pan, cast-iron skillet, unglazed quarry tiles, or heavy-gauge baking sheet
- Pizza peel

See Sources for Bread-Baking Products (page 398) to locate mail-order and Web-based vendors for harder-to-find items.

Equipment for Baking with Steam
(You Only Need One)

Metal broiler tray to hold boiling water for steam (and it must be metal): This is our first choice for creating the steam environment needed for breads to achieve a crisp and richly colored crust. Highly enriched breads (eg., challah, brioche, etc.) don't benefit from baking with steam, because fat in dough softens the crust anyway, and the egg wash provides the color. Pour hot tap water (or drop a handful of ice cubes) into the preheated metal broiler tray just before closing the oven door.

Some oven doors (and most professional ones) don't make a great seal for holding in steam. *If your oven allows steam to escape and you're not getting a beautiful crisp crust, or if you don't want to deal with water in the oven, try one of these three alternatives to the broiler tray method:*

1. Food-grade water sprayer: Spray the loaf with water before closing the oven door, then open at 30-second intervals for two more sprayings.

2. Roomy metal bowl or aluminum-foil roasting pan for covering free-form loaves in the oven: By trapping steam next to a loaf as it bakes, you can create the humid environment that produces a crisp crust without using a broiler tray or a sprayer. Whatever you use has to be heat-tolerant and tall enough so that the rising loaf won't touch it when it rises, but not so large that it hangs beyond the edge of the stone, or it won't trap the steam.

Two important warnings: 1. Do not use a glass pan to catch water for steam, or it will shatter on contact with the water! 2. Some of our readers have reported cracked oven window glass after spilling water on its hot surface. If you want extra assurance that this won't happen, protect the window with a towel before pouring water into the pan; remove the towel before closing the oven door. This tends to happen with older ovens built before manufacturers began using tempered glass.

3. Bake inside a *cloche* or a covered cast-iron pot: The clay baker (in French, *la cloche* [la klōsh] is a time-honored way to bake—the covered unglazed clay baking vessel traps steam inside, so the crackling crust forms without the need for a broiler tray or sprayer. Some cloches come with directions that recommend against preheating before use, but we've had best results in a preheated, ungreased *cloche*. We don't soak unglazed cloches in water before use as is sometimes advocated, and that obviously wouldn't help with glazed ones anyway. Unfortunately, we've found that the unglazed cloches aren't terribly durable—they tend to crack eventually, and the glazed ones aren't perfect either—we've had one where the handle cracked after just a little jostling. **Covered pots (Dutch oven)** also work well for much the same reason, but some of them will need a heat-resistant replacement knob. Check with the manufacturer about the temperature limit for any knob that looks to be made of a plastic instead of metal or ceramic. Most vessels won't need to be greased, but experiment with yours and grease it lightly after preheating the first time you try it. It's easiest (but not required) to rest the loaf on a sling of parchment paper before lowering it, paper and all, into the pot and covering it.

For a really professional crust result, the cloche or cast-iron pot can be preheated 50 degrees hotter than called for in the recipe. After a 20-minute preheat, reduce the oven to the recipe's specified temperature and add the rested dough. Uncover the vessel during the last third of the baking time. Don't try this if you're finding that the bottoms of your loaves are browning too much.

Other Equipment

Oven thermometer: Home ovens are often off by up to 75 degrees, so this is an important item. You need to know the actual oven temperature to get predictable bread-baking results. An inexpensive oven thermometer (less than $20.00) will help you get results just like the ones you see in our photos. Place your oven thermometer right on the stone for best results.

A hot oven drives excess water out of wet dough, but if it's too hot you'll burn the crust before fully baking the crumb (the bread's interior). Too low, and you'll end up with a pale crust and undercooked crumb unless you extend the baking time—but that can give you a thick, tough crust. Without the thermometer, your bread baking will have an annoying element of trial and error. If your oven runs significantly hot or cool, you may want to have it recalibrated by a professional. Otherwise, just compensate by adjusting your heat setting.

When a baking stone is in place, your oven may very well take longer to reach final temperature than the 30-minute preheat that we specify. And digital oven settings are no more accurate than old-fashioned dial displays, so rely on your oven thermometer. If you don't like the result you're getting with the short preheat, consider a longer one (45 or even 60 minutes).

Baking stone, cast-iron pizza pan, baking steel, cast-iron skillet, or unglazed quarry tiles: Bread turns out browner, crisper, and tastier when the dough is baked on one of these, especially in combination with a steam environment we describe on page 40 (this isn't important for the enriched breads in chapter 10).

Products may be labeled "pizza stones" (usually round), or "baking stones" (usually rectangular), but they're both made from the same kinds of materials and perform the same way. The larger, 14×16-inch models will keep flour, cornmeal, and other ingredients from falling to the oven floor. In our experience, ceramic stones don't last forever. Most are pretty durable, but we no longer find any manufacturers willing to guarantee them against cracking. Thick stones (½ inch) take longer to preheat compared to thin ceramic ones, cast-iron, or steel (see below). Thin ceramic are the least durable of the bunch, while cast-iron and steel are pretty much unbreakable.

Unglazed quarry tiles, available from home-improvement stores, are inexpensive and work well. The drawbacks: you'll need several of them to line an oven shelf, and stray cornmeal or flour may fall between the tiles onto the oven floor, where it will burn.

Traditionally, professionals have given two reasons to bake right on a ce-

Whole grain breads never get the same crackling crust as white breads:
Why? Oils from wheat germ in whole grains soften the crust and prevent crisping. That said, steam is very helpful in promoting a beautifully colored whole grain crust. For loaves where we call for a stone **and** steam, here's our advice: If you're going to omit one or the other, let it be the stone—if you omit the steam, you'll get a really dull-colored and unappealing bread (it will still taste good).

ramic stone. **First,** the stone promotes fast and even heat transfer because of its weight and density (versus, for example, a baking sheet), so it quickly dries and crisps the crust. That massive heat transfer also creates terrific "oven spring," especially in home ovens that don't deliver even heat. ("Oven spring" is the sudden expansion of gases within the bread—it occurs upon contact with the hot air and stone, and it prevents a dense, tough result.) **Second,** it's always been assumed that the stone's porosity allows it to absorb excess moisture from the dough (especially wet dough), encouraging crispness. It turns out that the effect must be mostly due to explanation number one, because we've found that dough baked on preheated cast-iron pizza pans, baking steels, or cast-iron skillets turns out as well as dough baked on stones, despite the fact that these metals aren't porous at all.

Having said all this, we must emphasize that you can make decent bread without a baking stone; just do it right on a heavy-gauge baking sheet (see

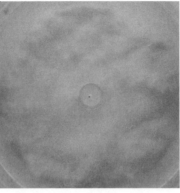

page 45). The crust won't be as crisp, but the result will be better than most any bread you can buy.

A 5- to 6-quart storage container or bucket with a lid—plastic, glass, stainless steel, crockery, or even a soup pot. You can mix and store the dough in the same vessel—this will save you from washing one more item (it all figures into the five minutes a day). Look for a food-grade container that holds 5 or 6 quarts to allow for the initial rise. Five-quart containers are just big enough, but gallon containers will probably let rising dough overflow (it's a mess). Round containers are easier to mix in than square ones (flour gets caught in corners). Great options are available on our website, or from Tupperware, King Arthur Flour's website, and kitchen-supply specialty stores, as well as discount chains, such as Costco and Target. Some food-storage buckets include a vented lid, which allows gases to escape during the fermentation process. You can usually close the vent (or seal the lid) after the first two days because gas production has really slowed by then. If your vessel has a plastic lid, you can drill a tiny hole in the lid to allow gas to escape. Avoid glass or crockery containers that create a truly airtight seal (with

a screw top, for example), because trapped gases could shatter them. If you don't have a vented container, just leave the lid open a crack for the first two days of storage. Soup pot lids aren't airtight and can be seated fully from day one if you go that route.

And of course, you can

always use a mixing bowl covered with plastic wrap (don't use a towel—it sticks horribly to high-moisture dough).

Pizza peel: This is a flat board with a long handle used to slide bread or pizza onto a hot surface. Wood or metal work well, but don't use anything made of plastic to transfer dough onto a stone—it could melt upon contact. Prepare the peel with cornmeal or parchment paper before putting dough on it, or everything will stick to it, and possibly to your stone. If you don't have a pizza peel, a flat, rimless baking or cookie sheet (no sides) will do, but it will be more difficult to handle. A thin wood or heat-resistant cutting board (not plastic) also works—some have handles that make them as easy to work with as peels.

Heavy-gauge baking sheets, jelly-roll pans, and cookie sheets: The highest-quality baking sheets are made of super-heavyweight aluminum and have short rims (They're sometimes called jelly-roll pans and our favorites are the ones made by Chicago Metallic). When well greased or lined with parchment paper or a silicone mat, they are a decent alternative to the pizza peel/baking stone method and let you avoid sliding dough off a pizza peel onto a stone.

Similar-gauge flat, round pans are available specifically for pizza. Avoid "air-insulated" baking sheets—they don't conduct heat well and won't produce a crisp crust. Thin cookie sheets can be used, but like air-insulated bakeware, they won't produce a great crust and can scorch bottom crusts due to their uneven heat delivery.

Silicone mats: Nonstick, flexible silicone baking mats are convenient and are reusable thousands of times. They're terrific for lower-temperature recipes (such as brioches and challahs), but we find that pizzas and other lean-dough specialties don't crisp as well on silicone. They're used on top of a baking sheet or dropped onto a hot stone, and don't need to be greased, so cleanup is a breeze. Be sure to get a mat that's temperature-rated to withstand what's called for in your recipe—many brands aren't rated for high-temperature baking.

Parchment paper: Parchment paper is an alternative to flour or cornmeal for preventing dough from sticking to the pizza peel as it's slid into the oven. Use a paper that's temperature-rated to withstand what's called for in your recipe. The paper goes along with the loaf, right onto the preheated stone, and can be removed halfway through the baking time to crisp up the bottom crust; otherwise the silcone coating on the paper prevents moisture transfer to the stone. Parchment paper can also be used to line baking sheets, Dutch ovens, and crock pots—this can substitute for greasing the sheet. Don't use products labeled as pastry parchment or butcher paper, and never use waxed paper—those will smoke, melt, or stick miserably to baked bread dough.

Baguette pan (metal or silicone): We usually bake French baguettes right on a stone, but metal or silicone baguette pans work nicely as an alternative, and can

help prevent sideways-spreading as they rise and bake. These pans are a great way to bake several beautifully shaped baguettes at once, without crowding. If you get the metal perforated version, use a sheet of parchment paper under the loaf to prevent our wetter-than-traditional dough from sticking to it. You won't need to do that with the silicone baguette pans.

Banneton/brotform: Wicker rising baskets (French = *banneton*, German = *brotform*) have long been favored by artisan bakers for the beautiful flour patterns they give the loaves, but we also found they are a great way to keep our soft doughs from spreading sideways while the loaves are rising. Smaller ones are the easiest to work with, preferably designed for one or one and a half pounds of dough (see Bavarian-Style Whole Grain Pumpernickel Bread, page 170).

Loaf pans: For sandwich loaves, we prefer smaller pans with approximate dimensions of 8½×4½ inches. With high-moisture dough, it can be difficult to get bigger loaves to bake through. This size pan is often labeled as holding 1 pound of dough, but we specify a more generous fill, to get taller slices—up to 2 pounds when the pan is filled three-quarters full.

Like baking sheets and silicone mats, loaf pans work well but don't promote the development of a crisp and beautifully colored crust—wherever the pan touches the bread, it's going to be pale compared to free-form loaves. One word of caution about loaf pans: When you're starting out with our wet doughs, use a pan with a nonstick coating, and even then, grease it. Traditional loaf pans (without the nonstick coating) are more challenging. We've had best success getting loaves to release from traditional uncoated pans when they're made from heavy-gauge aluminum or glazed ceramic—the thin ones don't do as well. Be sure to grease them well with butter or oil. And if you can't get a loaf to release from a loaf pan after loosening it with a spatula, wait ten minutes and the loaf will "steam" itself out.

Mini loaf pans: For smaller sandwich breads, and especially when baking with kids, it's fun to use mini loaf pans. They're sometimes labeled "number-1" loaf pans, measure about 6×3 inches, and take three-quarters of a pound of dough. The loaves bake faster than those in full-size loaf pans, so check for doneness sooner than called for when using them.

Brioche pans: Traditionally, brioche is baked either in a fluted brioche mold or in a loaf pan. Fluted molds are easy to find either online or in any baking supply store. They are available in several sizes, with or without a nonstick coating. Flexible silicone brioche molds are also available.

Bread knife: A serrated bread knife does a great job cutting through freshly baked bread without tearing or compressing it. Razor blades and French *lames* (lămm), are traditional and also work. With a bit of practice, you can use the lame to create artful designs in your crusts.

Kitchen shears or serrated steak knife: You'll need something to cut dough out of the storage bucket, and either of these works well. Shears are also handy for cutting pita bread, or even pizza, and you'll need a pair to cut the Pain d'Epí before baking (page 106).

Cooling rack: These are fashioned of wire or other thin metal and are usually intended for cake. They are very helpful in preventing the soggy bottom crust that can result when you cool bread on a plate or other non-porous surface.

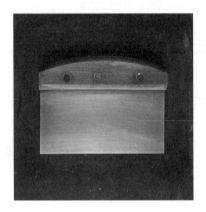

Dough scraper: The dough scraper (also called a bench scraper) makes it easier to work with wet dough, especially when you're just starting out. Without one, there'll be the temptation to use too much flour to prevent dough from sticking to the work surface. Keep our doughs wet by dusting lightly and scraping them off the work surface when they stick, rather than by working in additional flour. *Once you start making pizza and other rolled-out flatbreads, you really need to have one of these, because rolling them thin leads to sticking.* The scraper is also the easiest way to scrape excess cornmeal or flour off a hot baking stone. That's why we prefer the rigid steel scrapers over the flexible plastic ones—in part because you can't use plastic to scrape off a hot stone (be careful!).

Measuring cups: Avoid 2-cup measuring cups for flour, which are inaccurate when used with the scoop-and-sweep method specified in our recipes (pages 82–83). The 2-cup measures collect too much flour owing to excessive packing down into the cup. And be sure to use dry measuring cups for flour, which allow you to level off the flour by sweeping across the top of the cup with a knife; you can't level off a liquid measuring cup filled with flour.

Measuring spoons: Seek out a set that includes a half-tablespoon measure in addition to the usual suspects, which can be handy. If you can't find a ½-tablespoon measure, you can approximate a ½ tablespoon by using a rounded teaspoon, or, to be more exact, measure out 1½ teaspoons.

Pastry brush: These look like small paintbrushes, and are used to paint egg wash, water, or oil onto the surface of dough just before baking.

Scale: We love to weigh our ingredients rather than use measuring cups. It's faster and more accurate, and it's begun to catch on in the United States. Luckily, digital scales are getting cheaper all the time, so we now include weights for ingredients in all our dough recipes. Just press "tare" or "zero" after each ingredient is added to the dough vessel and you can use these scales without slowing down to do the arithmetic.

The scale is also a consistent way to measure out dough for loaves or flatbreads, but it isn't absolutely necessary because we also give you a visual cue for dough weight (for example, a grapefruit-size piece is 1 pound, and an orange-size piece is about ½ pound of dough).

Microplane zester: Microplane zesters or micro zesters are used for removing the zest from citrus fruit without including the bitter pith. In Chocolate Tangerine Bars (page 382), we use the coarse holes on an ordinary box grater to get a more assertive tangerine flavor.

Whisk: If you're not using a stand mixer, the best way to mix vital wheat gluten into the other dry ingredients before adding liquids is to use a wire or plastic whisk—the type intended for beating eggs. If you have a dough whisk, that works fine, too (see below). This is a crucial step for the doughs in this book that call for vital wheat gluten because whisking distributes the gluten and keeps it from clumping when the liquids are added. If use a stand mixer or dough whisk to make dough, you can use those to distribute the vital wheat gluten before adding liquids and you won't need the wire whisk. **Dough whisk:** Unlike flimsy eggbeating whisks, Danish-style dough whisks are made from strong non-bendable wire on a wood handle, and can be used to blend liquid and dry ingredients together quickly in the dough bucket. We find that they work faster and offer

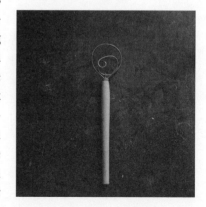

less resistance than a traditional wooden spoon (though a wooden spoon works fine). If you use one of these, you don't need a wire whisk to blend vital wheat gluten with the dry ingredients—just use the dough whisk.

Stand mixers—this is even easier than hand mixing: You can use a heavy-duty stand mixer, fitted with the paddle attachment (see photo), to speed mixing, and a 5-quart-capacity model will be large enough. **Note that some manufacturers call the paddle attachment the "flat beater."** So long as you're using a 5-quart-capacity mixer, we've found that the paddle/flat beater works better than the "dough hook" that manufacturers usually include—those are designed to simulate kneading (which we don't do), and they generally don't work well in our high-moisture dough. One complication: We found that in some high-capacity mixers—6 quarts or greater—the dough hook actually *does* work better, so experiment if you're having trouble getting your stand mixer to quickly incorporate the wet and dry ingredients with the paddle. Some readers have reported that especially with the larger mixers, dough can "climb up" the mixing attachment and avoid being mixed, or the dry ingredients pool at the bottom of the mixing bowl. If this happens, you can stop the mixer and scrape the dry ingredients into the dough, or briefly run the mixer on high.

Food processors: Also fast, but be sure that your food processor can handle a full batch of our dough, which weighs about 4 pounds and takes around 7 cups of flour—that means the food processor needs a capacity of about 14 cups, which is larger than most people have. Check with the manufacturer—if your machine doesn't have the capacity, mix a half batch at a time. Some food processors don't create a perfect seal at the bottom, so always add dry ingredients before liquids; otherwise it will leak a bit. Stop the machine as soon as the ingredients are uniformly mixed.

Immersion blenders are great for breaking up a lump of old dough, known in French as *pâte fermentée* (páht fair-mon-táy). Pâte fermentée can be used to jump-start the sourdough process in stored dough (see page 89). These blenders are also nice for breaking up pieces of whole tomatoes for pizza toppings. Be sure that the immersion blender is fully submerged in the liquid mixture before turning it on, otherwise you'll be spattered with ingredients. **Safety note:** Immersion blenders don't have a protective safety interlock, so it's possible to touch the sharp spinning blades while the unit is on. Be careful, and don't let children use an immersion blender.

Convection ovens: These produce a first-rate brown and crispy crust, and speed the baking time by circulating hot air around bread in the oven, which transfers heat more quickly. Convection can shorten baking time by about 15 percent in some ovens. Older convection models suggest lowering the temperature by 25 degrees to prevent over-browning, but many recent models make the correction automatically, so check your manual. In some, you'll need to turn the loaf around at the halfway point so that each side will brown evenly. Ignore convection oven instructions that suggest you can skip the preheat—the preheat is necessary for our method, especially if you're using a baking stone. As always, use an oven thermometer to check temperature; air circulation in convection ovens can "fool" thermostats in some ovens, sometimes driving the temperature up as much as 75 degrees.

These instructions apply only to range-based convection ovens, not microwaves with convection modes, which we have not tested. And never try to bake a loaf in a traditional microwave oven. It simply won't work.

4

TIPS AND TECHNIQUES

This chapter will help you perfect your whole grain breads made from our dough, with tips and techniques that will help you achieve breads with professional-quality crust (exterior) and crumb (interior).

Measuring Cups Versus Digital Scale?

Many readers of the first edition of this book asked us for weight measurements for every dough recipe, especially those outside the U.S., who commonly bake this way. So that's one of the major changes we've made—you won't need

conversion tables to weigh your ingredients, just read across the tables we provide and choose U.S. ounces or metric. Note that our recipes only require a fraction of an ounce of some ingredients (like salt and yeast). Since many scales for home use are accurate only to the nearest ⅛ of an ounce (3 or 4 grams), measuring small amounts this way can introduce inaccuracy—this becomes less important when measuring larger quantities for doubled recipes. **Unless you're confident of your scale's accuracy for very small amounts, or you're making a double batch or larger, measure salt and yeast with measuring spoons.**

CONVERSION TABLES FOR COMMON MEASURES

Volumes

U.S. Spoon and Cup Measures	U.S. Liquid Volume	Metric Volume
1 teaspoon	⅙ ounce	5 ml
1 tablespoon	½ ounce	15 ml
¼ cup	2 ounces	60 ml
½ cup	4 ounces	120 ml
1 cup	8 ounces	240 ml
2 cups	16 ounces	475 ml
4 cups	32 ounces	950 ml

U.S. and Metric Weight Conversion

U.S. Weight (Ounces)	U.S. Weight (Pounds)	Metric Weight
1 ounce	1/16 pound	28 grams
2 ounces	⅛ pound	56 grams
4 ounces	¼ pound	112 grams
8 ounces	½ pound	225 grams
16 ounces	1 pound	455 grams

Oven Temperature: Fahrenheit to Celsius Conversion

Degrees Fahrenheit	Degrees Celsius
350	180
375	190
400	200
425	220
450	230
475	240
500	250
550	288

Converting Recipes to 100% Whole Wheat

We've created a 100% whole wheat variation of our Master Recipe (page 81) that's a model for converting any of our recipes to 100% whole grain. Basically, whole wheat absorbs a little more water than all-purpose white flour. To convert recipes that use white flour into 100% whole wheat ones, just use an additional ¼ to ½ cup extra liquid and the recipe should work beautifully (the more whole wheat you're swapping in, the more water you'll need).

Omitting Vital Wheat Gluten

In the spirit of simplicity, we'll cut to the chase: the ¼ cup of vital wheat gluten that we use in the recipes absorbs about ½ cup of liquid. So if you omit vital wheat gluten in recipes calling for ¼ cup of it, you'll have to decrease the total liquids by about a half cup. The loaves won't rise as high, and they'll be denser, but they'll still be terrific. See page 12 for more on vital wheat gluten.

Too Salty? Not Salty Enough?

The recipes in the book were tested with Morton brand kosher salt (see page 26 for adjustments if you use other kinds of salt; it's the coarseness that varies). Readers of our first book will notice that the recipes in this, our health-oriented book, are less salty than they were in **Artisan Bread in Five Minutes a Day.** But you can adjust the salt to suit your own taste. If you find our recipes too salty, decrease the salt by 25 to 50 percent and see what you think. Below that threshold many people will find the bread flat-tasting. People accustomed to a low-salt diet can decrease the salt all the way to zero (or use potassium-based salt substitutes—see page 27).

If you find your bread to be too bland, you can adjust the salt upward by 25 to 50 percent, or up to 1½ tablespoons per 4- to 5-pound batch.

Can the Yeast Be Decreased?

Some experienced bakers prefer the more delicate flavor of a dough risen with less packaged yeast. Some traditionalists believe that rising the dough very slowly, with very little added yeast, builds better flavor. And if you really want to drop the packaged yeast, you can try our method with natural sourdough (see chapter 11, page 385).

We weren't convinced of this when we started writing bread cookbooks—many of our busy readers value the quicker rise that you get when you use the full amount of yeast that we call for in our recipes. And we think that our flavor is pretty darn good, especially when the dough ages a day or two.

But if you have more time, our recipes work beautifully with less yeast. We tested two ways, first halving the yeast (about ½ tablespoon), and then dropping it way down to ½ teaspoon for a whole batch. Both work, but they work slowly. For the ½-teaspoon version, you need to give the dough 6 to 12 hours for its initial rise in the bucket (4 to 5 hours for the ½-tablespoon version). But the 90-minute rest worked just as well for low-yeast dough as for high-yeast dough. *Active* time is still 5 minutes a loaf—it's just the passive rising time that escalates when you switch to the low-yeast version.

If you do this with egg-enriched dough, to be on the safe side, start your 2-hour rise on the counter and then finish in the refrigerator. The refrigerator rise will be very slow (see page 70). A long countertop rise could be risky due to spoilage of the eggs.

Dry Ingredients First?
Wet Ingredients First?

The reason our recipes always tell you to mix the flours, salt, yeast, and vital wheat gluten before adding any liquid is directly tied to the properties of vital wheat gluten—it clumps if it isn't distributed with the flour before it's hit with liquids. So, if you're making the variations without vital wheat gluten (see page 82), you can mix the traditional way, starting with the liquids and adding in yeast and the dry ingredients.

Dough Moisture Content:
How Wet Is Wet Enough?

Our recipes were carefully tested, and we arrived at the ratio of wet to dry ingredients with an eye toward creating a relatively slack and wet dough. But flours can vary in their protein content, the degree to which they're compacted into their containers, and in the amount of water they've absorbed from the environment. And environment changes; in most places, humidity will fluctuate over the course of the year. All of this means that our recipes may produce slightly variable results depending on humidity,

compaction, and the flour brand you're using. So you may have to adjust things—in the next batch, you can increase or decrease the water as needed.

If you find that your doughs are too stiff, especially if after storage they don't show good "oven spring" (the sudden rising seen soon after going into a hot oven), decrease the flour by ⅛ cup at a time in subsequent batches (or increase the water by a tablespoon). If they're too loose and wet, and don't hold a shape well for free-form loaves, increase the flour, again by ⅛ cup at a time.

You can vary the moisture level in our recipes based on your taste. Here's what you can expect:

If you modify a recipe, using . . .	
. . . more liquid or less flour (giving you wetter dough), you'll get . . .	. . . less liquid or more flour (giving you drier dough), you'll get . . .
Larger air holes and a desirable "custard" crumb (see below)	Smaller air holes, with denser crumb
Desirable "custard" crumb (interior, page 68); can become gummy if you go too far	Difficult to achieve custard effect; crumb will be drier
May be difficult for free-form loaf to hold shape, may spread sideways; will do well as flatbread or in loaf pans	Free-form loaves will hold shape well and remain high and domed
Requires less resting time before baking	Requires more resting time before baking

How to Mix More Flour (or Water) into Finished Dough

You can easily work a little more flour into dough that's too wet to shape easily, using your hands, a stand mixer, or a food processor (with dough attachment). Then allow the dough to rest again at room temperature for two hours to allow rising to occur again, otherwise you'll get dense loaves. If the dough's too dry, you can similarly work in some water, but you also need some flour to stimulate a new fermentation and rising since you'll be knocking all the gas out of the dough. Just use a little more water than you need, then add back some flour.

Sluggish Dough! Why Is It Taking So Long to Rise?

There are a number of possible explanations for a sluggish rise, but remember, this dough will continue to rise in the refrigerator during its storage time. So don't sweat about this. If you want to use the dough immediately after rising (before refrigeration), this may be more of an issue. Here are some things to try:

- **After mixing, just allow for a longer rise time before refrigeration:** So long as there's no egg or dairy in the recipe, you can go as long as necessary. If there are eggs or other perishables, you should complete the rise in the refrigerator after two hours on the counter.
- **Be sure you're using lukewarm, not cold water.**
- **If there are eggs in the recipe (such as in challah and, especially, in brioche), allow them to come to room temperature before using:** Egg doughs are where we get the most reports of a slow initial rise, because the cold eggs are cooling the dough mixture. The more eggs in a recipe, the more this is a problem.
- **If you're using active dry yeast, consider switching to "quick-rise" or "instant" yeast:** We've always said that our long storage method makes this unnecessary, but if you want to use the dough the day it's mixed, and room temperature is on the low side, this can make a difference.
- **Your yeast may be expired or otherwise inactive:** Though this is rarely the explanation, you can test your yeast with the old-fashioned "proofing" method. Mix a teaspoon of yeast with ¼ cup of lukewarm water and ½ teaspoon of sugar. If you don't see bubbles within 10 minutes, your yeast may be the problem.

STORING DOUGH TO DEVELOP FLAVOR

Our recipes are based on dough that can be stored for up to fourteen days in the refrigerator, depending on ingredients. That makes our method incredibly

convenient. But there's another benefit to storing the dough: Sourdough flavor develops over the lifespan of the batch, which means that your first loaves won't taste the same as your last ones. Some of our readers have taken to mixing staggered batches, so that they're never baking with brand-new dough.

How much to make and store: In order to have fresh-baked artisan bread with only five minutes a day of active preparation time, you'll want to make enough dough to last a week or more. Your initial time investment (mixing the dough) is the most significant one, though it generally takes no more than fifteen minutes.

By mixing larger batches, you can spread that investment over more days of bread making. So, we recommend mixing enough dough to last at least five to fourteen days (the limit is lower for egg-based and some other doughs). For larger households, that might mean doubling or even tripling the recipes. Choose a container large enough to accommodate the rising of the larger batch.

FLAVOR BOOSTERS

If you're finding that your loaves are a little bland-tasting, the easiest way to achieve richer flavor is to use a little leftover dough from the last batch in the new one (see Lazy Sourdough Shortcut, page 89). Another way to get this effect is to avoid baking newly mixed dough until it's aged for a few days and has had a chance to develop some sourdough flavor. Here are some things you can add to your dough that will bring out flavor in other ways:

- **More salt:** For this, our health-oriented book, we decided to go lighter on the salt, because some of our readers are on a low-salt diet. The default salt level in this book is 1 tablespoon of kosher (coarse) salt for approximately 4 pounds of dough. If you're finding that the flavor is bland, and your diet isn't salt-restricted, you can increase the salt to as much as 1½ tablespoons per 4-pound batch.
- **Whey:** Homemade cheese or yogurt makers can use leftover whey instead of water in our recipes. Experiment with how much, starting with about half whey and half water and see what you think.
- **Beer:** Yeasty flavors in beer can jump-start sourdough flavor. Don't worry about alcohol in the bread—virtually all of it boils off during baking.

What About Natural Sourdough?

Yes, it works with our method, and for the first time in our books we have developed a fast method for creating your own, to use instead of packaged yeast (or in concert with just a little). See chapter 11, page 385, for a full discussion of naturally fermented sourdough.

Can the Breads Be Made Vegan?

Most yeast breads are vegan. The exceptions are our enriched breads, which traditionally call for butter, eggs, and/or milk. Butter can be swapped out of recipes in many cases—see our long list of healthier (and vegan) oils listed on pages 28–29. Where we've used milk, you can swap soy, rice milk, almond milk, or water, but eggs are another story. Many of our readers have had success with egg replacers, but we've not tested them for this book.

Changes in the Dough Toward the End of Its Storage Life

Especially if you don't bake every day, you may find that toward the end of a batch's storage life, its entire surface darkens (or even turns gray) and it develops a more intense sourdough flavor; dark liquid may collect. None of this is mold or spoilage—don't toss it, just pour off the liquid, and work in enough flour to absorb excess moisture in the dough. Then rest the dough for two hours at room temperature before using. If you are not using it right away, refrigerate it again; you can keep it until the end of the dough's recommended life.

Discard any batch of dough that develops mold on its surface, which you can identify as dark or light patches, with or without a fuzzy appearance.

Strong Yeast or Alcohol Smell?

Some people detect a yeasty or alcohol aroma or flavor in the dough, and that's no surprise—yeast multiplies in dough, creating alcohol and carbon dioxide gas as it ferments sugars and starches. Alcohol boils off during baking, but our stored dough develops character from the by-products of yeast fermentation. Most people appreciate the flavor and aroma of this mild sourdough. But others want less of that, so here are some things to try:

- Always vent the rising container as directed, especially in the first two days of storage (see page 44). You can even drill a tiny hole in the lid to allow gas to escape.
- Consider a low-yeast version of our recipes (see page 56).
- Store your dough for shorter periods than we specify, freezing the remainder. Or make smaller batches so they're used up more quickly.

Freezing the Dough

Our dough can be frozen at any point in its batch-life, so long as the initial rise has been completed. It's best to divide it into loaf-size portions, then wrap it very well or seal it in airtight containers before freezing. Defrost overnight in the fridge when ready to use, then shape, rest, and bake as usual. How long you should freeze is partly a matter of taste—our dough loses some rising power when frozen and some people find the results dense if it's frozen for too long. That's especially true for enriched doughs, such as challah and brioche. Here are some basic guidelines for maximum freezing times:

- Lean dough (no eggs and minimal butter or oil): Four weeks
- Challah (see page 324): Three weeks
- Brioche (see page 343): Two weeks
- Gluten-free dough (see page 297): Two weeks

What Are "Lean" and "Enriched" Doughs?

"Lean" doughs are those made without significant amounts of eggs, fat, dairy, or sweetener. They bake well at high temperature without burning or drying out. Doughs "enriched" with lots of eggs, sweeteners, or milk (which contains milk sugar) require a lower baking temperature (and a longer baking time), because eggs and sweetener (especially in combination) can burn at high temperature.

Preparing the Pizza Peel—Grains or Parchment Paper?

Many of our recipes call for sliding the loaf off a pizza peel directly onto a hot baking stone. Cornmeal is the usual "lubricant," but it's only one of many options. We tend to use cornmeal on the peel for the more rustic, full-flavored loaves, and whole wheat flour for the more delicate breads with shorter resting times, like the

French baguette. Coarser grains like cornmeal are the most slippery, and fine-ground flours may require a heavier coating to prevent sticking (sometimes you'll have to nudge the loaves off with a metal spatula or dough scraper). Mostly though, the choice of grain on the pizza peel is a matter of taste. We've used Malt-O-Meal cereal or oatmeal in a pinch, and Zoë's mom once used grits. If you're really having trouble sliding loaves off a pizza peel prepared with grain, you can switch to parchment paper (see Equipment, page 46). Peel off the paper for the last third of the baking time to get a crisper bottom crust.

Sometimes a loaf, pizza, or flatbread will stick to the peel, especially if it has rested too long (pizzas in particular must go into the oven immediately after being topped). There's a simple solution. Before attempting a slide, we always shake the peel a bit to be sure that nothing is stuck. If it moves well on the peel, it will slide right onto the stone. If it's not moving well, sprinkle flour or cornmeal around the edge of the loaf and use a dough scraper to nudge some of it under the loaf, unsticking the stuck area. Now you should be able to slide the loaf easily into the oven. To prevent this, increase the amount of cornmeal or flour you're using under your loaves, or switch to parchment paper, which is fail-safe. This will also help if you're having trouble with smoking cornmeal on the stone or at the bottom of the oven. The paper slides into the oven with the bread.

Resting and Baking Times Are Approximate

All of our resting and baking times are approximate. Since artisan loaves are formed by hand, their size can vary from loaf to loaf (though you can weigh out the dough if you like). There can be significant changes in resting and baking time requirements with changes in loaf size. Although large flat loaves will rise and bake rapidly, large high-domed loaves will require dramatically longer resting and baking times. In general, flat or skinny loaves don't need much resting time, and will bake rapidly—pizza and many flatbreads need no resting time at all (for more on pizza and flatbread, see our book **Artisan Pizza** *and Flatbread in Five Minutes a Day*). Unless you're weighing out exact 1-pound loaves and forming the same shapes each time, your resting and baking times will vary, and our listed times should be seen only as a starting point. Here are some basic guidelines for varying resting and baking times based on what you're baking. **Increase resting and/or baking time if any of the following apply:**

- Your kitchen is cool: This only affects resting time, not baking.
- Larger loaf: A 3-pound loaf can also take nearly twice as long to bake, compared with a 1-pound loaf.
- You've overworked a loaf: This can happen if you spend too much time on the shaping step.

A good rule of thumb for resting time after shaping: If you want loaves to develop maximum rise and air holes, wait until the dough no longer feels dense and cold. A perfectly rested loaf will begin to feel "jiggly" when you shake it on its peel—like set Jell-O.

Not Much Rise While the Loaves Are Resting?

Compared with traditional doughs, our breads get more of their total rise from "oven spring" (sudden expansion of gases inside the loaf that occurs on contact with hot oven air and baking stone) and less from "proofing" (the resting time after a loaf is shaped, before baking). So don't be surprised if you don't see much rising during our resting step. You'll still get a nice rise from oven spring as long as you didn't overwork the dough while shaping. If you want to coax a little more rise during the resting period, try prolonging it (see Resting and Baking Times Are Approximate, page 64). And make sure your oven's temperature is

accurate by checking with a thermometer (see Equipment, page 42). If the oven is too cool or too hot, you won't get proper oven spring.

Are Your Loaves Spreading Sideways Rather than Rising Vertically?

Since our dough is wet, it's less structured than traditional dough. Even when loaves expanded well and had good air bubbles before baking, testers sometimes got free-form loaves that didn't hold their shape and spread sideways during baking rather than rising upward. The bread was delicious, but it couldn't make tall sandwich slices. The cause was often insufficient "gluten-cloaking," the stretching of the outside of the dough around itself during the shaping step. See chapter 5, step 4, and our videos on YouTube.com/BreadIn5, and be sure to use enough dusting flour when you shape loaves. If you continue to find that your loaves spread sideways, make sure you're using the right amounts of liquid and dry ingredients when you mix the dough, and that you're using a flour with adequate protein—not cake or pastry flour, which don't absorb water very well. Finally, you can dry out the dough by increasing the flour (start with ⅛ cup per batch)—see Dough Moisture Content, page 57.

And if your dough is nearing or exceeding the end of its storage life, when liquid is separating out from the dough and it's losing structure, consider using it for pizza or flatbread—those don't need much structure because they're flat in the first place and don't need to support the weight of a heavy loaf.

Oddly Shaped Loaves

The most common cause for oddly shaped loaves is inadequate resting after the shaping step. Be sure to let the shaped loaves rest long enough before baking—90 minutes for most of our recipes. Consider a longer resting time, especially if your environment is cool (see page 65) or your dough feels dry. If you're in a hurry, make baguettes (page 103) or flatbreads (chapter 8, page 261.)

Another cause of oddly shaped loaves, especially cracking along the bottom or bulging on the sides, is ineffective slashing. Slash at least ½ inch deep and keep the blade perpendicular to the crust. If you don't cut deeply enough, the bread will burst open oddly. View more tips by searching our YouTube channel (YouTube.com/BreadIn5) for "Slashing Dough."

If you haven't used enough cornmeal or flour on the pizza peel, a spot of dough may stick to it. As the loaf slides off the peel, the spot pulls, causing an oddly shaped loaf. Solution: Use more cornmeal or flour on the pizza peel, or switch to parchment paper, especially if the dough is particularly sticky. You can also add flour to the dough during the stretching and shaping step, which will require your loaf to rest longer before baking.

Finally, some readers have occasionally found that the edges of their loaves seemed to lift up off the stone, with an odd, almost bowl-like, rounded bottom crust. Turns out they weren't covering the shaped loaf with plastic wrap or a roomy, overturned bowl as it rested, and the top crust was drying out. That restricts expansion of the top crust, even if you've slashed (though deep slashing can help here). That dried-out, slightly shrunken top crust then literally pulls the bottom crust's edges off the stone—and there's some restriction in rise as well. In our first book (based mostly on white flour and calling for a very short resting time), you could get away with that. The loaves in this book, based on whole grains, generally need a 90-minute resting time, so they need to be covered after shaping.

How Long to Preheat the Baking Stone

Professionals sometimes suggest preheating the baking stone for an hour to absorb all the heat it possibly can, but we specify a shorter time in our recipes. Many of our readers expressed concern about wasted energy with a long preheat, not to mention the need for more advance planning. So we compromised— we know that some ovens will produce a better crust with a longer preheat, but we're pretty happy with the results we get at 30 minutes (even though many ovens equipped with a stone won't quite achieve target temperature that soon). If you find that the crust isn't as crisp as you like, or baking time is longer than expected, try increasing the preheating time to 45 or even 60 minutes. It's not essential but it can be useful, especially with a thicker stone.

Cast-iron or steel "stones" (see page 42) and ¼-inch-thick ceramic stones heat up faster than ½-inch-thick ceramic ones, so consider those if you're committed to the shortest possible preheat.

Baking Without a Stone

If you just don't have time to preheat a baking stone (or you don't have one), the next-best way to bake bread is a *heavy-gauge* aluminum baking sheet (see page 45). After shaping, set your bread to rest directly on the pan, which doesn't need to be preheated, but should be prepared with parchment paper, a silicone mat, butter, or oil. Your oven will only need a 10-minute preheat (or whatever your oven's manufacturer recommends).

What's "Custard" Crumb?

Perfectly baked high-moisture dough can produce a delightful "custard" crumb (interior). When mixed with water and then baked, wheat flour's protein, mostly gluten, traps the water and creates a chewy and moist texture, with air holes that have shiny walls. As you adjust flour amounts for your favorite recipes, you'll find that this is an effect you can manipulate. Too much flour, and you will lose the "custard" crumb character. Too little, and the dough will be difficult to shape and the crumb may be gummy.

What If the Loaves Are Dense?

If your bread is dense, doughy, or heavy, and has poor air-hole structure, read on. But before we start, let's talk about **expectations**. Homemade whole grain breads are denser than fluffy commercial breads, which are often laced with dough conditioners and other artificial ingredients. So don't expect the same loft and lightness.

1. Consider using our recipe versions that include vital wheat gluten: If you chose to omit vital wheat gluten (see chapter 5, page 80), and you're finding that the loaves are too dense, you may be happier with the versions that include vital wheat gluten—so make that switch.

2. Make sure that your dough is not too wet or too dry: Both extremes will result in a dense crumb. Some flours need a little extra water or you'll get a dry dough—see page 82 and page 92 for adjustments in the Master Recipe (versions with some white flour, and with none). If you're measuring flour by volume, make sure you are using the **scoop-and-sweep method** that we describe in chapter 5, step 1, page 82, and in our video (search our YouTube channel—YouTube.com/BreadIn5—for "How to Measure Flour"). And if you're getting inconsistent results, consider weighing the flour rather than measuring it with measuring cups (see Tips and Techniques, page 53).

3. Be quick and gentle when shaping loaves: We find that many bakers, especially experienced ones, want to knead the dough—but you can't do that with this kind of dough, or you will knock the gas out of it and the result will be a dense crumb. When shaping our doughs, you're trying to preserve air bubbles as much as possible—these bubbles create the holes in the bread. Shape your loaves in only 20 to 40 seconds. If you do overwork the dough, let it rest longer before baking.

4. Kitchen temperature, loaf size, and rest time: If your kitchen is much cooler than 68°F, you may need to let the dough rest for more time than specified in the recipe.

5. You may need to let the dough rise for longer than two hours. This is especially true if your kitchen is on the cold side, or if your ingredients were cold in the first place. Recipes that contain eggs can behave this way (the eggs can be allowed to come to room temperature to prevent this). If you're using the dough only after it's stored, you usually won't get this problem, because the dough will complete its initial rise in the refrigerator.

6. You may prefer longer-stored dough for pizza or flatbread: If you are using a dough that is nearing the end of its batch life, you may want to stick to pizza, pita, naan, or another option from the flatbread chapter (page 261), or from our third book, ***Artisan Pizza and Flatbread in Five Minutes a Day***. As the dough ages it produces denser results when you use it for loaves—many of our readers love it a little dense, but others use the older stuff for flatbreads. If you prefer your dough "younger," you can freeze it when it begins to produce denser loaves. Another option is to use overstored dough to start a new batch, using the *pâte fermentée* (páht fair-mon-táy) "old-dough" method (see Lazy Sourdough Shortcut, page 89). This will also jump-start complex flavors in your next batch.

7. Check your oven temperature with a thermometer: See Equipment, page 42; if your oven's temperature is off, whether too warm or too cool, you won't get proper "oven spring" and the loaf will be dense, with a pale or burnt crust.

8. Try the "refrigerator rise" trick: By using the refrigerator, you can shape your dough and then have it rise in the refrigerator for 8 to 14 hours. **First thing in the morning,** cut off a piece of dough and shape it as usual. Place the dough on a sheet of parchment paper, loosely wrap with plastic or cover it with an overturned bowl, and put it back in the refrigerator. **Right before dinner,** preheat your oven with a stone on a middle rack and take the loaf out of the refrigerator. You may find that it has spread slightly, and may not have risen much, but it will still have lovely oven spring. Because you don't handle the dough at all after the refrigerator rise, the bubbles in the dough should still be intact. A 30-minute rest on the counter while preheating is all you need. Then slash and bake as usual.

UNDERBAKING PROBLEMS

The crust is crispy when it comes out of the oven, but it softens as it comes to room temperature: This is most often a problem with very large breads, but it can happen with any loaf that's been slightly underbaked. Internal moisture, so high in wet dough, doesn't dissipate in underbaked bread, so it redistributes to the crust as the bread cools. You need to drive off that moisture with heat. As you gain experience, you'll be able to judge just how brown the loaf must be to prevent this problem with any given loaf size. We use brownness and crust firmness as our measure of doneness (there will be a few blackened bits on the loaf in non-egg breads). **If you have a crust that is initially crisp but softens as it cools, it can be returned to the oven until you achieve the desired result.**

The loaf has a soggy or gummy crumb (interior):

Don't slice or eat your loaves when they're still warm: We know, hot bread has a certain romance, so it's hard to wait for them to cool. But waiting will improve the texture—breads are at their peak two hours after they come out of the oven. Hot or warm bread cuts poorly and dries out quickly. When cool, loaves don't compress so easily when cut. Once the bread has cooled, use a sharp serrated bread knife, which will go right through the crisp crust and soft crumb.

Having said that, sometimes we just can't resist breaking into warm ones, especially with rolls or very small loaves where gumminess is less likely to be a problem.

- Check your oven temperature with a thermometer.
- Be sure that you're adequately preheating your stone and oven, and consider a longer preheat (page 67).
- Consider a longer baking time, but if the crust is browning more than you like, you can extend oven time with the heat turned to "Off."

Visit BreadIn5.com, where you'll find recipes, photos, videos, and instructional material.

- Make sure you are allowing the shaped loaf to rest before baking for the full time period we've recommended.
- Your dough may benefit from being a little drier. Increase the flour by ⅛ cup (or decrease the liquids a little) and check the result.
- If you're baking a large loaf (more than 1 pound), let it rest and bake longer.
- Be sure not to overwork dough when shaping, or you will compress the gas bubbles. If you think you've overworked the dough, let the loaf rest longer before baking.

The top crust won't crisp and brown nicely:

- Be sure you're using a baking stone where called for, and preheat it as recommended in the recipe, in an oven whose temperature has been checked with a thermometer.
- Bake with steam when called for. Use one of the methods described on page 40.
- Try the oven shelf switcheroo: If you're a crisp-crust fanatic, here's the ultimate approach for baking the perfect crust. Place the stone on the bottom shelf and start the loaf there. Two-thirds of the way through the baking time, transfer the loaf from the stone directly to the top rack of the oven (leave the stone where it is). Top crusts brown best on a high rack in the oven, and bottom crusts brown best near the bottom. This approach works beautifully with free-form loaves, but also helps crisp the crust of hard-crusted loaf-pan breads: Just pop the bread out of the pan before transferring to the top shelf—it makes a big difference. With this approach, you can permanently park your baking stone on the very lowest rack, where it will help even out the heat for everything you bake, not just bread. Then there'll be no need to shift around the stone or racks to accommodate your bread-baking habit.

Overbaking or Dryness Problems

Ounce for ounce, whole wheat flour has a little less gluten and a lot more fiber than white flour—both of which can make bread seem dry—but baking a moist loaf is just a matter of handling things right.

The crust is great, but the crumb (interior) is dry: We get this complaint primarily from people who are new to whole grain bread, are making the basic loaf in chapter 5 without any sweetener or oil, and using the lowest possible salt level (1 tablespoon per 4-pound batch). The first thing we suggest is adding in some of the "hygroscopic" (moisture-attracting) ingredients. Make the honey and oil variation of the Master Recipe (page 93) and you'll see what we mean. You can also increase the salt to up to 1½ tablespoons kosher salt for a 4- to 5-pound batch, because that's hygroscopic, too. And finally, making the versions that include vital wheat gluten also helps (gluten's hygroscopic). Other things to investigate:

- **Sometimes, the culprit in dry whole wheat bread is overbaking:** If you learned to bake by making white bread, you may have gotten used to a very firm crust, judging whether more baking time was needed by pressing the top crust. Whole grain breads don't get as firm, and some of our testers found that they were overbaking when they judged that way.
- **Oven temperature may be off:** Again, make sure your oven is calibrated properly, using an oven thermometer.
- **The dough was dry to begin with:** In traditional recipes, there's usually an instruction that reads something like "knead thoroughly, until the mass of dough is smooth, elastic, and less sticky, adding flour as needed." This often means too much flour gets added. Be careful not to work in much additional flour when shaping.

Flour blobs in the middle of the bread: Be sure to completely mix the initial batch. Using wet hands to incorporate the last bits of flour will often take care of this. The culprit is sometimes the shaping step—extra flour can get tucked up under and inside the loaf as it's formed. Use lots of dusting flour, but allow most of it to fall off.

Loaf-Pan Bread Stuck to the Pan

When making breads in a loaf pan using high-moisture dough, we recommend nonstick pans, but even then, we always coat with a thin layer of oil or butter. Wet dough tends to behave like glue during the resting/rising period for loaf-pan breads. Occasionally, a loaf will stick to a pan, but there's an easy way to get it out. After baking, simply wait about 10 minutes, and the loaf will steam itself free of the pan and you should be able to nudge it out easily. The crust that was in contact with the pan will be a bit moist and soft but it should dry out nicely, or you can put it back into the oven (out of the pan) for 3 to 5 minutes. Whatever you do, don't try to wrestle a hot loaf out of a stuck pan, or you'll end up tearing it.

What Is Dough Strength?

Gluten is "strengthened" and dough is made "strong" when the proteins align themselves into strands after water is added. Resilient, stretchy, gas-trapping gluten (with lined-up strands) can be formed in two ways:

- **The dough can be kneaded:** Not the way we like to spend our time. OR . . .
- **By using lots of water:** The gluten strands become mobile enough to *align themselves.*

Gluten alignment creates a protein network that traps gas bubbles and creates an airy crumb in the interior of bread. Without gluten (or something like it in gluten-free breads), loaves wouldn't rise; untrapped gas produced by yeast would just bubble out of the mixture.

Baking at High Altitude

There can be a big difference in how yeast behaves if you live much above 5,200 feet (1,585 meters). With less air pressure constraining the rising dough, it balloons up too quickly, and then collapses abruptly, giving you a dense crumb. The following adjustments can help you avoid that by slowing down the initial rise (the dough may not be ready for the refrigerator in the usual 2 hours):

- Decrease the yeast by half or even more (see page 56).
- Assuming you like the flavor and aren't on a salt-restricted diet, consider a saltier dough—salt inhibits fast yeast growth. You can increase to 1½ tablespoons of kosher (coarse) salt per 4- to 5-pound batch. And decrease sugar if there's any in the recipe—it feeds and stimulates yeast, which will speed up rising.
- Do the initial dough rise overnight in the refrigerator (see the refrigerator-rise trick, "Tips and Techniques," page 70), and consider mixing the dough using cold liquids (but allow for lots of rising time).

These techniques allow the dough to rise more slowly, giving it more time to achieve full height without collapsing.

How to Parbake Artisan Loaves

Parbaking means partially baking your loaves and finishing the baking later. Parbaked bread can even be frozen. The perfect opportunity for this approach? You are invited to your friends' home for dinner. Parbake the loaf at home and complete the baking in their oven—you'll be able to present absolutely fresh bread or rolls for the dinner party.

BAKING INSTRUCTIONS FOR PARBAKED BREAD:

1. Follow preparation steps for any recipe in this book.

2. Begin baking at the recipe's usual temperature.

3. Remove the loaf from the oven when it just begins to darken in color; the idea is to just set the center of the loaf. For most loaves, that means nearly 90 percent of the baking time.

4. Allow the loaf to cool on a rack, and then place in a plastic bag. Freeze immediately if you plan to wait more than half a day to finish baking.

TO COMPLETE THE BAKING:

1. If frozen, completely defrost the loaf, still wrapped, at room temperature. Unwrap the defrosted loaf, place it on a preheated baking stone or directly on the oven rack, and bake at the recipe's recommended temperature. Bake until browned and appealing, usually 5 to 10 minutes.

2. Cool on a rack as usual.

What's the Best Way to Store Baked Bread?

It's best to eat homemade bread on the day it's baked, because you won't be using any preservatives or chemical dough conditioners that delay staling. Once bread's been cut, we've found that best way to keep it fresher is to store it, cut side down, on a flat, non-porous surface like a plate or a clean counter-top. If you store it in foil or plastic, humidity will be trapped inside and the crust will soften, but you'll delay the inevitable drying-out process as bread goes stale. An exception is pita bread, which is supposed to have a soft crust and can be stored in a plastic bag or airtight container once completely cooled.

Breads made with whole grain flour and those made with dough that has been well aged stay fresh the longest. For the long-aged doughs, this works because by-products of fermentation are natural preservatives. Use stale bread for making bread crumbs in the food processor, recycle it into new loaves as *"altus"* (see sidebar, page 33), or use it in our recipe for Catalan Tomato Bread (*Pa amb tomàquet*) on page 115.

Baking on the Grill

For those hot summer days when you want fresh bread but can't stand the idea of turning on the oven, outdoor covered gas grills are one answer (or try slow cooker baking on page 98). When baking on a grill, thinner is better. Flatbreads are the easiest, but if you keep them skinny (like baguettes), loaf breads work, too. When you're first starting out with grilled breads, stick with lean doughs—they're more resistant to scorching. Once you get the knack of your grill's hot spots, you can broaden your repertoire.

1. **Form a free-form loaf (make it skinny and long) or an oblong-shaped flatbread with your favorite recipe.** Pay attention to the shape so it will fit between the gas grill burners and bake over *indirect* heat (the flames aren't right underneath the bread). If you keep it really thin (⅛ to ¼ inch thick), you don't need any resting time. And if you form an elongated flatbread so that it's narrow enough to fit mostly between the burner flames—then you can manipulate the amount of time the flatbread spends exposed to direct heat to get a little browning (but not too much).

2. **Preheat the grill** with burners set to high, but decrease to low just before placing the loaf right on the grates—between the gas grill burners so it isn't exposed to direct grill flames. Slash if you're doing a loaf bread.

Close the grill cover to retain heat. You may need to experiment with the heat setting—grill brands differ.

3. Open the grill in 4 to 15 minutes (depending on loaf thickness), **turn the loaf over,** and finish on the second side for another 4 to 15 minutes. You may need to briefly expose the loaf to direct heat in order to achieve browning.

If your grilled breads are burning, you can experiment with using a baking stone on the grill, which shields the loaf from scorching grill heat (cast-iron "stones" will be more crack-resistant on the grill). If you opt for a stone, you can achieve nice crust-browning with a moisture-trapping metal bowl or aluminum-foil roasting pan covering the loaf, but you'll probably still need to turn the loaf at the midpoint to get top-browning. Remove the bowl or pan for the last third of the baking time. You can also use covered cast-iron pots or cloches (see page 41) on the grill (preheat the top and bottom before putting the loaf in). If these scorch the bottom crust, line the pot or cloche with crumpled aluminum foil and use parchment paper between the loaf and the foil. Or, put a baking stone on the grill underneath the pot, to shield it from scorching heat. Bake two-thirds of the baking time closed, then uncover for the last third (but keep the grill cover closed).

5

THE MASTER RECIPE

A Whole Grain Artisan Free-Form Loaf

Our master recipe showcases a free-form loaf that's rich in whole wheat, shaped as an elongated oval, and topped with a delicious and nutritious seed mixture. By mixing dough in bulk without kneading, and baking loaves as they're needed, you'll truly be able to make this bread in five minutes a day of active preparation time (that is, excluding resting and oven time). Our standard loaf is over 70% whole grain, but you can make it with 100% whole wheat if you like (see page 91). If you're new to our whole wheat method, we recommend that you start with the 70% (standard) version that starts on the next page. Get used to working with this kind of dough before moving on to the 100% version (see page 91). And first time out, use the standard version **with** vital wheat gluten.

Our dough is stored for up to two weeks, and, over that time, it loses a bit of rising power and oven spring. Because of that, we found that many of our tasters preferred this bread with a little extra gluten—using a product called "vital wheat gluten," sometimes labeled "vital wheat gluten flour" (page 12). Vital wheat gluten helps whole grain doughs rise and produces a lighter loaf. If you can't find vital wheat gluten or prefer not to use it, we've given you information on how to adjust water depending on whether you're using vital wheat gluten or not (pages 12 or 82). Variations, starting on page 91, let you customize the loaves to your preferences: herbs, honey, oil, butter, sprouted wheat, Kamut (khorasan), or spelt flour are all delicious options, and this chapter shows you how to use them. It's just a matter of adjusting the water, and we tested with specific brands—so if you're using other brands, you'll have to experiment to re-create the consistency you get in our basic recipe made with Gold Medal whole wheat (or an equivalent like Pillsbury).

Our wet dough develops sourdough character during storage in the refrigerator, and that's the other fantastic advantage of making large stored batches. For the first time in our books, we've also included a fast and easy method for making authentic sourdough (it works with white flour, too). If you're willing to put in a little more time, you can have naturally fermented sourdough made the old-fashioned way—without packaged yeast (see page 385). But we strongly recommend that you get comfortable with the simpler method—packaged yeast—before you tackle natural sourdough.

This easy recipe and the variations that follow will give you the basic skills you need to complete the recipes in the rest of the book.

The Master Recipe

Makes enough dough for at least four 1-pound loaves. The recipe is easily doubled or halved.

Ingredient	Volume (U.S.)	Weight (U.S.)	Weight (Metric)
Gold Medal or Pillsbury whole wheat flour*	5¾ cups	1 pound, 10½ ounces	750 grams
All-purpose flour (see page 91 for 100% whole wheat version)	2 cups	10½ ounces	300 grams
Granulated yeast (can decrease to taste, see page 56)	1 tablespoon	0.35 ounce	10 grams
Kosher salt (can increase or decrease to taste, see page 56)	1 tablespoon	0.6 ounce	15 grams
Vital wheat gluten (see table page 82 to omit)	¼ cup	1⅜ ounces	40 grams
Lukewarm water (adjust based on flour choice*)	4 cups	2 pounds	910 grams
Cornmeal or parchment paper for the pizza peel			
1 to 2 tablespoons of whole seed mixture for sprinkling on top crust: sesame, flaxseed, caraway, raw sunflower, poppy, and/or anise (optional)			

*Some whole wheat flours require different total liquid amounts for this Master Recipe, shown in the chart on page 82**. For recipes that use different proportions of whole wheat flour, adjust water proportionally. **For best results when using flours other than Gold Medal or Pillsbury, it's best to weigh the flour, or the adjustments won't work as well.**

Total liquid amounts for various flours in this Master Recipe, with or without vital wheat gluten:		
Flour	Total Liquid (with vital wheat gluten)	Total Liquid (without vital wheat gluten)
Gold Medal or Pillsbury Whole Wheat	4 cups (2 lb./910 g.)	3½ cups (28 oz./795 g.)
King Arthur Whole Wheat	4¼ cups (34 oz./965 g.)	3¾ cups (30 oz./850 g.)
Bob's Red Mill Stone Ground Whole Wheat	4¼ cups (34 oz./965 g.)	3¾ cups (30 oz./850 g.)
Sprouted Wheat Flour: Arrowhead Mills brand	4¼ cups (34 oz./965 g.)	3¾ cups (30 oz./850 g.)
Kamut Flour: Bob's Red Mill Organic	3¾ cups (30 oz./850 g.)	3½ cups (28 oz./795 g.)
Spelt Flour: Bob's Red Mill		3¼ cups (26 oz./735 g.)
Hodgson Mill Stone Ground Whole Wheat	3½ cups (28 oz./795 g)	3¼ cups (26 oz./735 g.)

Mixing and Storing the Dough

1. **Measure the dry ingredients:** Use dry-ingredient measuring cups (avoid 2-cup measures, which compress the flour) to gently scoop the flour from a bin, then sweep the top level with a knife or spatula (or even

〜

Weighing your ingredients: We include weight equivalents for all our dough recipes, because many of our testers found it was easier to weigh ingredients than to use cup measures. Use a digital scale—they're becoming less expensive all the time. Simply press the "tare" (zeroing) button before adding an ingredient, then "tare" again to add the next ingredient. If you use any of the alternative flours, weighing is very important.

better, weigh your ingredients using the equivalents provided). Whisk together the flours, yeast, salt, and vital wheat gluten in a 5-quart bowl, or, preferably, in a resealable, lidded plastic food container or food-grade bucket (not airtight).

2. **Mix with water—kneading is unnecessary:** Warm the water until it feels slightly warmer than body temperature (about 100°F). Add all at once to the dry ingredients and mix without kneading—use a spoon, a dough whisk, a 14-cup food processor (with dough attachment), or a heavy-duty stand mixer (with paddle). If you're not using a machine, you might need to use wet hands to get the last bit of flour to incorporate. Using warm water will allow the dough to rise fully in about 2 hours. **Don't knead!** It isn't necessary. You're finished when everything is uniformly moist, without dry patches.

Visit BreadIn5.com, where you'll find recipes, photos, videos, and instructional material.

This step is done in a matter of minutes and will yield a dough that is wet and remains loose enough to conform to the shape of its container.

3. **Allow to rise:** Cover the dough with a lid (not airtight) that fits well to the container. If you are using a bowl, cover it loosely with plastic wrap. Lidded (or even vented) plastic buckets designed for dough storage are readily available (page 44); leave it open a crack for the first 48 hours to prevent buildup of gases; after that you can usually seal it. Allow the mixture to rise at room temperature until it begins to collapse (or at least flattens on the top), approximately 2 hours, depending on the room's temperature and the initial water temperature. Longer rising times, even overnight, will not harm the result, and if you're getting dense loaves, especially early in the batch-life, try 3 hours. After rising, refrigerate in the lidded (not airtight) container and use over the next 14 days. Fully refrigerated wet dough is less sticky and is easier to work with than dough at room temperature. So, the first time you try our method, it's best to refrigerate the dough overnight (or at least 3 hours) before shaping a loaf. Once refrigerated, the dough will have shrunk back upon itself. It will never rise again in the bucket, which is normal. Whatever you do, **do not punch down this dough.** With our method, you're trying to retain as much gas in the dough as possible, and punching it down knocks gas out and will make your loaves denser.

∽

WHAT WE *DON'T* HAVE TO DO: STEPS FROM TRADITIONAL ARTISAN BAKING THAT WE OMITTED

1. Mix a new batch of dough every time we want to make bread

2. Proof yeast

3. Knead dough

4. Rest/rise the loaves in a draft-free location—it doesn't matter.

5. Fuss over doubling or tripling of dough volume

6. Punch down and re-rise: ***Never*** punch down stored dough.

7. Poke rising loaves, leaving indentations to be sure they've proofed

Now you know why it only takes five minutes a day, not including resting and baking time.

On Baking Day

4. **Shape a loaf in 20 to 40 seconds.** First, prepare a pizza peel by sprinkling it liberally with cornmeal (or by lining it with parchment paper) to prevent your loaf from sticking to it when you slide it into the oven. Dust the surface of your refrigerated dough with flour. Pull up and cut off a 1-pound (grapefruit-size) piece of dough, using kitchen shears or a serrated knife. Hold the mass of dough in your hands and add a little more flour as needed so it won't stick to your hands. Gently stretch the surface of the dough around to the bottom, rotating a quarter turn as you go, to form a ball.

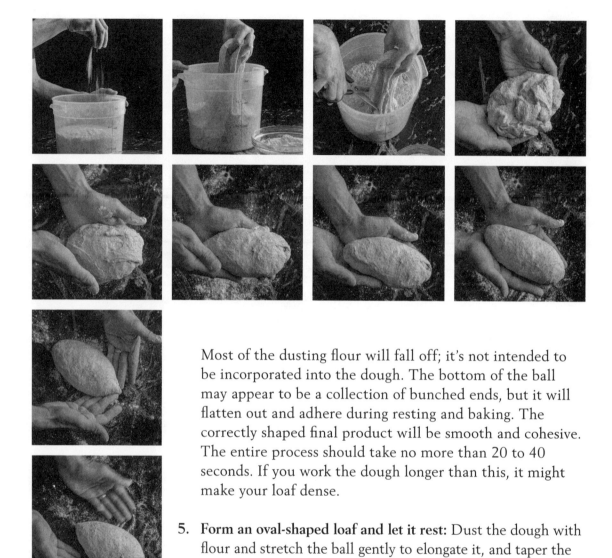

Most of the dusting flour will fall off; it's not intended to be incorporated into the dough. The bottom of the ball may appear to be a collection of bunched ends, but it will flatten out and adhere during resting and baking. The correctly shaped final product will be smooth and cohesive. The entire process should take no more than 20 to 40 seconds. If you work the dough longer than this, it might make your loaf dense.

5. **Form an oval-shaped loaf and let it rest:** Dust the dough with flour and stretch the ball gently to elongate it, and taper the ends by pinching them. For a really professional result, use the letter-fold method on page 102.

6. **Allow the loaf to rest,** loosely covered with plastic wrap or a roomy overturned bowl, on the prepared pizza peel for 90 minutes (40 minutes

if you're using fresh, unrefrigerated dough). Alternatively, you can rest the loaf on a silicone mat or on a greased cookie sheet without using a pizza peel. Depending on the age of the dough, you might not see much rise during this period; instead, it might spread sideways. More rising will occur during baking (oven spring).

7. **Thirty minutes before baking, preheat the oven to 450°F**, with a baking stone placed on a rack near the middle of the oven **(if you're not using a stone, the preheat can be short).** Place an empty **metal** broiler tray for holding water on any other rack that won't interfere with the rising bread. In step 9, you'll use the broiler tray to generate steam (see page 40 for steam alternatives).

> **Relax, you do not need to monitor doubling or tripling of volume as in traditional recipes. Our dough may not rise much after being shaped and rested, but when it goes into the oven you will see sudden rising ("oven spring").**

8. **Paint and slash:** Just before baking, use a pastry brush to paint the top with water. Sprinkle with the seed mixture if desired. Slash the loaf with ½-inch-deep parallel cuts crosswise across the top. Use a serrated bread knife held perpendicularly to the bread. View more tips by searching our YouTube channel (YouTube.com/BreadIn5) for "Slashing Dough."

> **The broiler tray *must* be metal:** Never use a glass pan to catch water for steam, or it will shatter!

⁊⁌

Why do we slash? When loaves undergo sudden "oven spring" upon contact with the hot stone and oven air, the expanding crumb can crack the crust in unattractive and uneven ways, or it can set early, preventing a full rise. Slashing ensures a beautiful, fully risen loaf.

9. **Baking with steam:** After a 30-minute preheat with the stone, you should be ready to bake, even though your oven thermometer might not yet be up to full temperature. For a crisper result, or if you're finding your loaves are underdone, preheat for as long as an hour. Place the tip of the peel a few inches beyond where you want the bread to land. Give the peel a few quick forward-and-back jiggles, then pull it sharply out from under the loaf. If you used parchment paper instead

of cornmeal, it will slide onto the stone with the loaf, and if you used a silicone mat or baking sheet, just place it on the stone. Quickly but carefully pour about 1 cup of hot water from the tap into the broiler tray and close the oven door to trap the steam. See safeguards on page 40 about water on oven glass, or use an alternative method to bake with steam, also on page 40). **Bake for about 30 minutes,** or until

Lazy Sourdough Shortcut: When your dough bucket is nearly empty, don't wash it. Immediately mix another batch in the same container. In addition to saving the cleanup step, you'll find that the bits of aged dough that remain stuck to the sides of the container will give your new batch a head start on sourdough flavor. Just scrape it down and it will hydrate and incorporate into the new dough. Don't do this with egg- or dairy-enriched dough; containers for those should be washed after each use.

Pâte fermentée: You can take that even further by adding a more sizable amount of old dough from your last batch. You can use up to 2 cups of old dough in the batch; just mix it with the water for your new batch and let it stand until it becomes soupy before you start mixing the new recipe, right on top of it (if the recipe calls for vital wheat gluten, whisk it into the flour before adding to the liquid). An immersion blender can be particularly helpful for blending the old dough with water. Add this mixture to your dry ingredients as in the recipe. Professionals call the old dough that you add to a new batch *pâte fermentée* (paht fair-mon-táy), which means nothing more than "fermented dough." **See safety note on immersion blenders, pages 50–51.**

the crust is richly browned and firm to the touch (smaller or larger loaves will require adjustments in baking time). If you used parchment paper, a silicone mat, or a cookie sheet under the loaf, carefully remove it two-thirds of the way through the baking time and bake the loaf directly on the stone or on an oven rack. When you remove the loaf from the oven, it may audibly crackle, or "sing." Allow the bread to cool completely, preferably on a wire cooling rack, for best flavor, texture, and slicing; this may take up to two hours. The crust may initially soften, but will firm up again when cooled (see cover photo).

10. **Store the remaining dough in the refrigerator in your lidded (not airtight) container and use it over the next 14 days.** You'll find that even 24 hours of storage improves the flavor and texture of your bread. The dough continues to ferment and will take on sourdough characteristics. **The dough can also be frozen**—wrap it well or place in an airtight container (see page 63 for guidelines on freezing time).

VARIATION: 100% Whole Wheat Master Recipe

Swap this table into the Master Recipe on page 79 for a 100% whole wheat version, but limit refrigerator storage to 5 days or you may find that the loaves are too dense. Vital wheat gluten can be omitted (see variation below). One-hundred-percent whole wheat dough may spread sideways more than you like. If so, use a loaf pan. If your kids resist 100% whole grain bread, try it with a little sweetener and oil (see variation on page 93).

Ingredient	Volume (U.S.)	Weight (U.S.)	Weight (Metric)
Gold Medal or Pillsbury Whole Wheat*	7⅔ cups	2 pounds, 3 ounces	1,000 grams
Granulated yeast (can decrease to taste, see page 56)	1 tablespoon	0.35 ounce	10 grams
Kosher salt (can increase or decrease to taste, see page 56)	1 tablespoon	0.6 ounce	15 grams
Vital wheat gluten (see table below to omit)	¼ cup	1⅜ ounces	40 grams
Lukewarm water (adjust based on flour choice*)	4¼ cups	2 pounds, 2 ounces	965 grams
Cornmeal or parchment paper for the pizza peel			
1 to 2 tablespoons of whole seed mixture for sprinkling on top crust: sesame, flaxseed, caraway, raw sunflower, poppy, and/or anise (optional)			

*Some whole wheat flours require different total liquid amounts for this Master Recipe, shown in the chart on page 92. You can use these guidelines to adjust the total liquids in other 100% whole wheat recipes in the book. For best results when using flours other than Gold Medal or Pillsbury, it's best to weigh the flour, or the adjustments won't work as well.

Total liquid amounts for various flours in this Master Recipe, with or without vital wheat gluten:		
Flour	Total Liquid (with vital wheat gluten)	Total Liquid (without vital wheat gluten)
Gold Medal or Pillsbury Whole Wheat	4¼ cups (34 oz./965 g)	3¾ cups (30 oz./850 g)
King Arthur Flour Whole Wheat	4¼ cups (34 oz./965 g)	3¾ cups (30 oz./850 g.)
Bob's Red Mill Stone Ground Whole Wheat	4¼ cups (34 oz./965 g)	3¾ cups (30 oz./850 g.)
Sprouted Wheat Flour: Arrowhead Mills brand	4 cups (2 lbs./910 g)	3½ cups (28 oz./795 g)
Kamut Flour: Bob's Red Mill Organic	4 cups (2 lbs./910 g)	3½ cups (28 oz./795 g)
Spelt Flour: Bob's Red Mill	4 cups (2 lbs./910 g)	3½ cups (28 oz./795 g)
Hodgson Mill Stone Ground Whole Wheat	3½ cups (28 oz./795 g)	3¼ cups (26 oz./735 g)

VARIATION: Honey Whole Wheat

Honey whole wheat is a standard American loaf, loved even by finicky eaters who object to whole grains. That's because the sugar in honey acts as a tenderizer, and the mellow sweetness of honey acts as a perfect foil to the slight bitterness of whole wheat.

Best of all, it's a simple variation: Just put ½ cup honey into the measuring cup for the water in step 2, then top it off to the required amount of water, decrease the baking temperature to 350°F, and increase the baking time to 45 minutes.

VARIATION: Oil and Sweetener, the Tenderizing Team

If your family shies from whole wheat bread because they like the softness and tenderness of white bread, here's the solution. A small amount of oil (or melted butter) plus sweetener tenderizes any whole grain bread. Just put 2 tablespoons each of oil (or melted unsalted butter) and honey into the measuring cup for the water in step 2, then top it off to the required amount of water. Baking time and temperature remain the same. Sugar will work as well as honey (but adds no flavor boost); you can add 2 tablespoons with the dry ingredients.

VARIATION: Naturally Fermented Sourdough (Levain) for Leavening

Our stored dough develops some of the character of sourdough as it ages. But if you have a hankering for authentic sourdough, made without packaged yeast, you can try our natural sourdough *levain*—instructions start on page 385. But try the basic yeast version here in chapter 5 before you try this—it's a bit more complicated, and we want you to understand what our dough looks like before you move on to the world of natural sourdough.

VARIATION: Herb Bread

This simple recipe shows off the versatility of our approach. Herb-scented breads are great favorites for appetizers and snacks. Follow the directions for mixing the Master Recipe dough and add 1 teaspoon dried thyme leaves (2 teaspoons fresh) and ½ teaspoon dried rosemary leaves (1 teaspoon fresh) to the water mixture. You can also use herbs with the other bread recipes in this chapter. This also works with sliced olives, chopped garlic, onions, seeds, nuts, or any other of your favorite ingredients.

Moon and Stars Bread (with Sesame Seeds)

"I've made this bread for my family when we're on vacation in the country and have the time and open spaces to notice the night sky. But out in the country, a full moon is a special cause for excitement. Granted, this loaf is really a crescent moon, not a full moon, but it's a pretty dramatic shape, with lots of crisp crust formed at the edge from the cuts, and sesame seeds for stars (see color photo)."—Jeff

Makes one 1-pound loaf

1 pound (grapefruit-size portion) Master Recipe dough (page 79)
Sesame seeds for sprinkling on top crust
Cornmeal, parchment paper, or silicone mat for the pizza peel

1. **On baking day,** dust the surface of the refrigerated dough with flour and cut off a 1-pound (grapefruit-size) piece. Dust the piece with more flour and quickly shape it into a ball by stretching the surface of the dough around to the bottom, rotating the ball a quarter turn as you go. Stretch the ball gently to elongate it, and taper the ends by rolling them between your palms and pinching them (or use the letter-fold method for a really professional result, page 103). Bend it into a semicircle—this will become your moon shape.

2. Allow the loaf to rest and rise on a pizza peel prepared with cornmeal or lined with parchment paper for 90 minutes (40 minutes if you're using fresh, unrefrigerated dough), loosely covered with plastic wrap or an overturned bowl. Alternatively, you can rest the loaf on a silicone mat or a greased cookie sheet without using a pizza peel.

3. **Thirty minutes before baking time, preheat the oven to 450°F,** with a baking stone placed on the middle rack. Place an empty metal broiler tray for holding water on any other rack that won't interfere with the rising bread.

4. Just before baking, use a pastry brush to paint the top with water, and sprinkle with the sesame seeds. Then use kitchen shears to snip 1- to 2-inch-deep cuts into the bread on the outside of the curve (see photo). There is no need to slash this loaf.

5. Slide the loaf directly onto the hot stone (or place the silicone mat or cookie sheet on the stone if you used one). Pour 1 cup of hot tap water into the broiler tray and quickly close the oven door (see page 40 for steam alternatives). Bake for about 30 minutes, or until richly browned and firm. If you used parchment paper, a silicone mat, or a cookie sheet under the loaf, carefully remove it and bake the loaf directly on the stone or on an oven rack two-thirds of the way through the baking time. Smaller or larger loaves will require adjustments in resting and baking time.

6. Allow the bread to cool on a rack before slicing.

Hearty Whole Wheat Sandwich Loaf

For our money, the best artisan loaves are shaped free-form and baked directly on a stone—the result is super-crusty. But, especially for children, sometimes a sandwich loaf is exactly what's needed. So here's a basic sandwich loaf from the whole grain master recipe. For this loaf, we especially like the Honey Whole Wheat variation (page 92) or the Oil and Sweetener version (page 93). Correct baking temperature as directed in the variation that you're using.

Makes one 2-pound loaf

2 pounds (cantaloupe-size portion) Master Recipe dough (page 79)

1. **On baking day,** lightly grease an 8½×4½-inch nonstick loaf pan. Dust the surface of the refrigerated dough with flour and cut off a 2-pound (cantaloupe-size) piece. Dust with more flour and quickly shape it into a ball by stretching the surface of the dough around to the bottom, rotating the ball a quarter turn as you go.

2. **Elongate the ball into an oval** and place it into the loaf pan; your goal is to fill the pan about three-quarters full. Cover loosely with plastic wrap or an overturned bowl. Allow the loaf to rest and rise for 1 hour and

45 minutes (60 minutes if you're using fresh, unrefrigerated dough). Don't be surprised if your dough doesn't rise much during the rest. That's normal for our dough, but you should see nice "oven spring."

3. **Thirty minutes before baking time, preheat the oven to 450°F,** with a baking stone placed on the middle rack. Place an empty metal broiler tray for holding water on any other rack that won't interfere with the rising bread. The baking stone is not essential for loaf-pan breads; if you omit it, the preheat can be as short as 5 minutes.

4. Just before baking, use a pastry brush to paint the top with water. Slash the loaf diagonally with ½-inch-deep parallel cuts, using a serrated bread knife. If you don't mind some irregular fracturing, you can skip the slashing when you bake in a loaf pan. The pan contains and controls the dough as the top crust develops random cracks—we think it's a beautiful effect.

5. Place the loaf on a rack near the center of the oven. Pour 1 cup of hot tap water into the broiler tray and quickly close the oven door (see page 40 for steam alternatives). Bake for 40 to 45 minutes, or until brown and firm.

6. Remove the loaf from the pan and allow it to cool completely on a rack before slicing or eating. If the loaf is difficult to remove, despite going around the edge with a spatula, allow it to sit in the pan for 10 minutes. The heat of the loaf will "steam" the stuck loaf right out. If the crust seems soft or overly damp where it was in contact with the pan, you can return it to the oven, out of the loaf pan, for about 5 minutes, to crisp the crust.

7. Allow the bread to cool on a rack before slicing.

Crock Pot Bread (Fast Bread in a Slow Cooker)

Over the years we've had requests for a method for baking our dough in an electric crock pot (slow cooker). **Bread in a crock pot? We had our doubts, lots of them.** We didn't think a slow cooker could get hot enough; thought it would take too long; didn't think it would bake through or have a nice crust. So we resisted trying it, convinced it would fail. **Oh, how wrong we were.** You don't have to preheat an oven, and your second rest/rise takes place right in the pot, so it's super-convenient for summer and holiday baking. The crock pot does indeed get hot enough, and it works. Straight out of the pot, the crust is soft and quite pale, but just a few minutes under the broiler and you have a gorgeous loaf. In the summer there is no need to heat up the oven to get great bread, and at the holidays it is a perfect way to free up much needed oven space. You could even amaze your friends at work by baking a loaf under your desk.

Makes 1 loaf

1 pound (grapefruit-size portion) Master Recipe dough (page 79)
Flour for dusting
Parchment paper for baking

∽

Check with your crock pot's manufacturer's instructions before trying this:
Some models' instructions specify that the crock pot has to be at least partially filled with a liquid to avoid safety or durability problems—which would mean that those manufacturers are saying you shouldn't use their product for bread baking. And never bake bread in an unattended crock pot.

1. **On baking day,** dust the surface of the refrigerated dough with flour and cut off a 1-pound (grapefruit-size) piece. Dust with more flour and quickly shape it into a ball by stretching the surface of the dough around to the bottom, rotating the ball a quarter turn as you go. Place it on a rectangular sheet of parchment paper.

2. Lower the dough into a 4-quart crock pot or other slow cooker. Be sure to follow the manufacturer's instructions for proper use.

3. Turn the temperature to high and put on the cover. **(Not all crock pots behave the same, so you should keep an eye on the loaf after about 45 minutes to make sure it is browning but not overbrowning on the bottom.**

4. Bake for 1 hour (this will depend on your crock pot; you may need to increase or decrease the time). **To check for doneness,** it should feel firm when you gently poke the top of the loaf.

5. The bottom crust should be nice and crisp, but the top of the loaf will be quite soft. For people who prefer a softer crust, this is a plus. But if you want a darker or crisper crust . . .

6. Remove the parchment paper and place the bread under the broiler for 5 minutes or until it is the color you like, with the rack positioned in the middle of the oven.

7. Allow the bread to cool on a rack before slicing.

Whole Grain Garlic Knots with Parsley and Olive Oil

Olive oil is our favorite oil flavor, and here's a recipe that really showcases it. It's rich in healthy monounsaturated fat, and olive oil is an authentically Italian way to enrich bread. Combined with parsley, garlic, and Parmigiano-Reggiano cheese, it's the essence of the Mediterranean.

Makes 5 garlic knots

1 pound (grapefruit-size portion) Master Recipe dough (page 79)
¼ cup (2 ounces/55 grams) extra-virgin olive oil
½ cup finely minced fresh flat-leaf parsley
4 garlic cloves, finely minced
2 tablespoons grated Parmigiano-Reggiano cheese

∽

Garlic: Eat this and you won't just ward off werewolves—garlic is full of calcium, potassium, and vitamin C. **Parsley** is a Mediterranean herb that's high in vitamins A, C, and K, as well as folic acid.

1. In a skillet, sauté the parsley and garlic in olive oil for about 4 minutes over medium heat, until the garlic is soft and the mixture is aromatic. Add more olive oil if mixture looks too dry, because you'll need to be able to drizzle this over the knots.

2. **On baking day,** dust the surface of the refrigerated dough with flour and divide the dough into 3-ounce pieces (about the size of small peaches). Dust each one with more flour and quickly shape into a ball by stretching the surface of the dough around to the bottom, rotating each ball a quarter turn as you go.

3. Elongate each ball into a rope a little less than ½ inch in diameter, and tie it into a knot. Allow the knots to rest for 30 minutes, loosely covered with plastic wrap or an overturned bowl, on an olive oil–greased cookie sheet, or a cookie sheet lined with a silicone mat or parchment paper.

4. **Preheat the oven to 425°F.** Place an empty metal broiler tray for holding water on any other rack that won't interfere with the rising knots.

5. Drizzle the knots with three-quarters of the olive oil, garlic, and parsley mixture. Sprinkle grated cheese over the knots.

6. Place the cookie sheet in the oven, pour 1 cup of hot tap water into the broiler tray, and quickly close the oven door. Bake for about 25 minutes, or until browned and firm. Drizzle the remaining olive oil mixture over the hot knots.

7. Serve slightly warm.

French Shapes Based on the Letter-Fold

We covered French bread shapes in our first book, but we were pretty laissez-faire about technique. Let's face it—most days, it just doesn't matter if the shape is perfect. You can continue to make baguettes and *ficelles* by simply elongating an oval of dough and rolling it between your palms to thin it out (the ends may be a bit knobby, but the taste will be scrumptious). But here's a more polished, professional loaf that will look just like the ones in the pictures. In addition to using this technique for the skinny baguettes and ficelles, you can use it to get professional tapered ends with your basic oval loaves, such as in the Master Recipe (page 79).

French Breads: Baguettes and Ficelles with Beautiful Tapers

Baguettes (see color photo) are a universal symbol of French artisan bread, and ficelles (fee-séll) (see color photo) are nothing more than really skinny baguettes. They're not at all hard to make, and using the letter-fold technique makes a big difference in getting a professional look. What's the difference between a baguette and a ficelle? Ficelles are just skinnier and crustier—almost a bread stick.

Makes 1 baguette or 2 ficelles

½ pound (orange-size portion) Master Recipe dough (page 79)
Egg white wash (1 egg white mixed with 1 teaspoon water)

1. **Thirty minutes before baking time, preheat the oven to 450°F,** with a baking stone placed on the middle rack. Place an empty metal broiler tray on any other rack that won't interfere with the rising bread.

2. Dust the surface of the refrigerated dough with flour and cut off a ½-pound (orange-size piece) for a baguette, and about half that for a ficelle. Dust the piece with more flour and quickly shape it into a ball by stretching the surface of the dough around to the bottom, rotating the ball a quarter turn as you go.

3. Gently stretch the dough into an oval. Fold the dough in thirds, like a letter. Bring in one side and gently press it into the center, taking care not to compress the dough too much.

4. Bring up the other side and pinch the seam closed. The letter-fold technique puts less dough into the ends and that's what gives you the nice taper.

5. Stretch very gently into a log, working the dough until you have a thin baguette. Don't compress the air out of the dough. If the dough resists pulling, let it rest for a moment to relax the gluten, then continue to stretch. Don't fight the dough. You can continue to stretch the dough during the 40-minute rest, until you achieve the desired thin result. The final width for a baguette should be about 1½ inches; for a ficelle, ¾ inch.

6. Allow the loaf to rest, loosely covered with plastic wrap or an over-turned bowl, on a pizza peel prepared with cornmeal or lined with parchment paper for 40 minutes (or just 20 minutes if you're using fresh, unrefrigerated dough). Alternatively, you can rest the loaf on a silicone mat, a greased cookie sheet, or perforated baguette pan without using a pizza peel.

7. Just before baking, use a pastry brush to paint the loaf with egg white wash or water. Slash the loaf with 3 slightly diagonal cuts ¼ inch deep, using a serrated bread knife.

8. Slide the loaf directly onto the hot stone (or place the silicone pad, cookie sheet, or baguette pan on the stone if you used one). Pour 1 cup of hot tap water into the metal broiler tray, and quickly close the oven door (see page 40 for steam alternatives). Bake for about 25 minutes for a baguette, or 15 to 20 minutes for a ficelle, until richly browned and firm.

9. Allow the bread to cool on a rack before slicing.

A Fancy French Bread: Pain d'Epi

If you start with a letter-folded baguette (page 103), you can create an *epi* (wheat stalk–shaped bread) with perfectly tapered "grains" of wheat that are the hallmark of this loaf (see color photo). This classic French shape is impressive and somewhat intimidating, until you see how easy it is to make. We love *pain d'epi* not only for its gorgeous appearance but also because it's the crustiest loaf there is. All of those cuts and angles offer more surface to crisp in the oven. It's a little more sophisticated to serve with dinner than ordinary rolls, and believe it or not, it's even easier to make.

Makes 1 pain d'epi

½ pound (orange-size portion) Master Recipe dough (page 79)
Parchment paper for lining the pizza peel

1. **Thirty minutes before baking time, preheat the oven to 450°F,** with a baking stone placed on the middle rack. Place an empty metal broiler tray on any other rack that won't interfere with the rising bread.

2. Dust the surface of the refrigerated dough with flour and cut off a ½-pound (orange-size) piece. Dust the piece with more flour and quickly shape it into a ball by stretching the surface of the dough around to the bottom, rotating the ball a quarter turn as you go.

3. To form the *epi*, gently stretch the dough into an oval. Fold the dough in thirds, like a letter. Bring in one side and gently press it into the center (see page 103).

4. Bring up the other side and pinch the seam closed. This will help you produce tapered ends.

5. Stretch very gently into a log, working the dough until you have a nice thin baguette about 1½ inches in diameter (see page 104). If the dough resists pulling, let it rest for a moment to relax the gluten, then continue to stretch. Don't fight the dough.

6. Lay the baguette on the edge of a prepared pizza peel. For the *epi*, parchment paper is preferred because it will allow the formed loaf to slide into the oven with a minimum of distortion and sticking. Allow the loaf to rest, loosely covered with plastic wrap or an overturned bowl, for 40 minutes (or just 20 minutes if you're using fresh, unrefrigerated dough).

7. Dust the loaf with flour and then, using kitchen shears and starting at one end of the loaf, cut into the dough at a very shallow angle. If you cut too vertically, the "wheat grains" won't be nice and pointy. Cut with a single snip all the way down to ¼ inch from the cutting board, but be careful not to cut all the way through the dough or you'll end up with individual rolls. Kitchen shears with long blades are best for this task.

8. Lay each piece that you've cut over to one side, alternating sides with each cut. Continue to cut in this fashion until you've reached the other end.

9. Slide the loaf directly onto the stone, parchment and all. Pour 1 cup of hot tap water into the metal broiler tray, and quickly close the oven door (see page 40 for steam alternatives). Bake for about 25 minutes, or until richly browned and firm. Peel off the parchment paper and finish the loaf directly on the stone or on an oven rack two-thirds of the way through the baking time.

10. Allow the bread to cool on a rack before serving.

The Easiest French Breads: Boule or Couronne

These are the easiest French shapes because they're basically just balls of dough: If you stop at the ball stage, that's a *boule* (pronounced *bool;* see color photo). If you poke your thumbs through and stretch a bit, you get a *couronne*, the crown-shaped bread of Lyon, France (if truth be told, it resembles a large bagel; see color photo). Use your hands to stretch the hole open so that it's about triple the width of the wall of the ring. Rest and bake the boule as for the Master Recipe (see color photo). For the couronne, follow resting and baking instructions for the baguette (page 105).

Wreath Bread

This is a gorgeous loaf to make during the holiday season (enriched breads from chapter 10 are a great option for this loaf; adjust the baking temperature as needed). Start with a *couronne* (page 109), and then make cuts as for the *pain d'epi* (page 106) all the way around (but always deflect the cut points to the **outside** of the circle), to create a festive wreath shape with dramatic points.

Soft Dinner Rolls, Brötchen, Baguette Buns, and Cloverleaf Rolls

Rolls are a delight to bake and they're adorable (see color photo). They're small, so they need very little resting time before they go into the oven. And they don't have to cool completely like larger loaves do—it's okay to eat them slightly warm. You can make any of the following recipes with the Master Recipe, or try these easy shapes with other lean doughs, or even the enriched challah (page 324) or brioche (page 343) doughs, which yield softer rolls. Be sure to decrease the oven temperature to 350°F when using egg-enriched dough, and increase the baking time about 25 percent.

Makes five 3-ounce rolls

1 pound (grapefruit-size portion) Master Recipe dough (page 79) or Egg
    White–Enriched Brötchen dough (see sidebar, page 113)
All-purpose flour for dusting
Egg white for glazing brötchen
Melted unsalted butter or oil for brushing dinner rolls
Unsalted butter, oil, or parchment paper for the baking sheet

Soft Dinner Rolls

1. **Preheat a baking stone near the middle of the oven to 450°F (20 to 30 minutes).**

2. Cut off 3-ounce (small peach-size) pieces of Master Recipe dough and quickly shape into balls. Allow to rest, 2 inches apart, on a baking sheet lined with parchment paper or a silicone mat for 20 minutes.

∽

To make soft pull-apart rolls: Cut off a 1-pound (grapefruit-size) piece of challah (page 324) or brioche (page 343), then divide the dough into 8 pieces and quickly shape them into balls. Place the dough balls in a greased 8×8-inch baking dish; they should be touching. Rest for 30 minutes. Preheat the oven to 350°F. Brush the tops of the rolls with melted butter before and after baking. Bake for about 30 minutes, or until golden brown. Serve slightly warm.

3. Cut a cross into the top of each roll, using a serrated knife or kitchen shears and keeping the shears perpendicular to the work surface when you cut.

4. Brush the tops with melted butter or oil and place the baking sheet in the oven. Bake for about 25 minutes, or until richly browned.

5. For the softest result, brush with more butter or oil when they come out of the oven. Serve slightly warm.

Brötchen (bro-chin)

On our website, people asked for German-style hard rolls, so we've included the most common: *brötchen* (German for "little bread"). They're traditionally made from dough enriched with egg whites, and then brushed with more egg white before baking at high temperature with steam. The egg white creates an incredible crust and crumb—see the sidebar (page 113) for an easy variation that turns the Master Recipe into brötchen dough for superb hard rolls.

*Master Recipe, 100% Whole Wheat Version with Vital Wheat Gluten
and without Vital Wheat Gluten (cross) page 79*

Moon and Stars Bread (with Sesame Seeds), page 94

Clockwise from top left: Whole Wheat Brioche, page 343, Ten-Grain Bread, page 164, Master Recipe, page 79, 100% Whole Grain Maple Oatmeal Bread, page 205, Bran Muffin Bread, page 340, Betsy's Seeded Oat Bread, page 208

Crock Pot Bread (Fast Bread in a Slow Cooker), page 98

Whole Grain Garlic Knots with Parsley and Olive Oil, page 100

Baguette, page 103, Garlic- or Tomato-Studded Baguette, page 216, and Rosemary Flax Baguette, page 128

Ficelle, page 103

Pain d'Epi, page 106, and Wreath Bread, page 106

Couronne, page 109

Baguette Buns, page 113, Soft Dinner Rolls, page 111, and Brötchen, page 112

Catalan Tomato Bread (*Pa amb tomàquet*), page 115

100% Whole Wheat Bread with Olive Oil in Dutch Oven, page 119

100% Whole Wheat and Flaxseed Bread in Cloche, page 125

Plain Bagels with Seeds, page 135

Soft Pretzels, page 140

Black-and-White Braided Pumpernickel and Rye Loaf, page 174

1. Preheat the oven to 450°F, with an empty metal broiler tray on any shelf that won't interfere with the rising brötchen.

2. Cut off 3-ounce (small peach-size) pieces of the Egg White-Enriched Dough for Brötchen (see sidebar) and quickly shape into balls, then pinch to form an oval shape. Allow to rest, 2 inches apart, on a baking sheet prepared with oil, butter, parchment paper, or a silicone mat for 20 minutes.

3. Brush the tops with egg white and cut a single lengthwise slash into the top of each roll, using a serrated knife.

4. Place the baking sheet in the oven, pour 1 cup of hot water into the broiler tray, and quickly close the oven door. Bake the rolls for about 25 minutes, or until richly browned. Serve slightly warm.

> ᧞
>
> **Egg White-Enriched Dough for Brötchen:**
> Put 3 egg whites into the bottom of a measuring cup, then top it off to the required amount of water in the Master Recipe (page 79). All other ingredient measurements are the same. Refrigerate for up to 5 days before freezing in 1-pound portions. This dough is great for brötchen, but you can use it for other rolls or bread as well.

Baguette Buns

1. Preheat a baking stone near the middle of the oven to 450°F (20 to 30 minutes), with an empty metal broiler tray on any other shelf.

2. Form a ½-pound baguette (see page 103) on a work surface; this will make about 6 buns. Using a dough scraper or a knife, make angled

parallel cuts about 2 inches apart along the length of the baguette to form rolls. Allow them to rest, 2 inches apart, on a baking sheet prepared with butter, oil, parchment paper, or a silicone mat for 20 minutes.

3. Place the baking sheet in the oven, pour 1 cup of hot water into the broiler tray, and quickly close the oven door. Bake the rolls for about 25 minutes, or until richly browned. Serve slightly warm.

Cloverleaf Buns

1. **Preheat a baking stone near the middle of the oven to 450°F (20 to 30 minutes),** with an empty metal broiler tray on any other shelf. Grease a muffin pan.

2. Cut off 3-ounce (small peach-size) pieces of dough. Cut each of these pieces into 4 smaller pieces. Shape each one into a smooth ball. Put the 4 balls together to form the cloverleaf and place in a cup of the prepared muffin pan. Continue with the remaining dough. Allow to rest for 30 minutes.

3. Slide the muffin pan into the oven, pour 1 cup of hot water into the broiler tray, and quickly close the oven door. Bake for about 25 minutes, or until richly browned.

4. Serve slightly warm.

Catalan Tomato Bread (*Pa amb tomàquet*)

This specialty from Catalonia, Spain, is served at just about every traditional meal in Barcelona (see color photo), and it answers the age-old question of what to do with stale bread. It's a simple but impressive preparation made with nothing but leftover hearty bread, tomato, olive oil, garlic, and salt, and it's closely related to the Italian *bruschetta* (though we haven't seen tomato pulp used this way in those Italian-style toasts). If the bread has gone stale, that's just fine. The most traditional recipes call for using very fresh, very ripe halved tomatoes from the garden, and simply rubbing the cut surface of the raw tomato onto the crisped bread. You can do that, but we like to deepen the flavor by roasting the tomatoes in the oven first, with some fresh herbs. If you grow your own tomatoes, by all means use them, but you can make this anytime of the year with canned tomato (it'll be very different with the canned stuff). The key is to go light with it—it takes just a kiss of tomato's richness and acidity to create a lovely effect. It's not meant to be a pizza.

Makes about 10 slices tomato bread

1 loaf whole grain bread
1 medium tomato, very ripe, halved
1 sprig fresh thyme
1 garlic clove, cut in half
Coarse salt

1. Sprinkle the tomato with the thyme leaves and roast in a 400°F oven for 25 minutes.

2. Using a sharp bread knife, cut the bread into ½-inch slices.

3. Crisp and brown the slices in the toaster, under the broiler, or on the grill, turning to brown on both sides if necessary.

4. Rub the bread slices with the garlic, then rub again with the roasted tomato, leaving just a sheet of tomato pulp. Drizzle with olive oil and sprinkle to taste with coarse salt.

5. Briefly heat through in a 350°F oven just before serving, if you like.

6

WHOLE GRAIN LOAF BREADS

Whole grains are better for you than white flour. They're loaded with fiber that comes from bran, the coating on the seeds that are ground to make flour. Whole grain flour also includes the germ, which contains a wealth of vitamins, antioxidants, and some vegetable-based fat, all destined to nourish the newly sprouted plant; that nourishment ends up in our bread when we leave it in the flour. White flour milling discards these two nutritionally crucial parts of the grain.

About bran: Somewhere in history, cultures decided that the inner white part of the grain was where the nutrition lived and that eating it was somehow more "refined." They decided that the outer shell (the bran), should be eaten only when we couldn't afford to throw it away and needed something to fill up on. Well, they were partly right. There's little protein, calories, or vitamins in bran. But bran is fiber, and a healthy digestive system requires it to function properly. Adults need about 30 grams of fiber per day, and our 100% whole wheat breads provide over 2 grams per 1½-ounce slice. White bread, on the other hand, contains less than ½ gram per slice, and near zero in many cases.

About the germ: Unlike bran, wheat germ contains nutritious vitamins and antioxidants. But before we even start on those, remember that wheat germ has fiber as well—over 14 grams per cup, which is more than whole wheat flour. In addition, a 2-tablespoon portion contains 20 percent of the recommended daily allowance (RDA) of vitamin E and folic acid, 15 percent of the thiamine, and 10 percent of the magnesium, phosphorus, and zinc. Not bad for something that people used to feed to farm animals.

100% Whole Wheat Bread with Olive Oil

Olive oil and whole wheat are perfect partners in bread. The oil is rich in monounsaturates, so it's a great way for healthy fats to complement the nutrients in whole wheat. The dough makes marvelous free-form loaves, pizza, and an Algerian flatbread that is unlike anything you've ever tried (page 290).

Makes enough dough for at least four 1-pound loaves. The recipe is easily doubled or halved.

Ingredient	Volume (U.S.)	Weight (U.S.)	Weight (Metric)
Whole wheat flour*	7 cups	2 pounds	910 grams
Granulated yeast (can decrease to taste, see page 56)	1 tablespoon	0.35 ounce	10 grams
Kosher salt (can increase or decrease to taste, see page 56)	1 tablespoon	0.6 ounce	15 grams
Vital wheat gluten*	¼ cup	1⅜ ounces	40 grams
Lukewarm water	3½ cups	1 pound, 12 ounces	795 grams
Olive oil	½ cup	3¾ ounces	105 grams
Cornmeal or parchment paper for the pizza peel			

*For whole wheat flours other than Gold Medal or Pillsbury, or for omitting vital wheat gluten, see page 92 for guidelines on adjustment.

1. **Mixing and storing the dough:** Whisk together the flour, yeast, salt, and vital wheat gluten in a 5-quart bowl, or a lidded (not airtight) food container.

2. Add the liquids and mix without kneading, using a spoon, a 14-cup food processor (with dough attachment), or a heavy-duty stand mixer (with paddle). You might need to use wet hands to get the last bit of flour to incorporate if you're not using a machine.

3. Cover (not airtight), and allow the dough to rest at room temperature until it rises and collapses (or flattens on top), approximately 2 hours.

4. The dough can be used immediately after the initial rise, though it is easier to handle when cold. Refrigerate it in a lidded (not airtight) container and use it over the next 7 days.

5. **On baking day,** dust the surface of the refrigerated dough with flour and cut off a 1-pound (grapefruit-size) piece. Dust the piece with more flour and quickly shape it into a ball by stretching the surface of the dough around to the bottom, rotating the ball a quarter turn as you go.

6. Elongate the ball into a narrow oval. Allow the loaf to rest, loosely covered with plastic wrap or an overturned bowl, on a pizza peel prepared with cornmeal or lined with parchment paper for 90 minutes (40 minutes if you're using fresh, unrefrigerated dough). Alternatively, you can rest the loaf on a silicone mat or greased cookie sheet without using a pizza peel.

7. **Thirty minutes before baking time, preheat the oven to 450°F,** with a baking stone placed on the middle rack. Place an empty metal broiler tray on any other rack that won't interfere with the rising bread.

8. Just before baking, use a pastry brush to paint the top with water. Slash the loaf with ½-inch-deep parallel cuts, using a serrated bread knife.

9. Slide the loaf directly onto the hot stone (or place the silicone mat or cookie sheet on the stone if you used one). Pour 1 cup of hot tap water into the broiler tray, and quickly close the oven door (see page 40 for

steam alternatives). Bake for about 30 minutes, or until richly browned and firm. If you used parchment paper, a silicone mat, or a cookie sheet under the loaf, carefully remove it and bake the loaf directly on the stone or an oven rack two-thirds of the way through the baking time. Smaller or larger loaves will require adjustments in resting and baking time.

10. Allow the bread to cool on a rack before slicing.

Vollkornbrot: 100% Whole Grain

Vollkornbrot is German for "whole kernel bread," so to make an authentic one, you need to find some wheat or rye berries—the whole, unbroken kernels of grain (they're not really berries). Rye berries are hard to find, but natural foods co-ops often carry wheat berries and whole rye flakes (flattened-out rye berries), or you can order these ingredients from King Arthur Flour. The result is a 100% whole grain loaf that is rustic, hearty, and moist—perfect when sliced thinly, slathered with butter, and topped with smoked fish, cold cuts, or cheese (see color photo).

Because of the high quantity of whole and unground grains, this dough is not worked like most. It has little resiliency, and you can't tightly shape it; just press the dough into the shape you want. Don't expect a lot of rising during the long (2-hour) resting time after shaping.

Makes enough dough for at least two 2-pound loaves. The recipe is easily doubled or halved. Any leftover dough can be made into buns (see page 111).

Ingredient	Volume (U.S.)	Weight (U.S.)	Weight (Metric)
Whole wheat flour*	5 cups	1 pound, 7 ounces	650 grams
Wheat berries	1 cup	6¼ ounces	180 grams
Rye flakes	1 cup	3 ounces	85 grams
Granulated yeast (can decrease to taste, see page 56)	1 tablespoon	0.35 ounce	10 grams
Kosher salt (can increase or decrease to taste, see page 56)	1 tablespoon	0.6 ounce	15 grams
Vital wheat gluten*	¼ cup	1⅜ ounces	40 grams

Ingredient	Volume (U.S.)	Weight (U.S.)	Weight (Metric)
Lukewarm water	3¾ cups	1 pound, 14 ounces	850 grams
Molasses	2 tablespoons	1¼ ounces	35 grams
Oil or butter for greasing the pan			

*For whole wheat flours other than Gold Medal or Pillsbury, or for omitting vital wheat gluten, see page 92 for guidelines on adjustment.

1. **Mixing and storing the dough:** Whisk together the flour, wheat berries, rye flakes, yeast, salt, and vital wheat gluten in a 5-quart bowl, or a lidded (not airtight) food container.

2. Combine the water and molasses and mix them with the dry ingredients without kneading, using a spoon, a 14-cup food processor (with dough attachment), or a heavy-duty stand mixer (with paddle). You might need to use wet hands to get the last bit of flour to incorporate if you're not using a machine.

3. Cover (not airtight), and allow the dough to rest at room temperature until it rises and collapses (or flattens on top), approximately 2 hours.

4. Refrigerate it in a lidded (not airtight) container and use over the next 7 days, but **do not use the dough until it has aged at least 24 hours (to give the whole kernels a chance to absorb water).**

5. **On baking day,** lightly grease an 8½×4½-inch nonstick loaf pan. Dust the surface of the refrigerated dough with flour and cut off a 2-pound (cantaloupe-size) piece. Dust the piece with more flour and quickly shape it into a ball by stretching the surface of the dough around to the bottom, rotating the ball a quarter turn as you go.

6. Elongate the ball into an oval and place it into a loaf pan; your goal is to fill the pan about three-quarters full. Cover loosely with plastic wrap or an overturned bowl. Allow the loaf to rest for 2 hours.

7. **Thirty minutes before baking time, preheat the oven to 450°F,** with a baking stone placed on the middle rack. Place an empty metal broiler tray on any other rack that won't interfere with the rising bread.

8. Just before baking, use a pastry brush to paint the top with water. You don't need to slash this loaf—it's not going to rapidly expand like ordinary breads.

9. Place the loaf on a rack near the center of the oven. Pour 1 cup of hot tap water into the broiler tray, and quickly close the oven door (see page 40 for steam alternatives). Bake for about 45 minutes, or until richly browned and firm.

10. Remove the loaf from the pan and allow the bread to cool on a rack before slicing thinly.

100% Whole Wheat and Flaxseed Bread

This is a book about healthy breads, and we would be remiss not to include those made with flaxseed, which has some powerful health effects (see sidebar on page 126) and a mild and nutty flavor. If you'd rather downplay the flavor of flax, try our aromatic Rosemary-Flaxseed Baguette (page 128), in which the herb dominates the grain flavors.

Makes enough dough for at least four 1-pound loaves. The recipe is easily doubled or halved.

Ingredient	Volume (U.S.)	Weight (U.S.)	Weight (Metric)
Ground flaxseed	½ cup	2½ ounces	70 grams
Whole wheat flour*	7 cups	2 pounds	910 grams
Granulated yeast (can decrease to taste, see page 56)	1 tablespoon	0.35 ounce	10 grams
Kosher salt (can increase or decrease to taste, see page 56)	1 tablespoon	0.6 ounce	15 grams
Vital wheat gluten*	¼ cup	1⅜ ounces	40 grams
Lukewarm water	3¾ cups	1 pound, 14 ounces	850 grams
Cornmeal or parchment paper for the pizza peel			

*For whole wheat flours other than Gold Medal or Pillsbury, or for omitting vital wheat gluten, see page 92 for guidelines on adjustment.

1. **Mixing and storing the dough:** Whisk together the flaxseed, flour, yeast, salt, and vital wheat gluten in a 5-quart bowl, or a lidded (not airtight) food container.

Omega-3 fatty acids are a super-healthy type of polyunsaturated fat. The Inuit peoples of Alaska experience low levels of heart disease, and some researchers have suggested that it may result from their high intake of fish and marine animals rich in omega-3 fatty acids; this despite an otherwise high-calorie, high-fat, and high-cholesterol diet. But some of our readers don't like fish, and others are vegans. People have also told us that they just can't eat enough fish to provide much of an omega-3 boost in their diets.

So, short of moving to Alaska and gorging on the local cuisine, how can you get more omega-3 fatty acids in your diet? One word: **flaxseed!** It's a concentrated vegetarian source of omega-3.

2. Add the water and mix without kneading, using a spoon, a 14-cup food processor (with dough attachment), or a heavy-duty stand mixer (with paddle). You might need to use wet hands to get the last bit of flour to incorporate if you're not using a machine.

3. Cover (not airtight), and allow the dough to rest at room temperature until it rises and collapses (or flattens on top), approximately 2 hours.

4. The dough can be used immediately after its initial rise, though it is easier to handle when cold. Refrigerate it in a lidded (not airtight) container and use over the next 10 days. The flavor will be best if you wait for at least 24 hours of refrigeration.

5. **On baking day,** dust the surface of the refrigerated dough with flour and cut off a 1-pound (grapefruit-size) piece. Dust the piece with more flour and quickly shape it into a ball by stretching the surface of the dough around to the bottom, rotating the ball a quarter turn as you go.

6. Allow the loaf to rest, loosely covered with plastic wrap or an over-turned bowl, on a pizza peel prepared with cornmeal or lined with parchment paper for 90 minutes (40 minutes if you're using fresh, unrefrigerated dough). Alternatively, you can rest the loaf on a silicone mat or a greased cookie sheet without using a pizza peel.

7. **Thirty minutes before baking time, preheat the oven to 450°F,** with a baking stone placed on the middle rack. Place an empty metal broiler tray on any other rack that won't interfere with the rising bread.

8. Just before baking, dust the top of the loaf with flour and then slash the loaf with ½-inch-deep parallel cuts, using a serrated bread knife.

9. Slide the loaf directly onto the hot stone (or place the silicone mat or cookie sheet on the stone if you used one). Pour 1 cup of hot tap water into the broiler tray, and quickly close the oven door (see page 40 for steam alternatives). Bake for 30 to 35 minutes, or until richly browned and firm. If you used parchment paper, a silicone mat, or a cookie sheet, carefully remove it and bake the loaf directly on the hot stone or an oven rack two-thirds of the way through the baking time. Smaller or larger loaves will require adjustments in resting and baking time.

10. Allow the bread to cool on a rack before slicing or eating.

Rosemary Flaxseed Baguette

Flaxseed has a strong flavor that some people love, but it is an acquired taste for others. For those folks, we wanted to create something that had all the health benefits without an obvious flaxseed flavor (see sidebar on page 126). The addition of rosemary and olive oil makes this an aromatic and absolutely delicious loaf (you can swap in flaxseed oil to boost the omega-3s). To accentuate the rosemary's presence in the bread we added a few sprigs to the outside of the baguette—gorgeous! For those of you who love the taste of flaxseed, you can add a couple more tablespoons to the dough without throwing off the recipe (see color photo).

Like turmeric (see sidebar, page 290) **rosemary contains antioxidants,** and has been studied as an ingredient in marinades for protein-rich grilled foods. So this is delicious news—Indian spices and Mediterranean herbs both have health benefits in addition to great flavors. Kansas State University researchers found that naturally occurring rosmarinic acid in rosemary (and other herbs) inhibits the formation of heterocyclic amines (HCAs) that build up in food during grilling. HCAs have been implicated as carcinogenic (cancer-causing) agents.

Makes enough dough for at least eight ½-pound loaves. The recipe is easily doubled or halved.

Ingredient	Volume (U.S.)	Weight (U.S.)	Weight (Metric)
Ground flaxseed	½ cup	2½ ounces	70 grams
Whole wheat flour	3 cups	14 ounces	390 grams
All-purpose flour	4 cups	1 pound, 4 ounces	565 grams
Wheat germ	½ cup	2 ounces	55 grams
Granulated yeast (can decrease to taste, see page 56)	1 tablespoon	0.35 ounce	10 grams
Kosher salt (can increase or decrease to taste, see page 56)	1 tablespoon	0.6 ounce	15 grams
Vital wheat gluten*	¼ cup	1⅜ ounces	40 grams
Lukewarm water	3½ cups	1 pound, 12 ounces	795 grams
Olive or flaxseed oil	½ cup	3¾ ounces	105 grams
3 tablespoons minced fresh rosemary, plus sprigs to decorate the top			
Egg white wash (1 egg white beaten with 1 teaspoon water)			
Cornmeal or parchment paper for the pizza peel			

*If omitting vital wheat gluten, decrease water to 3 cups.

1. **Mixing and storing the dough:** Whisk together the flaxseed, flours, wheat germ, yeast, salt, and vital wheat gluten in a 5-quart bowl, or a lidded (not airtight) food container.

2. Add the water, olive oil, and minced rosemary and mix without kneading, using a spoon, a 14-cup food processor (with dough attachment),

or a heavy-duty stand mixer (with paddle). You might need to use wet hands to get the last bit of flour to incorporate if you're not using a machine.

3. Cover (not airtight), and allow the dough to rest at room temperature until it rises and collapses (or flattens on top), approximately 2 hours.

4. The dough can be used immediately after its initial rise, though it is easier to handle when cold. Refrigerate it in a lidded (not airtight) container and use over the next 10 days. The flavor will be best if you wait for at least 24 hours of refrigeration.

5. **On baking day,** dust the surface of the refrigerated dough with flour and cut off a ½-pound (orange-size) piece. Dust the piece with more flour and quickly shape it into a ball by stretching the surface of the dough around to the bottom, rotating the ball a quarter turn as you go.

6. Elongate the ball into a baguette shape, or use the letter-fold technique to get a perfect tapered result (see page 103). Allow to rest, loosely covered with plastic wrap or an overturned bowl, on a pizza peel prepared with cornmeal or lined with parchment paper for 40 minutes (20 minutes if you're using fresh, unrefrigerated dough). Alternatively, you can rest the loaf on a silicone mat, a greased cookie sheet, or a baguette pan (see chapter 3, Equipment, page 46), without using a pizza peel.

7. **Thirty minutes before baking time, preheat the oven to 450°F,** with a baking stone placed on the middle rack. Place an empty metal broiler tray on any other rack that won't interfere with the rising bread.

8. Just before baking, use a pastry brush to paint the top with egg white wash and then slash the loaf with ½-inch-deep parallel cuts, using a serrated bread knife. Decorate the top of the loaf by poking a few rosemary sprigs into the cut part of the dough, laying them flat against the loaf.

9. Slide the loaf directly onto the hot stone (or place the silicone mat, baguette pan, or cookie sheet on the stone if you used one). Pour 1 cup of hot tap water into the broiler tray, and quickly close the oven door (see page 40 for steam alternatives). Bake for about 25 minutes, or until richly browned and firm. If you used parchment paper, a silicone mat, or a cookie sheet, carefully remove it and bake the loaf directly on the stone or an oven rack two-thirds of the way through the baking time. Smaller or larger loaves will require adjustments in resting and baking time.

10. Allow the bread to cool on a rack before slicing or eating.

Soft Whole Wheat Sandwich Bread

This is the bread your kids will want in their school lunch boxes every day. It's nice and soft, with sweetness from honey. You'll love that it is made with whole wheat and your kids will think it's perfect with everything from peanut butter and jelly to ham and cheese. When formed into flat buns and sprinkled with sesame seeds it makes the best hamburger buns ever; see page 144 for instructions.

Makes enough dough for at least two 2-pound loaves. The recipe is easily doubled or halved.

Ingredient	Volume (U.S.)	Weight (U.S.)	Weight (Metric)
Whole wheat flour*	5 cups	1 pound, 6½ ounces	640 grams
All-purpose flour	2½ cups	12½ ounces	355 grams
Granulated yeast (can decrease to taste, see page 56)	1 tablespoon	0.35 ounce	10 grams
Kosher salt (can increase or decrease to taste, see page 56)	1 tablespoon	0.6 ounce	15 grams
Vital wheat gluten*	¼ cup	1⅜ ounces	40 grams
Lukewarm water	2½ cups	1 pound, 4 ounces	565 grams
Honey	½ cup	6 ounces	170 grams
Eggs	5	10 ounces	280 grams
Vegetable oil, olive oil, or melted unsalted butter or coconut oil (see page 28 for options)	⅔ cup	5 ounces	140 grams
Oil or butter for greasing the pan			

*For whole wheat flours other than Gold Medal or Pillsbury, or for omitting vital wheat gluten, see page 82 for guidelines on adjustment.

1. **Mixing and storing the dough:** Whisk together the flours, yeast, salt, and vital wheat gluten in a 5-quart bowl, or a lidded (not airtight) food container.

2. Combine the liquid ingredients and mix them with the dry ingredients without kneading, using a spoon, a 14-cup food processor (with dough attachment), or a heavy-duty stand mixer (with paddle). You might need to use wet hands to get the last bit of flour to incorporate if you're not using a machine.

3. Cover (not airtight), and allow the dough to rest at room temperature until it rises and collapses (or flattens on top), approximately 2 hours.

4. The dough can be used immediately after its initial rise, though it is easier to handle when cold. Refrigerate it in a lidded (not airtight) container and use over the next 5 days. The flavor will be best if you wait for at least 24 hours of refrigeration.

5. **On baking day,** lightly grease an 8½×4½-inch nonstick loaf pan. Dust the surface of the refrigerated dough with flour and cut off a 2-pound (cantaloupe-size) piece. Dust the piece with more flour and quickly shape it into a ball by stretching the surface of the dough around to the bottom, rotating the ball a quarter turn as you go.

6. Elongate the ball into an oval and place it in the loaf pan; your goal is to fill the pan about three-quarters full. Cover it loosely with plastic wrap or an overturned bowl. Allow the loaf to rest for 90 minutes (40 minutes if you're using fresh, unrefrigerated dough).

7. **Thirty minutes before baking time, preheat the oven to 350°F,** with a baking stone placed on the middle rack. The baking stone is not essential for loaf-pan breads; if you omit it, the preheat can be as short as 5 minutes.

8. Place the loaf on a rack near the center of the oven and bake for 45 to 50 minutes, or until golden brown. Smaller or larger loaf pans will require adjustments in baking time.

9. Remove the bread from the pan and allow it to cool completely on a rack before slicing

Cinnamon-Raisin Whole Wheat Bagels
(or Plain Bagels)

"Two things that a transplanted New York bagel snob like me doesn't like to admit: 1) New York bagels aren't quite what they used to be, and 2) I like cinnamon-raisin bagels, even though they're newfangled—because they're delicious, and gorgeous to look at. Just as French readers of our blog tell us that baguettes in France aren't what they used to be, some New Yorkers say that their local bagels have become mass-produced and bland, without the chew and crispy crust that they remember (there are exceptions but you have to seek them out). So here's how to hand-shape, boil, and bake your own. **If you're really a traditionalist, skip the cinnamon, sugar, and raisins and you'll have a terrific plain whole-grain bagel. Leaving out the sugar and raisins allows you to bake at 450°F.** *If you're not so enamored of tradition, check out the non-boiled variation at the end of the recipe, or even the gluten-free version."*—Jeff

Makes about 10 bagels

2 pounds (cantaloupe-size portion) Master Recipe dough (page 79), Soft
    Whole Wheat Sandwich Bread (page 132), 100% Whole Wheat Bread
    with Olive Oil (page 119), or other non-enriched dough
2 tablespoons sugar (brown or white)
1½ teaspoons ground cinnamon
¾ cup (4½ ounces/130 grams) raisins

The Boiling Pot

8 quarts boiling water
¼ cup (2 ounces/55 grams) granulated sugar
1 teaspoon baking soda

Visit BreadIn5.com, where you'll find recipes, photos, videos, and instructional material.

1. Mix the sugar and cinnamon in a small bowl. Using your hands and a rolling pin, flatten the dough to a thickness of ¼ inch. Sprinkle the dough with the cinnamon-sugar and raisins. Roll up the dough, jelly-roll style, to incorporate the raisins. Shape into a ball and dust with flour.

2. Cut off a 3-ounce piece of dough from the ball (about the size of a small peach). Dust the piece with flour and quickly shape it into a ball by stretching the surface of the dough around to the bottom, rotating the ball a quarter turn as you go.

3. Punch your thumb through a dough ball to form the hole. Stretch it open with your fingers until the hole's diameter is about triple the width of the bagel wall. Repeat with the rest of the dough balls, cover them loosely with plastic wrap or an overturned bowl, and allow them to rest at room temperature for 20 minutes.

4. **Thirty minutes before baking time, preheat the oven to 425°F,** with a baking stone placed on the middle rack. Place an empty metal broiler tray on any other rack that won't interfere with the rising bagels.

5. **Prepare the boiling pot:** Bring a large saucepan or stockpot full of water to a boil. Reduce to a simmer and add the sugar and baking soda.

6. Drop the bagels into the simmering water one at a time, making sure they are not crowding one another. They need enough room to float without touching or they will be misshapen. Let them simmer for 2 minutes, flip them over with a slotted spoon, and simmer for another minute on the other side.

7. Remove them from the water, using the slotted spoon, and place them on a clean kitchen towel that has been lightly dusted with whole wheat

flour. This will absorb some of the excess water from the bagels. Then place them on a peel covered with whole wheat flour. Alternatively, you can place the bagels on a baking sheet prepared with parchment paper, or a silicone mat without using a pizza peel.

8. Slide the bagels directly onto the hot stone (unless you used parchment paper or a silicone mat, in which case you'll just place the baking sheet in the oven). Pour 1 cup of hot tap water into the broiler tray, and quickly close the oven door (see page 40 for steam alternatives). Bake for 20 to 25 minutes, or until deeply browned and firm. If you used parchment paper or a silicone mat, peel the bagels off to finish the baking on an oven shelf or a stone for the last third of the baking time.

9. Serve these a bit warm—they're fantastic.

If your bagels are coming out with a craggy and uneven surface . . . don't worry about it. The perfectly smooth, glass-like surface of commercial bagels is the result of very high-protein white flour and lots of machine kneading. That creates a very "strong" dough that stands up to hot water better than ours. Your bagels will look more even as you gain experience shaping them, but frankly—it doesn't matter—ours aren't all that perfect either.

VARIATION: Non-Boiled Bagels

While traditional bagels are boiled before baking, it turns out that you can make a credible bagel without that step. Simply shape them, place on a baking sheet prepared with parchment paper, rest for 20 minutes, then bake with steam. You won't have to deal with absorbing the excess water in step 7. If you want seeds or other toppings, brush with water just before baking and sprinkle on the toppings. Peel the bagels off the parchment paper or silicone mat to finish the baking on an oven shelf or a stone for the last third of the baking time.

VARIATION: Onion, Sesame, Poppy Seed, or Plain Bagels

Skip the raisin and cinnamon-sugar roll-in and use any non-enriched dough from this book. Shape the bagels, and if you're boiling them, sprinkle with seeds (see color photo) or dried onion flakes just before baking (or skip the toppings for plain bagels). If you're omitting the boiling step, bake the bagels on parchment paper or a silicone mat and brush with water before sprinkling so the flakes or seeds will stick, and drain any excess water by lifting the edge of each bagel while tilting the pan. Onion flakes burn at high temperature, so bake onion bagels at 400°F for 25 to 30 minutes. Sesame, poppy seed, or plain bagels (without raisins) can be baked at 450°F for 20 to 25 minutes. Peel the bagels off the parchment paper or silicone mat to finish the baking on an oven shelf or a stone for the last third of the baking time.

And don't try to make onion bagels with sautéed onions, as we, regrettably, once did—their texture is all wrong. Believe it or not, nothing says "New York bagel" like dried onion flakes.

VARIATION: Gluten-Free Bagels

Use any of the non-sweet doughs from the Gluten-Free chapter (page 297), and skip the boiling step (gluten-free dough does poorly with boiling). Gently pat out flattened dough balls and place the balls on a flour-dusted surface. Gently work your thumb into the center to form a hole, then stretch with your fingers until the diameter of the hole is about triple the width of the bagel wall. If the bagel breaks while you are opening the hole, you can press it gently back together (gluten-free dough has no "stretch" at all). Carefully transfer the bagels to a baking sheet prepared with parchment paper, cover loosely with plastic wrap, and allow to rest at room temperature for 20 minutes. Bake with steam at 475°F for 20 minutes.

Soft Pretzels

You can make fantastic soft pretzels with our dough by twisting it into the classic pretzel shape—a very old baker's symbol (see color photo)—or as a bun for sandwiches. A brief bath in a boiling alkaline solution (we use baking soda, instead of lye) transforms ordinary bread crust into the essence of pretzels, but you can take a shortcut with a pastry brush that's much quicker, and creates almost as impressive a crust (see variation on page 143). We love them warm, with mustard.

Makes about 5 pretzels

The Pretzels

1 pound (grapefruit-size portion) Master Recipe dough (page 79), Soft
    Whole Wheat Sandwich Bread (page 132), 100% Whole Wheat Bread
    with Olive Oil (page 119), or other non-enriched dough
Extra flour for dusting the kitchen towel
Coarse salt or "pretzel" salt
Whole wheat flour for the pizza peel

The Boiling Pot

8 quarts boiling water
¼ cup baking soda
2 tablespoons sugar

1. **On baking day,** dust the surface of the refrigerated dough with flour
    and cut off a 1-pound (grapefruit-size) piece. Divide the dough into 5
    equal pieces. Dust each piece with more flour and quickly shape it into
    a ball by stretching the surface of the dough around to the bottom,
    rotating the ball a quarter turn as you go. Elongate the ball, dusting
    with additional flour as necessary. Roll it back and forth with your

hands on a flour-dusted surface to form a rope about 20 inches long, approximately ½ inch in diameter at the center, and tapered on the ends.

2. Twist the dough rope into a pretzel shape by first forming a horseshoe with the ends facing away from you. Fold the tapered ends down to the thick part of the rope, crossing them, one over the other. Extend the ends an inch beyond the bottom loop and gently press them together.

3. **Preheat a baking stone near the middle of the oven to 450°F (20 to 30 minutes),** with an empty metal broiler tray on any shelf that won't interfere with rising pretzels.

4. Keep the pretzels covered loosely with plastic wrap as you repeat the process to shape the remaining dough. Let the pretzels rest at room temperature for 20 minutes. If you prefer to skip the boiling step, rest the pretzels on a baking sheet prepared with parchment paper and read the variation on page 143 before proceeding to step 6 for salting.

5. **Prepare the boiling pot:** Bring a large saucepan or stockpot full of water to a boil. Reduce to a simmer and add the baking soda and sugar. Drop the pretzels into the simmering water one at a time, making sure they are not crowding one another. They need enough

We didn't use lye in the boiling pot: When we published our pretzel recipe in the first edition, a few people wrote to express their dismay that we didn't use lye in the boiling pot—that's right, the same chemical used in drain cleaner. They claimed that it's the crucial ingredient to get the absolutely authentic German-style pretzel crust they craved. They may have a point, but we doubted we'd be able to convince home bakers to try this particularly wacky ingredient. We actually went so far as to purchase food-grade lye, but then we read the label: "... *wear chemical-resistant gloves. Wear protective clothing. Wear goggles...*" And our favorite, advising users to watch out for *"digestive tract burns"* (though the manufacturer helpfully advises against swallowing the lye). We found that baking soda makes a terrific substitute—it's alkaline enough. We must admit, we never opened that container of lye.

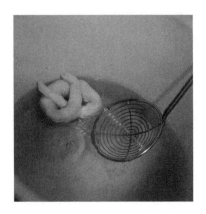

room to float without touching or they will be misshapen. Let them simmer for 1 minute and then flip them over with a slotted spoon or skimmer to cook the other side for another 30 seconds.

6. Remove them from the water using the slotted spoon or skimmer and place on a clean kitchen towel that has been dusted with flour. This will absorb some of the excess water from the pretzels. Then place them on a peel covered with whole wheat flour. Sprinkle with coarse salt.

7. Slide the pretzels directly onto the hot stone (or place the baking sheet in the oven if you skipped the boiling step). Pour 1 cup of hot water into the broiler tray and quickly close the oven door (see page 40 for steam alternatives). Bake for about 15 minutes, or until deeply browned and firm. If you want crisp pretzels, bake 5 to 10 minutes longer.

8. Serve these a bit warm, with a hefty stein of beer.

VARIATION: A Shortcut: Brushing on Baking Soda Instead of Boiling the Pretzels

You can create a reasonable approximation of authentic pretzels even if you skip the boiling step. Just mix 1 teaspoon baking soda with ¼ cup water, and brush the pretzels with the mixture just before baking. This method is particularly nice if you're making pretzels with a softer dough.

VARIATION: Pretzel Buns

Divide a 1-pound ball of dough (see ingredients list) into 8 smooth balls, then allow to rest for 20 minutes. Boil as above but shorten the boil to 20 seconds on each side, drain as above, and space 2 inches apart on a baking sheet prepared with oil, butter, parchment paper, or a silicone mat. Sprinkle with coarse salt and bake with steam for 20 minutes at 450°F.

Hamburger (or Hot Dog) Buns

Hamburger and hot dog buns present a special challenge for home artisan bakers. We're always going for the perfect crisp crust in our breads. But we really don't want a crisp or firm crust in hamburger or hot dog buns. If you make these buns with a hard or crisp crust, you can really bruise the roof of your mouth. What to do? There are two choices: You can either stick with enriched dough, and the oil or butter will soften the crust. Or, you can use non-enriched ("lean") dough and brush with egg wash or melted butter to create a softer crust.

Makes 6 buns

Use any of these refrigerated pre-mixed doughs: Soft Whole Wheat Sandwich
   Bread dough is our first choice (page 132), or any of the enriched doughs
   (chapter 10, page 323)
1½ pounds (small cantaloupe-size portion) of any pre-mixed dough listed
   above
Egg wash (1 egg beaten with 1 tablespoon water) or melted unsalted butter
Sesame seeds (optional)

1. **On baking day,** dust the surface of the refrigerated dough with flour and cut off a 1½-pound (small cantaloupe-size) piece. Dust the piece with more flour and quickly shape it into a ball by stretching the surface of the dough around to the bottom, rotating the ball a quarter turn as you go.

2. **To form hamburger buns,** divide the ball into 6 roughly equal portions (each about the size of a plum). Shape each one into a smooth ball as you did above. Place the buns at least 2 inches apart on two cookie sheets lined with parchment paper. Press them so that they are slightly flattened. Allow to rest, loosely covered with plastic wrap or an overturned bowl, for 40 minutes (20 minutes if you're using fresh, unrefrigerated

dough). Alternatively, you can rest the buns on a silicone mat or a greased cookie sheet.

3. **To form hot dog buns,** divide the ball into 6 roughly equal portions (each about the size of a plum). Shape each one into a smooth ball. Stretch each ball into a 6-inch-long rope. Allow to rest as above.

4. **Thirty minutes before baking time, preheat the oven to 350°F.** The baking stone is not essential for this recipe; if you omit it, the preheat can be as short as 5 minutes.

5. Just before baking, use a pastry brush to paint the tops of the buns with egg wash or melted unsalted butter, and sprinkle with sesame seeds if desired. Slide the cookie sheet into the oven. Bake for about 20 minutes, or until richly browned and firm.

6. Allow the buns to cool on a rack before slicing.

♺

Yogurt is a terrific source of the important trace element zinc, but its real claim to fame is its **calcium** content. It's the most calcium-rich dairy food. Between zinc and calcium, yogurt may be the mineral king.

Olive Spelt Bread

This is one of our favorite breads in the book. We've fallen in love with spelt flour and it's made all the better here by the addition of yogurt. It gives the bread a tanginess right from the start that we've waited days for in other doughs. We've used a whole milk yogurt, which gives the bread richness, but the bread is also excellent with nonfat yogurt.

Makes enough dough for at least four 1-pound loaves. The recipe is easily doubled or halved.

Ingredient	Volume (U.S.)	Weight (U.S.)	Weight (Metric)
Spelt flour	4 cups	1 pound, 2 ounces	515 grams
All-purpose flour	2 cups	10 ounces	285 grams
Granulated yeast (can decrease to taste, see page 56)	1 tablespoon	0.35 ounce	10 grams
Kosher salt (can increase or decrease to taste, see page 56)	1 tablespoon	0.6 ounce	15 grams
Vital wheat gluten*	¼ cup	1⅜ ounces	40 grams
Lukewarm water	2 cups	1 pound	455 grams
Yogurt, whole or nonfat	2 cups	1 pound	455 grams
Green olives, pitted and chopped	1 cup	5 ounces	140 grams
Cornmeal or parchment paper for the pizza peel			

*If omitting vital wheat gluten, decrease water to 1½ cups.

1. **Mixing and storing the dough:** Whisk together the flours, yeast, salt, and vital wheat gluten in a 5-quart bowl, or a lidded (not airtight) food container.

2. Combine the water, yogurt, and olives and mix them with the dry ingredients without kneading, using a spoon, a 14-cup food processor (with dough attachment), or a heavy-duty stand mixer (with paddle). You might need to use wet hands to get the last bit of flour to incorporate if you're not using a machine.

3. Cover (not airtight), and allow the dough to rest at room temperature until it rises and collapses (or flattens on top), approximately 2 hours.

4. The dough can be used immediately after its initial rise, though it is easier to handle when cold. Refrigerate it in a lidded (not airtight) container and use over the next 7 days. The flavor will be best if you wait for at least 24 hours of refrigeration.

5. **On baking day,** dust the surface of the refrigerated dough with flour and cut off a 1-pound (grapefruit-size) piece. Dust the piece with more flour and quickly shape it into a ball by stretching the surface of the dough around to the bottom, rotating the ball a quarter turn as you go.

6. Allow the loaf to rest, loosely covered with plastic wrap or an overturned bowl, on a pizza peel prepared with cornmeal or parchment paper for 90 minutes (40 minutes if you're using fresh, unrefrigerated dough). Alternatively, you can rest the loaf on a silicone mat or a greased cookie sheet without using a pizza peel.

7. **Thirty minutes before baking time, preheat the oven to 450°F,** with a baking stone placed on the middle rack. Place an empty metal broiler tray on any other rack that won't interfere with the rising bread.

8. Just before baking, dust the top with flour. Slash the loaf diagonally with ½-inch-deep parallel cuts, using a serrated bread knife.

9. Slide the loaf directly onto the hot stone (or place the silicone mat or cookie sheet on the stone if you used one). Pour 1 cup of hot tap water into the broiler tray, and quickly close the oven door (see page 40 for steam alternatives). Bake for about 35 minutes, or until richly browned and firm. If you used parchment paper, a silicone mat, or a cookie sheet under the loaf, carefully remove it and bake the loaf directly on the stone or an oven rack two-thirds of the way through the baking time. Smaller or larger loaves will require adjustments in resting and baking time.

10. Allow the bread to cool on a rack before slicing.

Pesto and Pine Nut Bread

The basil, cheese, and pine nuts are so fragrant while this bread is baking that it's a chore to wait for it to cool down and cut into it. We've made this dough with both fresh pesto and the jarred stuff, both are terrific. Serve the bread with fresh mozzarella, a drizzle of olive oil, and a really great red wine. *Bellissimo!*

Makes enough dough for at least four 1-pound loaves. The recipe is easily doubled or halved.

Ingredient	Volume (U.S.)	Weight (U.S.)	Weight (Metric)
Spelt flour	2 cups	9 ounces	255 grams
Whole wheat flour	2 cups	9 ounces	255 grams
All-purpose flour	3 cups	15 ounces	425 grams
Granulated yeast (can decrease to taste, see page 56)	1 tablespoon	0.35 ounce	10 grams
Kosher salt (can increase or decrease to taste, see page 56)	1 tablespoon	0.6 ounce	15 grams
Vital wheat gluten*	2 tablespoons	⅔ ounce	18 grams
Lukewarm water	3½ cups	1 pound, 12 ounces	795 grams
Pesto (for homemade, see Pesto Pizza, page 272, or use a jarred variety)	¾ cup	7 ounces	200 grams
Pine nuts	½ cup	2½ ounces	70 grams
Cornmeal or parchment paper for the pizza peel			

*If omitting vital wheat gluten, decrease water to 3¼ cups.

1. **Mixing and storing the dough:** Whisk together the flours, yeast, salt, and vital wheat gluten in a 5-quart bowl, or a lidded (not airtight) food container.

2. Combine the water, pesto, and pine nuts and mix them with the dry ingredients without kneading, using a spoon, a 14-cup food processor (with dough attachment), or a heavy-duty stand mixer (with paddle). You might need to use wet hands to get the last bit of flour to incorporate if you're not using a machine.

3. Cover (not airtight), and allow the dough to rest at room temperature until it rises and collapses (or flattens on top), approximately 2 hours.

4. The dough can be used immediately after its initial rise, though it is easier to handle when cold. Refrigerate it in a lidded (not airtight) container and use over the next 10 days. The flavor will be best if you wait for at least 24 hours of refrigeration.

5. **On baking day,** dust the surface of the refrigerated dough with flour and cut off a 1-pound (grapefruit-size) piece. Dust the piece with more flour and quickly shape it into a ball by stretching the surface of the dough around to the bottom, rotating the ball a quarter turn as you go.

6. Elongate the ball into a narrow oval. Allow the loaf to rest, loosely covered with plastic wrap or an overturned bowl, on a pizza peel prepared with cornmeal or lined with parchment paper for 90 minutes (40 minutes if you're using fresh, unrefrigerated dough). Alternatively, you can rest the loaf on a silicone mat or a greased cookie sheet without using a pizza peel.

7. **Thirty minutes before baking time, preheat the oven to 450°F,** with a baking stone placed on the middle rack. Place an empty metal broiler tray on any other shelf that won't interfere with the rising bread.

8. Just before baking, use a pastry brush to paint the top crust with water. Slash the loaf diagonally with ½-inch-deep parallel cuts, using a serrated bread knife.

9. Slide the loaf directly onto the hot stone (or place the silicone mat or cookie sheet on the stone if you used one). Pour 1 cup of hot tap water into the broiler tray, and quickly close the oven door (see page 40 for steam alternatives). Bake for about 30 minutes, or until richly browned and firm. If you used parchment paper, a silicone mat, or a cookie sheet under the loaf, carefully remove it and bake the loaf directly on the stone or an oven shelf two-thirds of the way through the baking time. Smaller or larger loaves will require adjustments in resting and baking time.

10. Allow the bread to cool on a rack before slicing.

Roasted Garlic Bread

〰

Garlic won't ward off vampires, but it's a terrific source of the minerals manganese and selenium, plus vitamins B_6 and C. Other phytochemicals (beneficial plant chemicals) in garlic appear to lower cholesterol and, hopefully, heart risk as well.

Spelt flour, ground flaxseed, and *lots* of garlic are not only good for you, but create an incredible flavor. For the best garlic bread of your life, split the loaf lengthwise after baking and fill it with parsley butter. Two heads of garlic might sound like a lot, but roasting the cloves mellows their pungent bite.

Makes enough dough for at least four 1-pound loaves. The recipe is easily doubled or halved.

Ingredient	Volume (U.S.)	Weight (U.S.)	Weight (Metric)
Garlic, 2 heads			
Ground flaxseed	¼ cup	1¼ ounces	35 grams
Spelt flour	3½ cups	1 pound	455 grams
All-purpose flour	4 cups	1 pound, 4 ounces	565 grams
Granulated yeast (can decrease to taste, see page 56)	1 tablespoon	0.35 ounce	10 grams
Kosher salt (can increase or decrease to taste, see page 56)	1 tablespoon	0.6 ounce	15 grams
Vital wheat gluten*	2 tablespoons	¾ ounce	20 grams
Lukewarm water	4 cups	2 pounds	910 grams
Cornmeal or parchment paper for the pizza peel			

*If omitting vital wheat gluten, decrease water to 3¾ cups.

PARSLEY BUTTER (OPTIONAL)

¼ cup (2 ounces/55 grams) unsalted butter, softened, or zero trans fat, zero
   hydrogenated oil margarine, softened
2 tablespoons finely chopped fresh flat-leaf parsley
Salt and freshly ground black pepper

1. **Roasting the garlic:** Wrap the garlic heads in aluminum foil and bake
   for 45 minutes at 400°F. Allow to cool, and cut off the tops of the
   heads. Squeeze out the roasted garlic pulp and set aside.

2. **Mixing and storing the dough:** Whisk together the flaxseed, flours,
   yeast, salt, and vital wheat gluten in a 5-quart bowl, or a lidded (not
   airtight) food container.

3. Add the water and roasted garlic and mix without kneading, using a
   spoon, a 14-cup food processor (with dough attachment), or a heavy-
   duty stand mixer (with paddle). You might need to use wet hands to
   get the last bit of flour to incorporate if you're not using a machine.

4. Cover (not airtight), and allow the dough to rest at room temperature
   until it rises and collapses (or flattens on top), approximately 2 hours.

5. The dough can be used immediately after its initial rise, though it is
   easier to handle when cold. Refrigerate it in a lidded (not airtight)
   container and use over the next 10 days. The flavor will be best if you
   wait for at least 24 hours of refrigeration.

6. **On baking day,** dust the surface of the refrigerated dough with flour
   and cut off a 1-pound (grapefruit-size) piece. Dust the piece with more
   flour and quickly shape it into a ball by stretching the surface of the
   dough around to the bottom, rotating the ball a quarter turn as you go.

7. Elongate the ball into a narrow oval. Allow the loaf to rest, loosely covered with plastic wrap or an overturned bowl, on a pizza peel prepared with cornmeal or lined with parchment paper for 90 minutes (40 minutes if you're using fresh, unrefrigerated dough). Alternatively, you can rest the loaf on a silicone mat or a greased cookie sheet without using a pizza peel.

8. **Thirty minutes before baking time, preheat the oven to 450°F,** with a baking stone placed on the middle rack. Place an empty metal broiler tray on any other rack that won't interfere with the rising bread.

9. Just before baking, use a pastry brush to paint the top crust with water. Slash the loaf diagonally with ½-inch-deep parallel cuts, using a serrated bread knife.

10. Slide the loaf directly onto the hot stone (or place the silicone mat or cookie sheet on the stone if you used one). Pour 1 cup of hot tap water into the broiler tray, and quickly close the oven door (see page 40 for steam alternatives). Bake for 30 to 35 minutes, or until richly browned and firm. If you used parchment paper, a silicone mat, or a cookie sheet under the loaf, carefully remove it and bake the loaf directly on the stone or an oven rack two-thirds of the way through the baking time. Smaller or larger loaves will require adjustments in resting and baking time.

11. Mix together the ingredients for the parsley butter, if using. Set aside.

12. Allow the bread to cool on a rack before slicing. Split the loaf while slightly warm and fill with parsley butter, if desired. Wrap in foil, and return to the oven for 10 minutes.

100% Whole Grain Herbed Potato and Roasted Garlic Bread

This fragrant loaf is made with an entire head of roasted garlic and herbed potatoes. The potatoes add moistness to the bread, and leaving the skins on increases their fiber and nutrient content. This bread is perfect for soups and salads or dipped in olive oil.

◌◌

Potatoes, with skins, please: Potatoes are terrifically high in the essential mineral potassium, which may help control blood pressure, especially for those eating too much salt. But leave the skin on the potatoes—that's where most of the potato's fiber lives.

Makes enough dough for at least four 1-pound loaves. The recipe is easily doubled or halved.

Ingredient	Volume (U.S.)	Weight (U.S.)	Weight (Metric)
Garlic, 1 head			
Spelt flour	3½ cups	1 pound	455 grams
Whole wheat flour	3 cups	14 ounces	395 grams
Ground flaxseed	¼ cup	1¼ ounces	35 grams
Herbes de Provence, 1 teaspoon: Use a prepared herb mix or make your own with equal amounts of dried marjoram, thyme, rosemary, basil, and savory, plus a little lavender if it's available.			

(continued)

Visit BreadIn5.com, where you'll find recipes, photos, videos, and instructional material.

Ingredient	Volume (U.S.)	Weight (U.S.)	Weight (Metric)
Granulated yeast (can decrease to taste, see page 56)	1 tablespoon	0.35 ounce	10 grams
Kosher salt (can increase or decrease to taste, see page 56)	1 tablespoon	0.6 ounce	15 grams
Vital wheat gluten*	¼ cup	1⅜ ounces	40 grams
Potato, 1 large, cut raw into ¼-inch cubes. Clean but don't peel the potato.			
Lukewarm water	3½ cups	1 pound, 12 ounces	795 grams
Cornmeal or parchment paper for the pizza peel			

*If omitting vital wheat gluten, decrease water to 3¼ cups.

1. **Roasting the garlic:** Wrap the garlic head in aluminum foil and bake for 45 minutes at 400°F. Allow to cool and cut off the top of the head. Squeeze out the roasted garlic and set aside.

2. **Mixing and storing the dough:** Whisk together the flours, flaxseed, herbes de Provence, yeast, salt, and vital wheat gluten in a 5-quart bowl, or a lidded (not airtight) food container.

3. Add the potato, water, and roasted garlic and mix without kneading, using a spoon, a 14-cup food processor (with dough attachment), or a heavy-duty stand mixer (with paddle). You might need to use wet hands to get the last bit of flour to incorporate if you're not using a machine.

4. Cover (not airtight), and allow the dough to rest at room temperature until it rises and collapses (or flattens on top), approximately 2 hours.

5. The dough can be used immediately after its initial rise, though it is easier to handle when cold. Refrigerate it in a lidded (not airtight)

container and use over the next 10 days. The flavor will be best if you wait for at least 24 hours of refrigeration.

6. **On baking day,** dust the surface of the refrigerated dough with flour and cut off a 1-pound (grapefruit-size) piece. Dust the piece with more flour and quickly shape it into a ball by stretching the surface of the dough around to the bottom, rotating the ball a quarter turn as you go.

7. Elongate the ball into a narrow oval. Allow the loaf to rest, loosely covered with plastic wrap or an overturned bowl, on a pizza peel prepared with cornmeal or lined with parchment paper for 90 minutes (40 minutes if you're using fresh, unrefrigerated dough). Alternatively, you can rest the loaf on a silicone mat or a greased cookie sheet without using a pizza peel.

8. **Thirty minutes before baking time, preheat the oven to 450°F,** with a baking stone placed on the middle rack. Place an empty metal broiler tray on any other rack that won't interfere with the rising bread.

9. Just before baking, use a pastry brush to paint the top crust with water. Slash the loaf diagonally with ½-inch-deep parallel cuts, using a serrated bread knife.

10. Slide the loaf directly onto the hot stone (or place the silicone mat or a cookie sheet on the stone if you used one). Pour 1 cup of hot tap water into the broiler tray, and quickly close the oven door (see page 40 for steam alternatives). Bake for 30 to 35 minutes, or until richly browned and firm. If you used parchment paper, a silicone mat, or a cookie sheet under the loaf, carefully remove it and bake the loaf directly on the stone or an oven rack two-thirds of the way through the baking time. Smaller or larger loaves will require adjustments in resting and baking time.

11. Allow the bread to cool on a rack before slicing.

Emmer (Farro) Bread

Emmer (farro) is hot among adventurous restaurant chefs, who are using it in its whole-kernel form to create incredible pilaf dishes (it's usually known by its Italian name, *farro,* when used this way). The flavor is marvelous, and the grain has much more protein than regular wheat—16 to 18 percent compared with wheat's 9 to 12 percent. Emmer contains gluten, so it can't be eaten by people with celiac disease, but its gluten content is lower than wheat's.

Emmer is a marvelous grain—it's a wheat variety with a great flavor. We developed terrific flavor by adding a small amount of white vinegar and beer to the mix. Sesame seeds in the crumb itself make a nice counterpoint to the flavors that develop in the dough. Emmer flour can be ordered in the U.S. from Bluebird Grain Farms (see Sources for Bread-Baking Products page 398). Be sure to order the fine-milled emmer flour (which is milled from whole grain), not "whole grain emmer," which is the unground whole kernel of emmer.

Makes enough dough for at least five 1-pound loaves. The recipe is easily doubled or halved.

Ingredient	Volume (U.S.)	Weight (U.S.)	Weight (Metric)
Emmer flour, fine-milled	4½ cups	1 pound, 3 ounces	540 grams
Whole wheat flour*	4½ cups	1 pound, 4 ounces	575 grams
Sesame seeds, plus additional for sprinkling on top crust	2 tablespoons	0.6 ounces	17 grams
Granulated yeast (can decrease to taste, see page 56)	1 tablespoon	0.35 ounce	10 grams

Ingredient	Volume (U.S.)	Weight (U.S.)	Weight (Metric)
Kosher salt (can increase or decrease to taste, see page 56)	1 tablespoon	0.6 ounce	15 grams
Vital wheat gluten*	¼ cup	1⅜ ounces	40 grams
Lukewarm water	4 cups	2 pounds	910 grams
Beer, any type except porter, stout, or other strongly flavored brews	½ cup	4 ounces	115 grams
White vinegar	2 tablespoons	1 ounce	28 grams
Cornmeal or parchment paper for the pizza peel			

*For whole wheat flours other than Gold Medal or Pillsbury, or for omitting vital wheat gluten, see page 92 for guidelines on adjustment.

1. **Mixing and storing the dough:** Whisk together the flours, sesame seeds, yeast, salt, and vital wheat gluten in a 5-quart bowl, or a lidded (not airtight) food container.

2. Combine the liquid ingredients and mix them with the dry ingredients without kneading, using a spoon, a 14-cup food processor (with dough attachment), or a heavy-duty stand mixer (with paddle). You might need to use wet hands to get the last bit of flour to incorporate if you're not using a machine.

3. Cover (not airtight), and allow the dough to rest at room temperature until it rises and collapses (or flattens on top), approximately 2 hours.

4. The dough can be used immediately after its initial rise, though it is easier to handle when cold. Refrigerate it in a lidded (not airtight) container and use over the next 7 days. The flavor will be best if you wait for at least 24 hours of refrigeration.

5. **On baking day,** dust the surface of the refrigerated dough with flour and cut off a 1-pound (grapefruit-size) piece. Dust the piece with more flour and quickly shape it into a ball by stretching the surface of the dough around to the bottom, rotating the ball a quarter turn as you go.

6. Elongate the ball into a narrow oval. Allow the loaf to rest, loosely covered with plastic wrap or an overturned bowl, on a pizza peel prepared with cornmeal or lined with parchment paper for 90 minutes (40 minutes if you're using fresh, unrefrigerated dough). Alternatively, you can rest the loaf on a silicone mat or a greased cookie sheet without using a pizza peel.

7. **Thirty minutes before baking time, preheat the oven to 450°F,** with a baking stone placed on the middle rack. Place an empty metal broiler tray on any other rack that won't interfere with the rising bread.

8. Just before baking, slash the loaf diagonally with ½-inch-deep parallel cuts, using a serrated bread knife.

9. Slide the loaf directly onto the hot stone (or place the silicone mat or cookie sheet on the stone if you used one). Pour 1 cup of hot tap water into the broiler tray, and quickly close the oven door (see page 40 for steam alternatives). Bake for about 30 minutes, or until richly browned and firm. If you used parchment paper, a silicone mat, or a cookie sheet under the loaf, carefully remove it and bake the loaf directly on the stone or an oven rack two-thirds of the way through the baking time. Smaller or larger loaves will require adjustments in resting and baking time.

10. Allow the loaf to cool on a rack before slicing.

Cracked Wheat Bread

By blending crunchy cracked wheat with whole wheat flour, we produced a bread with wonderful texture, great flavor, and lots of nutrition. Because we don't soak the cracked whole wheat, you must let this dough sit for at least 8 hours before using it. This allows the cracked wheat to soften, and gives the dough more complexity and the desired sourdough characteristics.

Makes enough dough for at least four 1-pound loaves. The recipe is easily doubled or halved.

Ingredient	Volume (U.S.)	Weight (U.S.)	Weight (Metric)
Whole wheat flour*	4½ cups	1 pound, 4¼ ounces	575 grams
All-purpose flour	2 cups	10 ounces	285 grams
Cracked whole wheat	1 cup	5½ ounces	155 grams
Granulated yeast (can decrease to taste, see page 56)	1 tablespoon	0.35 ounce	10 grams
Kosher salt (can increase or decrease to taste, see page 56)	1 tablespoon	0.6 ounce	15 grams
Vital wheat gluten*	¼ cup	1⅜ ounces	40 grams
Lukewarm water	4¼ cups	2 pounds, 2 ounces	965 grams
Cornmeal or parchment paper for the pizza peel			

*For whole wheat flours other than Gold Medal or Pillsbury, or for omitting vital wheat gluten, see page 55 for guidelines on adjustment.

1. **Mixing and storing the dough:** Whisk together the flours, cracked wheat, yeast, salt, and vital wheat gluten in a 5-quart bowl, or a lidded (not airtight) food container.

2. Add the water and mix without kneading, using a spoon, a 14-cup food processor (with dough attachment), or a heavy-duty stand mixer (with paddle). You might need to use wet hands to get the last bit of flour to incorporate if you're not using a machine.

3. Cover (not airtight), and allow the dough to rest at room temperature until it rises and collapses (or flattens on top), approximately 2 hours.

4. Refrigerate it in a lidded (not airtight) container and use over the next 10 days. **Wait at least 8 hours to use the dough because the cracked wheat needs to absorb water before it is baked.**

5. **On baking day,** dust the surface of the refrigerated dough with flour and cut off a 1-pound (grapefruit-size) piece. Dust the piece with more flour and quickly shape it into a ball by stretching the surface of the dough around to the bottom, rotating the ball a quarter turn as you go, then elongate into an oval.

6. Allow the loaf to rest, loosely covered with plastic wrap or an overturned bowl, on a pizza peel prepared with cornmeal or lined with parchment paper for 90 minutes. Alternatively, you can rest the loaf on a silicone mat or a greased cookie sheet without using a pizza peel.

7. **Thirty minutes before baking time, preheat the oven to 450°F,** with a baking stone placed on the middle rack. Place an empty metal broiler tray on any other rack that won't interfere with the rising bread.

8. Just before baking, use a pastry brush to paint the top with water. Slash the loaf with ½-inch-deep parallel cuts, using a serrated bread knife.

9. Slide the loaf directly onto the hot stone (or place the silicone mat or cookie sheet on the stone if you used one). Pour 1 cup of hot tap water into the broiler tray, and quickly close the oven door (see page 40 for steam alternatives). Bake for about 30 minutes, or until richly browned and firm. If you used parchment paper, a silicone mat, or a cookie sheet under the loaf, carefully remove it and bake the loaf directly on the stone or an oven rack two-thirds of the way through the baking time. Smaller or larger loaves will require adjustments in resting and baking time.

10. Allow the loaf to cool on a rack before slicing.

Ten-Grain Bread

We thought about scouring our local natural food co-op for individual flours for our ten-grain bread recipe, but we soon realized we'd have an infinite number of combinations to choose from. So instead we decided on a nationally available ten-grain hot cereal from Bob's Red Mill. The wheat, corn, rye, triticale, oats, soy, millet, barley, brown rice, oat bran, and flaxseed that are featured in Bob's Red Mill ten-grain cereal create a rich and complex flavor with a wonderful flavor harmony that would be difficult to re-create with individual flours.

Makes enough dough for at least four 1-pound loaves. The recipe is easily doubled or halved.

Ingredient	Volume (U.S.)	Weight (U.S.)	Weight (Metric)
Ten-grain hot cereal (Bob's Red Mill brand), uncooked	2 cups	11½ ounces	325 grams
Whole wheat flour	3 cups	13½ ounces	385 grams
All-purpose flour	2 cups	10 ounces	285 grams
Granulated yeast (can decrease to taste, see page 56)	1 tablespoon	0.35 ounce	10 grams
Kosher salt (can increase or decrease to taste, see page 56)	1 tablespoon	0.6 ounce	15 grams
Vital wheat gluten*	¼ cup	1⅜ ounces	40 grams
Lukewarm water	3½ cups	1 pound, 12 ounces	795 grams
Cornmeal or parchment paper for the pizza peel			
1 to 2 tablespoons of whole seed mixture for sprinkling on top crust: sesame, flaxseed, caraway, raw sunflower, poppy, and/or anise (optional)			

*If omitting vital wheat gluten, decrease water to 3 cups.

1. **Mixing and storing the dough:** Whisk together the cereal, flours, yeast, salt, and vital wheat gluten in a 5-quart bowl, or a lidded (not airtight) food container.

2. Add the water and mix without kneading, using a spoon, a 14-cup food processor (with dough attachment), or a heavy-duty stand mixer (with paddle). You might need to use wet hands to get the last bit of flour to incorporate if you're not using a machine.

3. Cover (not airtight), and allow the dough to rest at room temperature until it rises and collapses (or flattens on top), approximately 2 hours.

4. The dough can be used immediately after the initial rise, though it is easier to handle when cold. Refrigerate it in a lidded (not airtight) container and use over the next 10 days.

5. **On baking day,** dust the surface of the refrigerated dough with flour and cut off a 1-pound (grapefruit-size) piece. Dust the piece with more flour and quickly shape it into a ball by stretching the surface of the dough around to the bottom, rotating the ball a quarter turn as you go.

6. Elongate the ball into an oval. Allow the loaf to rest, loosely covered with plastic wrap or an overturned bowl, on a pizza peel prepared with cornmeal or lined with parchment paper for 90 minutes (40 minutes if you're using fresh, unrefrigerated dough). Alternatively, you can rest the loaf on a silicone mat or a greased cookie sheet without using a pizza peel.

7. **Thirty minutes before baking time, preheat the oven to 450°F,** with a baking stone placed on the middle rack. Place an empty metal broiler tray on any other rack that won't interfere with the rising bread.

8. Just before baking, use a pastry brush to paint the top crust with water. Sprinkle with the seed mixture and slash the loaf with ½-inch-deep parallel cuts, using a serrated bread knife.

9. Slide the loaf directly onto the hot stone (or place the silicone mat or cookie sheet on the stone if you used one). Pour 1 cup of hot tap water into the broiler tray, and quickly close the oven door (see page 40 for steam alternatives). Bake for about 30 minutes, or until richly browned and firm. If you used parchment paper, a silicone mat, or a cookie sheet under the loaf, carefully remove it and bake the loaf directly on the stone or an oven rack two-thirds of the way through the baking time. Smaller or larger loaves will require adjustments in resting and baking time.

10. Allow to cool on a rack before slicing.

Whole Grain Rye Bread

This loaf is not your grandmother's rye bread, delicious as it was. Most of us who grew up with great fresh rye were eating bread that was very low in whole grains. Our version here is bursting with whole grain flavors; it's much heartier than Grandma's was. These days, U.S. shoppers will find only high-bran rye in stores. Avoid "light" or "medium" rye (which are only available through mail order anyway), and you'll end up with the very high whole grain result we have in mind here.

Makes enough dough for at least four 1-pound loaves. The recipe is easily doubled or halved.

Ingredient	Volume (U.S.)	Weight (U.S.)	Weight (Metric)
Whole wheat flour	2½ cups	11¼ ounces	320 grams
Rye flour	2¾ cups	11⅔ ounces	330 grams
All-purpose flour	2½ cups	12½ ounces	355 grams
Granulated yeast (can decrease to taste, see page 56)	1 tablespoon	0.35 ounce	10 grams
Kosher salt (can increase or decrease to taste, see page 56)	1 tablespoon	0.6 ounce	15 grams
Vital wheat gluten*	¼ cup	1⅜ ounces	40 grams
Caraway seeds (plus additional for sprinkling on top crust)	1½ tablespoons	0.35 ounce	10 grams
Lukewarm water	4 cups	2 pounds	910 grams
Cornmeal or parchment paper for the pizza peel			

*If omitting vital wheat gluten, decrease water to 3½ cups.

---

1. **Mixing and storing the dough:** Whisk together the flours, yeast, salt, vital wheat gluten, and caraway seeds in a 5-quart bowl, or a lidded (not airtight) food container.

2. Add the water and mix without kneading, using a spoon, a 14-cup food processor (with dough attachment), or a heavy-duty stand mixer (with paddle). You might need to use wet hands to get the last bit of flour to incorporate if you're not using a machine.

3. Cover (not airtight), and allow the dough to rest at room temperature until it rises and collapses (or flattens on top), approximately 2 hours.

4. The dough can be used immediately after the initial rise, though it is easier to handle when cold. Refrigerate it in a lidded (not airtight) container and use over the next 7 days. The flavor will be better if you wait for at least 24 hours of refrigeration.

5. **On baking day,** dust the surface of the refrigerated dough with flour and cut off a 1-pound (grapefruit-size) piece. Dust the piece with more flour and quickly shape it into a ball by stretching the surface of the dough around to the bottom, rotating the ball a quarter turn as you go.

6. Elongate the ball into a narrow oval. Allow the loaf to rest, loosely covered with plastic wrap or an overturned bowl, on a pizza peel prepared with cornmeal or lined with parchment paper for 90 minutes (40 minutes if you're using fresh, unrefrigerated dough). Alternatively, you can rest the loaf on a silicone mat or a greased cookie sheet without using a pizza peel.

7. **Thirty minutes before baking time, preheat the oven to 450°F,** with a baking stone placed on the middle rack. Place an empty metal broiler tray on any other rack that won't interfere with the rising bread.

8. Just before baking, use a pastry brush to paint the top with water, and then sprinkle with the additional caraway seeds. Slash the loaf with ½-inch-deep parallel cuts, using a serrated bread knife.

9. Slide the loaf directly onto the hot stone (or place the silicone mat or cookie sheet on the stone if you used one). Pour 1 cup of hot tap water into the broiler tray, and quickly close the oven door. Bake for 30 to 35 minutes, or until richly browned and firm. If you used parchment paper, a silicone mat, or a cookie sheet under the loaf, carefully remove it two-thirds of the way through the baking time and bake the loaf directly on the stone or an oven rack. Smaller or larger loaves will require adjustments in resting and baking time.

10. Allow the bread to cool on a rack before slicing.

VARIATION: Onion Rye

Thinly slice a medium onion and sauté in oil, butter, or coconut oil until brown and nicely caramelized. Allow to cool and use the roll-in technique (see page 136) to incorporate the onions into 1 pound of Whole Grain Rye dough. Form a loaf and bake as above.

Bavarian-Style Whole Grain Pumpernickel Bread

On our website, people asked us whether they could use wicker rising baskets (*banneton* in French, or *brotform* in German) to contain the dough and prevent it from spreading sideways during prolonged rising. We were a bit skeptical, fearing that dough this wet might stick to the wicker. But so long as you coat the wicker heavily with white flour, it's not a problem. And it can be a gorgeous solution when you've mixed the dough a little too wet, or it's near the end of its storage life. The traditional Bavarian-style pumpernickel rises in a brotform, and it's designed to be a very rustic bread, ringed with scorched flour. It's perfect with butter or for dipping into hearty soups. The smaller bannetons are a bit difficult to find, but it's worth seeking out a 6½-inch one. If you use a larger banneton (like the commonly available 9-inch model), it's going to take 3 pounds of dough and require a very long baking time (at least an hour). If you don't have a banneton, this dough bakes up beautifully as a free-form or loaf bread (see color photo).

೧೯

Altus: Traditional pumpernickel recipes call for the addition of altus, which is stale rye or pumpernickel bread crumbs, soaked in water, squeezed dry, and blended into the dough. If you want to find a use for some stale rye or pumpernickel bread, you can experiment with this approach, which some say adds moisture and flavor to many traditional rye breads. Add up to a cup of altus with the liquid ingredients. You may need to adjust flour to end up with dough of your usual consistency.

Makes enough dough for at least four 1-pound loaves. The recipe is easily doubled or halved.

Ingredient	Volume (U.S.)	Weight (U.S.)	Weight (Metric)
Whole wheat flour	2½ cups	11¼ ounces	320 grams
Rye flour	2¾ cups	11⅔ ounces	330 grams
All-purpose flour	2½ cups	12½ ounces	355 grams
Granulated yeast (can decrease to taste, see page 56)	1 tablespoon	0.35 ounce	10 grams
Kosher salt (can increase or decrease to taste, see page 56)	1 tablespoon	0.6 ounce	15 grams
Caramel color powder*	1 tablespoon	0.35 ounce	10 grams
Vital wheat gluten**	¼ cup	1⅜ ounces	40 grams
Caraway seeds (plus additional for sprinkling on top crust)	1 tablespoon	¼ ounce	7 grams
Molasses	2 tablespoons	1¼ ounces	35 grams
Lukewarm water	4 cups	2 pounds	910 grams
Cornmeal or parchment paper for the pizza peel, or flour for the banneton			

*Can substitute ¼ cup of homemade liquid caramel color (see page 33).
**If omitting vital wheat gluten, decrease water to 3½ cups.

1. **Mixing and storing the dough:** Whisk together the flours, yeast, salt, caramel color, vital wheat gluten, and caraway seeds in a 5-quart bowl, or a lidded (not airtight) food container. If you make your own caramel color, it's going to be a liquid, so add it in step 2 and decrease water by ¼ cup.

Visit BreadIn5.com, where you'll find recipes, photos, videos, and instructional material.

2. Combine the molasses and water, and your own caramel if using, and mix them with the dry ingredients without kneading, using a spoon, a 14-cup food processor (with dough attachment), or a heavy-duty stand mixer (with paddle). You might need to use wet hands to get the last bit of flour to incorporate if you're not using a machine.

3. Cover (not airtight), and allow the dough to rest at room temperature until it rises and collapses (or flattens on top), approximately 2 hours.

4. The dough can be used immediately after the initial rise, though it is easier to handle when cold. Refrigerate it in a lidded (not airtight) container and use over the next 7 days.

5. **On baking day,** prepare a 6½-inch banneton or brotform by generously sprinkling it with flour; shake it all around so it coats the sides. **Be generous with the flour.** Dust the surface of the pumpernickel dough with flour and cut off a 1-pound (grapefruit-size) piece of dough. Dust the piece with more flour and quickly shape it into a ball by stretching the surface of the dough around to the bottom, rotating the ball a quarter turn as you go.

6. Place the loaf into the banneton or brotform **with the irregular side up;** the smooth, tightly shaped side stays in contact with the basket. The dough should come about two-thirds of the way up the sides of the banneton. Cover loosely with plastic wrap and allow the loaf to rest at room temperature for 90 minutes (40 minutes if you are using fresh, unrefrigerated dough). You might not see impressive rising during this time.

7. **Thirty minutes before baking time, preheat the oven to 450°F,** with a baking stone placed on the middle rack. Place an empty metal broiler tray on any other rack that won't interfere with the rising bread.

8. After the dough is rested, gently use your fingers to be sure that it isn't sticking to the banneton. Don't dig way down or you may deflate the loaf. Gently turn the basket over onto your preheated stone; it should unmold and drop gently. If it doesn't, help it out with your fingers and make the best of it **(be careful—don't burn yourself on the hot stone).** It should be fine even if it deflates a bit, thanks to oven spring. Using a serrated knife, make ½-inch-deep slashes in a cross pattern, which will create a beautiful effect with the concentric circles of flour.

9. Pour 1 cup of hot tap water into the broiler tray, and quickly close the oven door (see page 40 for steam alternatives). Bake for about 30 minutes, or until firm. Smaller or larger loaves will require adjustments in resting and baking time.

10. Allow the bread to cool on a rack before slicing.

Black-and-White Braided Pumpernickel and Rye Loaf

This festive loaf is a New York classic. Pumpernickel and rye doughs are braided together to create a delicious showpiece that is great for sandwiches, or just schmeared with butter (see color photo).

Makes one 1-pound braided loaf

½ pound (orange-size portion) Bavarian-Style Whole Grain Pumpernickel Bread dough (page 170)
½ pound (orange-size portion) Whole Grain Rye Bread dough (page 167)
Caraway seeds for sprinkling on top crust

1. Dust the surface of the pumpernickel dough with flour and cut off an orange-size piece. Dust the piece with more flour and quickly shape it into a ball by stretching the surface of the dough around to the bottom, rotating the ball a quarter turn as you go.

2. Dust the surface of the rye dough with flour and cut off an orange-size piece. Dust the piece with more flour and quickly shape it into a ball by stretching the surface of the dough around to the bottom, rotating the ball a quarter turn as you go. Cut the ball in half and form 2 balls.

3. Roll each ball between your hands (or on a board), stretching to form 3 long ropes of equal length (the pumpernickel rope will be thicker because its dough ball was twice as large). If the balls resist shaping, let them rest for 5 minutes and try again—don't fight the dough.

4. Line up the 3 ropes, keeping the pumpernickel rope in the center. Braid the ropes, starting from the center and working to one end. If you've never done a 3-stranded braid before, it's simple—just remember to

drape one of the outside strands over the center one, then do the same with the other outside strand (see challah photo, page 324). Repeat until you reach the end and then pinch the strands together. Flip the loaf over, rotate it, braid from the center out to the remaining end, and pinch the ends of the strands together. This produces a loaf with a more uniform thickness than when braided from end to end.

5. Allow the loaf to rest, loosely covered with plastic wrap or an over-turned bowl, on a pizza peel prepared with cornmeal or lined with parchment paper for 90 minutes (40 minutes if you're using fresh, unrefrigerated dough). Alternatively, you can rest the loaf on a silicone mat or a greased cookie sheet without using a pizza peel.

6. **Thirty minutes before baking time, preheat the oven to 450°F**, with a baking stone placed on the middle rack. Place an empty metal broiler tray on any other rack that won't interfere with the rising bread.

7. Just before baking, use a pastry brush to paint the loaf with water, and then sprinkle with the caraway seeds.

8. Slide the loaf directly onto the hot stone (or place the silicone mat or cookie sheet directly on the stone if you used one). Pour 1 cup of hot tap water into the broiler tray, and quickly close the oven door (see page 40 for steam alternatives). Bake for about 35 minutes, or until richly browned and firm. If you used parchment paper, a silicone mat, or a cookie sheet under the loaf, carefully remove it and bake the loaf directly on the stone or an oven rack two-thirds of the way through the baking time. Smaller or larger loaves will require adjustments in resting and baking time.

9. Allow the bread to cool on a rack before slicing.

Bradley Benn's Beer Bread

"My friend Bradley Benn is a talented potter in Minneapolis, and, as it turns out, an accomplished bread baker. Much to my surprise and delight, he delivered a loaf of his fabulous beer bread, which he'd adapted for our Bread in Five method. The flavor had sourdough characteristics, the crumb was wonderful, and the onions and walnuts added the perfect touch. The whole wheat beer dough makes a wonderful loaf without the addition of the onions and walnuts as well. He was kind enough not only to share the bread, but also his recipe, which I deliver to you. Thank you, Bradley."—Zoë

The fats in walnuts have a terrific beneficial effect on cholesterol, plus they're loaded with fiber and vitamin E.

Makes enough dough for at least three 1-pound loaves. The recipe is easily doubled or halved.

Ingredient	Volume (U.S.)	Weight (U.S.)	Weight (Metric)
Rye flour	¾ cup	3¼ ounces	90 grams
Whole wheat flour*	5 cups	1 pound, 6½ ounces	640 grams
Granulated yeast (can decrease to taste, see page 56)	1 tablespoon	0.35 ounce	10 grams
Kosher salt (can increase or decrease to taste, see page 56)	1 tablespoon	0.6 ounce	15 grams
Vital wheat gluten*	¼ cup	1⅜ ounces	40 grams

*For whole wheat flours other than Gold Medal or Pillsbury, or for omitting vital wheat gluten, see page 92 for guidelines on adjustment.

Ingredient	Volume (U.S.)	Weight (U.S.)	Weight (Metric)
Lukewarm water	1¼ cups	10 ounces	285 grams
Beer	1½ cups	12 ounces	340 grams
Vegetable oil, olive oil, or melted unsalted butter or coconut oil (see page 28 for options)	¼ cup	2 ounces	55 grams
Honey	1 tablespoon	¾ ounce	20 grams
Cornmeal or parchment paper for the pizza peel			

THE ONION MIXTURE, PER LOAF

½ medium sweet onion, chopped

2 tablespoons olive oil

Salt and freshly ground black pepper

1 teaspoon fresh rosemary (½ teaspoon dried), plus ½ teaspoon fresh rosemary (¼ teaspoon dried) for sprinkling on the top crust

½ cup (2 ounces/60 grams) walnuts, chopped

½ teaspoon coarse salt for sprinkling on the top crust

1. **Mixing and storing the dough:** Whisk together the flours, yeast, salt, and vital wheat gluten in a 5-quart bowl, or a lidded (not airtight) food container.

2. Combine the water, beer, oil, and honey and mix them with the dry ingredients without kneading, using a spoon, a 14-cup food processor (with dough attachment), or a heavy-duty stand mixer (with paddle). You might need to use wet hands to get the last bit of flour to incorporate if you're not using a machine.

3. Cover (not airtight), and allow the dough to rest at room temperature until it rises and collapses (or flattens on top), approximately 2 hours.

4. The dough can be used immediately after initial rise, though it is easier to handle when cold. Refrigerate it in a lidded (not airtight) container and use over the next 10 days. The flavor will be best if you wait for at least 24 hours of refrigeration.

5. **Preparing the onion mixture:** In a sauté pan over medium heat, cook the onion, olive oil, salt and pepper to taste, and the rosemary until the onion has wilted, but not darkened. Remove from heat and set aside.

6. **On baking day,** dust the surface of the refrigerated dough with flour and cut off a 1-pound (grapefruit-size) piece. Dust with more flour and quickly shape it into a ball by stretching the surface of the dough around to the bottom, rotating the ball a quarter turn as you go.

7. With a rolling pin, roll out the dough until it is a ¼-inch-thick rectangle. As you roll out the dough, use enough flour to prevent it from sticking to the work surface, but not so much as to make the dough dry.

8. Spread the sautéed onion mixture and walnuts evenly over the rolled-out dough, leaving a ½-inch border all around. Roll the dough into a log starting at the long end. Pinch the ends closed. Allow the loaf to rest, loosely covered with plastic wrap or an overturned bowl, and rise on a pizza peel prepared with cornmeal or lined with parchment paper for 90 minutes (40 minutes if you're using fresh, unrefrigerated dough). Alternatively, you can rest the loaf on a silicone mat or a greased cookie sheet without using a pizza peel.

9. **Thirty minutes before baking time, preheat the oven to 400°F,** with a baking stone placed on the middle rack. Place an empty metal broiler tray on any other rack that won't interfere with the rising bread.

10. Just before baking, use a pastry brush to paint the top with water, and then sprinkle with additional rosemary and coarse salt. Slash the loaf with ½-inch-deep parallel cuts, using a serrated bread knife.

11. Slide the loaf directly onto the hot stone. Pour 1 cup of hot tap water into the broiler tray, and quickly close the oven door (see page 40 for steam alternatives). Bake for about 45 minutes, or until deeply browned and firm. If you used parchment paper, a silicone mat, or a cookie sheet under the loaf, carefully remove it and bake the loaf directly on the stone or an oven rack two-thirds of the way through the baking time. Smaller or larger loaves will require adjustments in resting and baking time.

12. Allow the bread to cool on a rack before slicing.

Dilled Rye Bread

Dill is a traditional ingredient in Scandinavian-style breads, and if you haven't tried it, you're in for a treat. The recipe works with dried dill, but it will lack the clarity of flavor that you get with the fresh herb.

Makes enough dough for at least four 1-pound loaves. The recipe is easily doubled or halved.

Ingredient	Volume (U.S.)	Weight (U.S.)	Weight (Metric)
Whole wheat flour	2½ cups	11¼ ounces	320 grams
Rye flour	2¾ cups	11⅔ ounces	330 grams
All-purpose flour	2½ cups	12½ ounces	355 grams
Granulated yeast (can decrease to taste, see page 56)	1 tablespoon	0.35 ounce	10 grams
Kosher salt (can increase or decrease to taste, see page 56)	1 tablespoon	0.6 ounce	15 grams
Vital wheat gluten*	¼ cup	1⅜ ounces	40 grams
Lukewarm water	4 cups	2 pounds	910 grams
2 tablespoons chopped fresh dill (2 teaspoons dried), plus additional for sprinkling the top			
Cornmeal or parchment paper for the pizza peel			

*If omitting vital wheat gluten, decrease water to 3½ cups.

1. **Mixing and storing the dough:** Whisk together the flours, yeast, salt, and vital wheat gluten in a 5-quart bowl, or a lidded (not airtight) food container.

2. Add the water and dill and mix without kneading, using a spoon, a 14-cup food processor (with paddle), or a heavy-duty stand mixer (with paddle). You might need to use wet hands to get the last bit of flour to incorporate if you're not using a machine.

3. Cover (not airtight), and allow the dough to rest at room temperature until it rises and collapses (or flattens on top), approximately 2 hours.

4. The dough can be used immediately after the initial rise, though it is easier to handle when cold. Refrigerate it in a lidded (not airtight) container and use over the next 7 days.

5. **On baking day,** dust the surface of the refrigerated dough with flour and cut off a 1-pound (grapefruit-size piece). Dust the piece with more flour and quickly shape it into a ball by stretching the surface of the dough around to the bottom, rotating the ball a quarter turn as you go.

6. Elongate the ball into an oval. Allow the loaf to rest, loosely covered with plastic wrap or an overturned bowl, on a pizza peel prepared with cornmeal or lined with parchment paper for 90 minutes (40 minutes if you're using fresh, unrefrigerated dough). Alternatively, you can rest the loaf on a silicone mat or a greased cookie sheet without using a pizza peel.

7. **Thirty minutes before baking time, preheat the oven to 450°F,** with a baking stone placed on the middle rack. Place an empty metal broiler tray on any other rack that won't interfere with the rising bread.

8. Just before baking, use a pastry brush to paint the top with water, and then sprinkle with the additional dill. Slash the loaf with ½-inch-deep parallel cuts, using a serrated bread knife.

9. Slide the loaf directly onto the hot stone (or place the silicone mat or cookie sheet on the stone if you used one.). Pour 1 cup of hot tap water into the broiler tray, and quickly close the oven door (see page 40 for steam alternatives). Bake for about 30 minutes, or until richly browned and firm. If you used parchment paper, a silicone mat, or a cookie sheet under the loaf, carefully remove it and bake the loaf directly on the stone or an oven rack two-thirds of the way through the baking time. Smaller or larger loaves will require adjustments in resting and baking time.

10. Allow the bread to cool on a rack before slicing.

100% Whole Grain Rosemary-Potato Dinner Rolls with a Salt Crust

These crusty whole grain rosemary rolls (with soy flour for extra protein) have a lovely soft-textured crumb because of the potatoes. We admit that our inspiration for these salty rolls are French fries. Not everyone loves salt as much as we do, so feel free to cut back. This is also true for anyone on a low-sodium diet—you can eliminate the salt crust altogether.

Makes enough dough for at least five batches of 8 rolls (40 rolls)

Ingredient	Volume (U.S.)	Weight (U.S.)	Weight (Metric)
Rye flour	1 cup	4¼ ounces	120 grams
Whole wheat flour*	5 cups	1 pound, 6½ ounces	640 grams
Soy flour	¼ cup	1 ounce	30 grams
Granulated yeast (can decrease to taste, see page 56)	1 tablespoon	0.35 ounce	10 grams
Kosher salt (can increase or decrease to taste, see page 56)	1 tablespoon	0.6 ounce	15 grams
Vital wheat gluten*	¼ cup	1⅜ ounces	40 grams
Fresh rosemary, finely chopped	2 tablespoons		
Lukewarm water	3 cups	1 pound, 8 ounces	680 grams
Olive oil	¼ cup	2 ounces	55 grams

*For whole wheat flours other than Gold Medal or Pillsbury, or for omitting vital wheat gluten, see page 92 for guidelines on adjustment.

(continued)

Visit BreadIn5.com, where you'll find recipes, photos, videos, and instructional material.

Ingredient	Volume (U.S.)	Weight (U.S.)	Weight (Metric)
Diced raw potatoes, cut into ¼-inch cubes; clean the potatoes but don't peel	3 cups	1 pound	455 grams
Coarse sea salt for the top crust (can substitute kosher salt)	1 teaspoon		
Fresh rosemary, coarsely chopped, for the top crusts	1 tablespoon		

1. **Mixing and storing the dough:** Whisk together the flours, yeast, salt, vital wheat gluten, and 2 tablespoons rosemary in a 5-quart bowl, or a lidded (not airtight) food container.

2. Add the liquid ingredients and potatoes and mix without kneading, using a spoon, a 14-cup food processor (with dough attachment), or a heavy-duty stand mixer (with paddle). You might need to use wet hands to get the last bit of flour to incorporate if you're not using a machine.

3. Cover (not airtight), and allow the dough to rest at room temperature until it rises and collapses (or flattens on top), approximately 2 hours.

4. The dough can be used immediately after its initial rise, though it is easier to handle when cold. Refrigerate it in a lidded (not airtight) container and use over the next 7 days. The flavor will be best if you wait for at least 24 hours of refrigeration.

5. **On baking day,** dust the surface of the refrigerated dough with flour and cut off a 1-pound (grapefruit-size) piece. Dust the piece with more flour and quickly shape it into a ball by stretching the surface of the dough around to the bottom, rotating the ball a quarter turn as you go.

6. **To form the rolls:** Divide the ball into 8 roughly equal portions (each about the size of a golf ball). Shape each one into a smooth ball. Allow them to rest, loosely covered with plastic wrap or an overturned bowl, on a baking sheet lined with parchment paper for 40 minutes (20 minutes if you're using fresh, unrefrigerated dough). Alternatively, you can rest the rolls on a silicone mat–lined cookie sheet or on a greased cookie sheet.

7. **Thirty minutes before baking time, preheat the oven to 450°F,** with a baking stone placed on the middle rack. Place an empty metal broiler tray on any other rack that won't interfere with the rising rolls.

8. Just before baking, use a pastry brush to paint the top crusts of the rolls with water, and sprinkle the rolls with the sea salt and chopped rosemary.

9. Slide the cookie sheet directly onto the hot stone. Pour 1 cup of hot tap water into the broiler tray, and quickly close the oven door (see page 40 for steam alternatives). Bake for about 20 minutes, or until richly browned and firm.

10. Allow the rolls to cool on a rack before eating.

Buckwheat Bread

"The flavor of buckwheat reminds me of being freezing cold and soaked to the bone. My husband and I were in Normandy, touring the magical Mont-Saint-Michel in spring. It was glorious but rainy and cold. We found comfort in a café with Calvados and buckwheat crêpes. The flavor of the grain is so wonderful in this bread that you won't mind whatever weather conditions you may find yourself in while you eat. The unground buckwheat groats (grains) add a lovely texture to the bread, and it doesn't matter whether you buy them raw, or toasted (in which case they may be labeled 'kasha'). You can find them in your local co-op or on the web."—Zoë

Makes enough dough for at least four 1-pound loaves. The recipe is easily doubled or halved.

Ingredient	Volume (U.S.)	Weight (U.S.)	Weight (Metric)
Buckwheat groats	½ cup	3½ ounces	100 grams
Lukewarm water	4½ cups	2 pounds, 4 ounces	1,020 grams
All-purpose flour	2 cups	10 ounces	285 grams
Whole wheat flour	4 cups	1 pound, 2 ounces	515 grams
Buckwheat flour	1 cup	4¼ ounces	120 grams
Granulated yeast (can decrease to taste, see page 56)	1 tablespoon	0.35 ounce	10 grams
Kosher salt (can increase or decrease to taste, see page 56)	1 tablespoon	0.6 ounce	15 grams
Vital wheat gluten*	¼ cup	1⅜ ounces	40 grams
Cornmeal or parchment paper for the pizza peel			

*If omitting vital wheat gluten, decrease water to 4 cups.

1. Soak the groats in 1 cup of the lukewarm water for 30 minutes.

2. **Mixing and storing the dough:** Whisk together the flours, yeast, salt, and vital wheat gluten in a 5-quart bowl, or a lidded (not airtight) food container.

3. Add the groats (including the soaking water) and the remaining 3½ cups water and mix without kneading, using a spoon, a 14-cup food processor (with dough attachment), or a heavy-duty stand mixer (with paddle). You might need to use wet hands to get the last bit of flour to incorporate if you're not using a machine.

4. Cover (not airtight), and allow the dough to rest at room temperature until it rises and collapses (or flattens on top), approximately 2 hours.

5. The dough can be used immediately after the initial rise, though it is easier to handle when cold. Refrigerate it in a lidded (not airtight) container and use over the next 10 days. The flavor will be best if you wait for at least 24 hours of refrigeration.

6. **On baking day,** dust the surface of the refrigerated dough with flour and cut off a 1-pound (grapefruit-size) piece. Dust with more flour and quickly shape it into a ball by stretching the surface of the dough around to the bottom, rotating the ball a quarter turn as you go.

7. Allow the loaf to rest, loosely covered with plastic wrap or an overturned bowl, on a pizza peel prepared with cornmeal or lined with parchment paper for 90 minutes (40 minutes if you're using fresh, unrefrigerated dough). Alternatively, you can rest the loaf on a silicone mat or a greased cookie sheet without using a pizza peel.

8. **Thirty minutes before baking time, preheat the oven to 450°F**, with a baking stone placed on the middle rack. Place an empty metal broiler tray on any other rack that won't interfere with the rising bread.

9. Just before baking, use a pastry brush to paint the top with water. Slash the loaf with ½-inch-deep parallel cuts across the top, using a serrated bread knife.

10. Slide the loaf directly onto the hot stone (or place the silicone mat or cookie sheet on the stone if you used one). Pour 1 cup of hot tap water into the broiler tray, and quickly close the oven door (see page 40 for steam alternatives). Bake for about 30 minutes, or until richly browned and firm. If you used parchment paper, a silicone mat, or a cookie sheet under the loaf, carefully remove it and bake the loaf directly on the stone or an oven rack two-thirds of the way through the baking time. Smaller or larger loaves will require adjustments in resting and baking time.

11. Allow the bread to cool on a rack before slicing.

Anadama Corn Bread

Pretty much every traditional American cookbook contains a recipe for this bread, a Native American–inspired loaf that's sweetened with molasses. The corn and molasses are perfect at Thanksgiving or served with a hearty stew. Newer books seem to ignore anadama bread, and that's a shame, because this classic is a winner. This loaf spreads and bakes flatter than most—you could really think of this as a flatbread.

Molasses is an unrefined sweetener that imparts a complexity that white sugar lacks. There are actually some bitter and caramel notes to savor—it beautifully rounds out the whole wheat we used to boost the fiber and vitamin content of the bread.

Makes enough dough for at least four 1-pound loaves. The recipe is easily doubled or halved.

Ingredient	Volume (U.S.)	Weight (U.S.)	Weight (Metric)
All-purpose flour	3 cups	15 ounces	425 grams
Whole wheat flour	2¼ cups	10 ounces	285 grams
Wheat germ	¼ cup	1 ounce	30 grams
Cornmeal	1½ cups	8½ ounces	245 grams
Granulated yeast (can decrease to taste, see page 56)	1 tablespoon	0.35 ounce	10 grams
Kosher salt (can increase or decrease to taste, see page 56)	1 tablespoon	0.6 ounce	15 grams
Vital wheat gluten*	¼ cup	1⅜ ounces	40 grams

*If omitting vital wheat gluten, decrease water to 3 cups.

(continued)

Ingredient	Volume (U.S.)	Weight (U.S.)	Weight (Metric)
Lukewarm water	3½ cups	1 pound, 12 ounces	795 grams
Molasses	½ cup	5 ounces	140 grams
Cornmeal or parchment paper for the pizza peel			

1. **Mixing and storing the dough:** Whisk together the flours, wheat germ, 1½ cups cornmeal, yeast, salt, and vital wheat gluten in a 5-quart bowl, or a lidded (not airtight) food container.

2. Combine the water and molasses and mix them with the dry ingredients without kneading, using a spoon, a 14-cup food processor (with dough attachment), or a heavy-duty stand mixer (with paddle). You might need to use wet hands to get the last bit of flour to incorporate if you're not using a machine.

3. Cover (not airtight), and allow the dough to rest at room temperature until it rises and collapses (or flattens on top), approximately 2 hours.

4. The dough can be used immediately after the initial rise, though it is easier to handle when cold. Refrigerate it in a lidded (not airtight) container and use over the next 7 days.

5. **On baking day,** dust the surface of the refrigerated dough with flour and cut off a 1-pound (grapefruit-size) piece. Dust the piece with more flour and quickly shape it into a ball by stretching the surface of the dough around to the bottom, rotating the ball a quarter turn as you go.

6. Allow the loaf to rest, loosely covered with plastic wrap or an overturned bowl, on a pizza peel prepared with cornmeal or lined with parchment paper for 90 minutes (40 minutes if you're using fresh, unrefrigerated dough). Alternatively, you can rest the loaf on a silicone mat or a greased cookie sheet without using a pizza peel.

7. **Thirty minutes before baking time, preheat the oven to 450°F**, with a baking stone placed on the middle rack. Place an empty metal broiler tray on any other rack that won't interfere with the rising bread.

8. Just before baking, use a pastry brush to paint the top crust with water. Slash the loaf with ½-inch-deep parallel cuts, using a serrated bread knife.

9. Slide the loaf directly onto the hot stone (or place the silicone mat or cookie sheet on the stone if you used one). Pour 1 cup of hot tap water into the broiler tray, and quickly close the oven door (see page 40 for steam alternatives). Bake for about 30 minutes, or until richly browned and firm. If you used parchment paper, a silicone mat, or a cookie sheet under the loaf, carefully remove it and bake the loaf directly on the stone or an oven rack two-thirds of the way through the baking time. Smaller or larger loaves will require adjustments in resting and baking time.

10. Allow the bread to cool on a rack before slicing.

Quinoa Bread

Quinoa (pronounced *keen-wah*) is something of a wonder grain. It's high in protein, calcium, and fiber. Native cultures of South America made this grain a staple millennia ago, and it's been rediscovered by natural food fans after years of neglect.

Makes enough dough for at least four 1-pound loaves. The recipe is easily doubled or halved.

Ingredient	Volume (U.S.)	Weight (U.S.)	Weight (Metric)
Whole wheat flour	3 cups	13½ ounces	385 grams
All-purpose flour	3½ cups	1 pound, 1½ ounces	495 grams
Quinoa, whole grain unground, uncooked	1 cup	6½ ounces	185 grams
Granulated yeast (can decrease to taste, see page 56)	1 tablespoon	0.35 ounce	10 grams
Kosher salt (can increase or decrease to taste, see page 56)	1 tablespoon	0.6 ounce	15 grams
Vital wheat gluten*	¼ cup	1⅜ ounces	40 grams
Lukewarm water	3¾ cups	1 pound, 14 ounces	850 grams
Cornmeal or parchment paper for the pizza peel			

*If omitting vital wheat gluten, decrease water to 3¼ cups.

1. **Mixing and storing the dough:** Whisk together the flours, quinoa, yeast, salt, and vital wheat gluten in a 5-quart bowl, or a lidded (not airtight) food container.

2. Add the water and mix without kneading, using a spoon, a 14-cup food processor (with dough attachment), or a heavy-duty stand mixer (with paddle). You might need to use wet hands to get the last bit of flour to incorporate if you're not using a machine.

3. Cover (not airtight), and allow the dough to rest at room temperature until it rises and collapses (or flattens on top), approximately 2 hours.

4. The dough can be used immediately after the initial rise, though it is easier to handle when cold. Refrigerate it in a lidded (not airtight) container and use over the next 10 days. The flavor will be best if you wait for at least 24 hours of refrigeration.

5. **On baking day,** dust the surface of the refrigerated dough with flour and cut off a 1-pound (grapefruit-size) piece. Dust the piece with more flour and quickly shape it into a ball by stretching the surface of the dough around to the bottom, rotating the ball a quarter turn as you go.

6. Elongate the ball into a narrow oval. Allow the loaf to rest on a pizza peel prepared with cornmeal or lined with parchment paper for 90 minutes (40 minutes if you're using fresh, unrefrigerated dough). Alternatively, you can rest the loaf on a silicone mat or a greased cookie sheet without using a pizza peel.

7. **Thirty minutes before baking time, preheat the oven to 450°F,** with a baking stone placed on the middle rack. Place an empty metal broiler tray on any other rack that won't interfere with the rising bread.

8. Just before baking, use a pastry brush to paint the top with water. Slash the loaf with ½-inch-deep parallel cuts, using a serrated bread knife.

9. Slide the loaf directly onto the hot stone (or place the silicone mat or cookie sheet on the stone if you used one). Pour 1 cup of hot tap water into the broiler tray, and quickly close the oven door (see page 40 for

steam alternatives). Bake for about 30 minutes, or until richly browned and firm. If you used parchment paper, a silicone mat, or a cookie sheet under the loaf, carefully remove it and bake the loaf directly on the stone or an oven rack two-thirds of the way through the baking time. Smaller or larger loaves will require adjustments in resting and baking time.

10. Allow the bread to cool on a rack before slicing.

Toasted Millet and Fruit Bread

Whole millet has a very subtle flavor, so we like to toast it first. This gives the grain a more complex taste that comes through in the bread. Because the dough is quite wet and will be refrigerated (giving the millet seeds a chance to absorb water), there's no need to precook the hard grain; it will soften just enough. The chewy sweetness of all the dried fruit adds a wonderful contrast to the crunch of the millet, but you can make a plain millet version by leaving out the fruit if you like.

Millet is a major component of bird seed. Adorable songbirds just seem to love these tiny, bead-like grains.* But it turns out that millet is very nutritious for humans as well, with as much protein as wheat, and it's particularly high in niacin, vitamin B$_6$, folic acid, calcium, iron, potassium, magnesium, and zinc. Because it's a drought-resistant crop, it's important for basic survival all over arid parts of the African continent.

*Speaking of which, follow us on Twitter @artisanBreadIn5.

Makes enough dough for five 1-pound loaves. The recipe is easily doubled or halved.

Ingredient	Volume (U.S.)	Weight (U.S.)	Weight (Metric)
Whole millet seed	1 cup	6½ ounces	185 grams
Whole wheat flour	4 cups	1 pound, 2 ounces	515 grams

(continued)

Ingredient	Volume (U.S.)	Weight (U.S.)	Weight (Metric)
All-purpose flour	2 cups	10 ounces	285 grams
Brown sugar, packed	½ cup	3¾ ounces	105 grams
Granulated yeast (can decrease to taste, see page 56)	1 tablespoon	0.35 ounce	10 grams
Kosher salt (can increase or decrease to taste, see page 56)	1 tablespoon	0.6 ounce	15 grams
Vital wheat gluten*	¼ cup	1⅜ ounces	40 grams
Lukewarm water	3¾ cups	1 pound, 14 ounces	850 grams
Mixed dried fruit (raisins, dried cranberries, dried cherries, dried currants)	3 cups	16 ounces	455 grams
Cornmeal or parchment paper for the pizza peel			

*If omitting vital wheat gluten, decrease water to 3¼ cups.

1. **Mixing and storing the dough:** Before mixing, toast the millet in a dry skillet over medium heat, stirring and shaking constantly until it turns golden brown. Whisk together the millet, flours, brown sugar, yeast, salt, and vital wheat gluten in a 5-quart bowl, or a lidded (not airtight) food container.

2. Add the water and fruit and mix without kneading, using a spoon, a 14-cup food processor (with dough attachment), or a heavy-duty stand mixer (with paddle). You might need to use wet hands to get the last bit of flour to incorporate if you're not using a machine.

3. Cover (not airtight), and allow the dough to rest at room temperature until it rises and collapses (or flattens on top), approximately 2 hours.

4. The dough must be refrigerated for at least 24 hours before use. Refrigerate it in a lidded (not airtight) container and use over the next 7 days.

5. **On baking day,** dust the surface of the refrigerated dough with flour and cut off a 1-pound (grapefruit-size) piece. Dust with more flour and quickly shape it into a ball by stretching the surface of the dough around to the bottom, rotating the ball a quarter turn as you go. Because of the millet and dried fruit the loaf will never be perfectly smooth.

6. Elongate the ball into a narrow oval. Allow the loaf to rest, loosely covered with plastic wrap or an overturned bowl, on a pizza peel prepared with cornmeal or lined with parchment paper for 90 minutes. Alternatively, you can rest the loaf on a silicone mat or a greased cookie sheet without using a pizza peel.

7. **Thirty minutes before baking time, preheat the oven to 375°F,** with a baking stone placed on the middle rack. Place an empty metal broiler tray on any other rack that won't interfere with the rising bread.

8. Just before baking, use a pastry brush to paint the top with water. Slash the loaf with ½-inch-deep parallel cuts, using a serrated bread knife.

9. Slide the loaf directly onto the hot stone (or place the silicone mat or cookie sheet on the stone if you used one). Pour 1 cup of hot tap water into the broiler tray, and quickly close the oven door (see page 40 for steam alternatives). Bake for about 40 minutes, or until richly browned and firm. If you used parchment paper, a silicone mat, or a cookie sheet under the loaf, carefully remove it and bake the loaf directly on the stone or an oven rack two-thirds of the way through the baking time. Smaller or larger loaves will require adjustments in resting and baking time.

10. Allow the loaf to cool on a rack before slicing.

100% Whole Grain Brown Rice Bread (Get Rid of Those Leftovers!)

"I grew up on brown rice. When I cook with it today, I am transported straight back to the commune where I grew up in Vermont. Back then it was pure hippie fare, but today you find it everywhere, and for good reason—it's good for you, and it tastes great. The nutty flavor and chewy texture are so much richer and more complex than white rice."—Zoë

Makes enough dough for at least four 1-pound loaves. The recipe is easily doubled or halved.

Ingredient	Volume (U.S.)	Weight (U.S.)	Weight (Metric)
Whole wheat flour*	5½ cups	1 pound, 9 ounces	710 grams
Flaxseed, ground	½ cup	2½ ounces	70 grams
Granulated yeast (can decrease to taste, see page 56)	1 tablespoon	0.35 ounce	10 grams
Kosher salt (can increase or decrease to taste, see page 56)	1 tablespoon	0.6 ounce	15 grams
Vital wheat gluten*	¼ cup	1⅜ ounces	40 grams
Lukewarm water	3½ cups	1 pound, 12 ounces	795 grams
Brown rice, cooked	1 cup	6½ ounces	185 grams
Cornmeal or parchment paper for the pizza peel			

*For whole wheat flours other than Gold Medal or Pillsbury, or for omitting vital wheat gluten, see page 92 for guidelines on adjustment.

1. **Mixing and storing the dough:** Whisk together the flour, flaxseed, yeast, salt, and vital wheat gluten in a 5-quart bowl, or a lidded (not airtight) food container.

2. Combine the water and rice and mix into the dry ingredients without kneading, using a spoon, a 14-cup food processor (with dough attachment), or a heavy-duty stand mixer (with paddle). You might need to use wet hands to get the last bit of flour to incorporate if you're not using a machine.

3. Cover (not airtight), and allow the dough to rest at room temperature until it rises and collapses (or flattens on top), approximately 2 hours.

4. The dough can be used immediately after its initial rise, though it is easier to handle when cold. Refrigerate it in a lidded (not airtight) container and use over the next 7 days. The flavor will be best if you wait for at least 24 hours of refrigeration.

5. **On baking day,** dust the surface of the refrigerated dough with flour and cut off a 1-pound (grapefruit-size) piece. Dust the piece with more flour and quickly shape it into a ball by stretching the surface of the dough around to the bottom, rotating the ball a quarter turn as you go.

6. Elongate the ball into a narrow oval. Allow to rest, loosely covered with plastic wrap or an overturned bowl, on a pizza peel prepared with cornmeal or lined with parchment paper for 90 minutes (40 minutes if you're using fresh, unrefrigerated dough). Alternatively, you can rest the loaf on a silicone mat or a greased cookie sheet without using a pizza peel.

7. **Thirty minutes before baking time, preheat the oven to 450°F,** with a baking stone placed on the middle rack. Place an empty metal broiler tray on any other rack that won't interfere with the rising bread.

8. Just before baking, use a pastry brush to paint the top with water. Slash the loaf with ½-inch-deep parallel cuts, using a serrated bread knife.

9. Slide the loaf directly onto the hot stone (or place the silicone mat or cookie sheet on the stone if you used one). Pour 1 cup of hot tap water into the broiler tray, and quickly close the oven door (see page 40 for steam alternatives). Bake for 35 to 40 minutes, or until richly browned and firm. If you used parchment paper, a silicone mat, or a cookie sheet under the loaf, carefully remove it and bake the loaf directly on the stone or an oven rack two-thirds of the way through the baking time. Smaller or larger loaves will require adjustments in resting and baking time.

10. Allow the bread to cool on a rack before slicing.

Wild Rice Pilaf Bread

Wild rice is a North Woods staple, an ancient Native American crop that is still traditionally grown in paddies in Minnesota and Wisconsin, and sometimes gathered by hand. It is the gluten-free seed of a wild North American grass. Cultivated varieties available in supermarkets are a less expensive alternative to the wild product and work well in this recipe. A classic Minnesota side dish is a delicious pilaf made with wild rice, mushrooms, and onions—that mixture inspired this bread.

You must fully cook the wild rice according to its package directions before using it in the recipe, or you'll end up with hard, uncooked grains in the bread.

Makes enough dough for at least five 1-pound loaves. The recipe is easily doubled or halved.

Ingredient	Volume (U.S.)	Weight (U.S.)	Weight (Metric)
Olive oil	½ cup	4 ounces	115 grams
2 medium onions, chopped coarsely			
Mushrooms, thinly sliced	1½ cups	5 ounces	135 grams
Thyme, dried	½ teaspoon (or 1 teaspoon fresh thyme)		
Whole wheat flour	4½ cups	1 pound, 4½ ounces	580 grams
All-purpose flour	4 cups	1 pound, 4 ounces	565 grams
Granulated yeast (can decrease to taste, see page 56)	1 tablespoon	0.35 ounce	10 grams
Kosher salt (can increase or decrease to taste, see page 56)	1 tablespoon	0.6 ounce	15 grams

(continued)

Ingredient	Volume (U.S.)	Weight (U.S.)	Weight (Metric)
Vital wheat gluten*	¼ cup	1⅜ ounces	40 grams
Lukewarm water	3½ cups	1 pound, 1½ ounces	495 grams
Eggs, large	2	4 ounces	115 grams
Wild rice, cooked and drained, or with cooking liquid fully absorbed	1 cup	5 ounces	140 grams
Cornmeal or parchment paper for the pizza peel			

*If omitting vital wheat gluten, decrease water to 3 cups.

Wild rice is a great source of the minerals potassium and phosphorus and the B vitamins. Mushrooms are incredibly rich in **niacin,** and are also a great source of potassium, an essential mineral that may lower blood pressure. **Onions** are a good source of antioxidant flavonoids.

1. **Preparing the vegetables:** In a skillet, sauté the onions in the olive oil over medium-high heat until lightly browned. Add the mushrooms and thyme and continue to cook until the mushrooms give off their liquid. Set aside to cool.

2. **Mixing and storing the dough:** Whisk together the flours, yeast, salt, and vital wheat gluten in a 5-quart bowl, or a lidded (not airtight) food container.

3. Add the liquid ingredients, the onion-mushroom mixture, and the wild rice, and mix without kneading, using a spoon, a 14-cup food

processor (with dough attachment), or a heavy-duty stand mixer (with paddle). You might need to use wet hands to get the last bit of flour to incorporate if you're not using a machine.

4. Cover (not airtight), and allow the dough to rest at room temperature until it rises and collapses (or flattens on top), approximately 2 hours. The flavor will be best if you wait for at least 24 hours of refrigeration.

5. The dough can be used immediately after its initial rise, though it is easier to handle when cold. Refrigerate it in a lidded (not airtight) container and use over the next 5 days.

6. **On baking day,** dust the surface of the refrigerated dough with flour and cut off a 1-pound (grapefruit-size) piece. Dust the piece with more flour and quickly shape it into a ball by stretching the surface of the dough around to the bottom, rotating the ball a quarter turn as you go.

7. Elongate the ball into a narrow oval. Allow the loaf to rest, loosely covered with plastic wrap or an overturned bowl, on a pizza peel prepared with cornmeal or lined with parchment paper for 90 minutes (40 minutes if you're using fresh, unrefrigerated dough). Alternatively, you can rest the loaf on a silicone mat or a greased cookie sheet without using a pizza peel.

8. **Thirty minutes before baking time, preheat the oven to 450°F,** with a baking stone placed on the middle rack. Place an empty metal broiler tray on any other rack that won't interfere with the rising bread.

9. Just before baking, use a pastry brush to paint the top crust with water. Slash the loaf diagonally with ½-inch-deep parallel cuts, using a serrated bread knife.

10. Slide the loaf directly onto the hot stone or place the silicone mat or cookie sheet on the stone if you used one. Pour 1 cup of hot tap water into the broiler tray, and quickly close the oven door (see page 40 for steam alternatives). Bake for about 35 minutes, or until richly browned and firm. If you used parchment paper, a silicone mat, or a greased cookie sheet under the loaf, carefully remove it and bake the loaf directly on the stone or an oven rack two-thirds of the way through the baking time. Smaller or larger loaves will require adjustments in resting and baking time.

11. Allow the bread to cool on a rack before slicing.

100% Whole Grain Maple Oatmeal Bread

This version of our favorite oatmeal bread has the sweet flavor of maple and cinnamon together with the hearty warm comfort of wheat and oats. You will love it toasted with jam or with your favorite sandwich fillings.

Makes enough dough for at least two 2-pound loaves. The recipe is easily doubled or halved.

Ingredient	Volume (U.S.)	Weight (U.S.)	Weight (Metric)
Whole wheat flour*	5 cups	1 pound, 6½ ounces	640 grams
Old-fashioned rolled oats	2 cups	6⅔ ounces	190 grams
Wheat germ	½ cup	2 ounces	55 grams
Granulated yeast (can decrease to taste, see page 56)	1 tablespoon	0.35 ounce	10 grams
Kosher salt (can increase or decrease to taste, see page 56)	1 tablespoon	0.6 ounce	15 grams
Vital wheat gluten*	¼ cup	1⅜ ounces	40 grams
Ground cinnamon	2 teaspoons		
Lukewarm water	3 cups	1 pound, 8 ounces	680 grams
Maple syrup	¾ cup	6 ounces	170 grams
Oil	¼ cup	2 ounces	55 grams
Egg wash (1 egg beaten with 1 tablespoon water) for brushing on the top crust			
Raw sugar for sprinkling on top			

*For whole wheat flours other than Gold Medal or Pillsbury, or for omitting vital wheat gluten, see page 92 for guidelines on adjustment.

1. **Mixing and storing the dough:** Whisk together the flour, oats, wheat germ, yeast, salt, vital wheat gluten, and cinnamon in a 5-quart bowl, or a lidded (not airtight) food container.

2. Add the liquid ingredients and mix without kneading, using a spoon, a 14-cup food processor (with dough attachment), or a heavy-duty stand mixer (with paddle). You might need to use wet hands to get the last bit of flour to incorporate if you're not using a machine.

3. Cover (not airtight), and allow the dough to rest at room temperature until it rises and collapses (or flattens on top), approximately 2 hours.

4. The dough can be used immediately after its initial rise, though it is easier to handle when cold. Refrigerate it in a lidded (not airtight) container and use over the next 7 days.

5. **On baking day,** lightly grease an 8½×4½-inch nonstick loaf pan. Dust the surface of the refrigerated dough with flour and cut off a 2-pound (cantaloupe-size) piece. Dust with more flour and quickly shape it into a ball by stretching the surface of the dough around to the bottom, rotating the ball a quarter turn as you go.

6. Elongate the ball into an oval and place it into the loaf pan; your goal is to fill the pan about three-quarters full. Cover loosely with plastic wrap or an overturned bowl. Allow the loaf to rest and rise for 1 hour 45 minutes (60 minutes if you're using fresh, unrefrigerated dough).

7. **Preheat the oven to 375°F,** with the rack in the middle of the oven. The baking stone is not essential for loaf pan breads; if you omit it, the preheat can be as short as 5 minutes.

8. Just before baking, use a pastry brush to paint the top crust with egg wash, then sprinkle it with sugar.

9. Slide the loaf directly onto the hot stone or on a rack near the middle of the oven. Bake for 45 to 50 minutes, or until richly browned and firm.

10. Remove the bread from the pan and allow to cool on a rack before slicing.

Betsy's Seeded Oat Bread

This bread was developed for Betsy, whom we met on our website. She requested a hearty loaf full of tasty and nutritious seeds. We loved the idea and came up with a recipe. We figured there was no one better to test it than Betsy herself. We wanted to make sure it was just what she wanted. Together we fine-tuned it and came up with a fabulous bread packed with pumpkin, sunflower, sesame, and flaxseed. These seeds are sometimes called "brain food" because of their high content of vitamin B (see Appendix, page 395, for more on the B vitamins). They are also an excellent source of omega-3 oils and protein. All that, combined with rolled oats and whole grains, makes this bread seriously delicious and seriously good for you.

Seeds are nature's perfect packaging for vitamins and healthy oils: The oils in seeds are packed inside the seeds' skin, which protects them from spoilage. The oil is high in healthy monounsaturated and polyunsaturated fats.

Makes enough dough for at least four 1-pound loaves. The recipe is easily doubled or halved.

Ingredient	Volume (U.S.)	Weight (U.S.)	Weight (Metric)
Whole wheat flour	2 cups	9 ounces	260 grams
All-purpose flour	3 cups	15 ounces	425 grams
Old-fashioned rolled oats	1½ cups	5 ounces	140 grams
Ground flaxseed	2 tablespoons	½ ounce	13 grams
Pumpkin seeds, plus more for sprinkling on top crust	¾ cup	2¼ ounces	65 grams
Sunflower seeds, plus more for sprinkling on top crust	¾ cup	3½ ounces	100 grams

Ingredient	Volume (U.S.)	Weight (U.S.)	Weight (Metric)
Sesame seeds, plus more for sprinkling on top crust	¼ cup	1¼ ounces	35 grams
Granulated yeast (can decrease to taste, see page 56)	1 tablespoon	0.35 ounce	10 grams
Kosher salt (can increase or decrease to taste, see page 56)	1 tablespoon	0.6 ounce	15 grams
Vital wheat gluten*	¼ cup	1⅜ ounces	40 grams
Lukewarm water	3 cups	1 pound, 8 ounces	680 grams
Barley malt syrup, honey, or agave syrup	½ cup	6 ounces	170 grams
Vegetable oil, olive oil, or melted unsalted butter or coconut oil (see page 28 for options)	¼ cup	2 ounces	55 grams

*If omitting vital wheat gluten, decrease water to 2½ cups.

1. **Mixing and storing the dough:** Whisk together the flours, rolled oats, seeds, yeast, salt, and vital wheat gluten in a 5-quart bowl, or a lidded (not airtight) food container.

2. Combine the liquid ingredients and mix them with the dry ingredients without kneading, using a spoon, a 14-cup food processor (with dough attachment), or a heavy-duty stand mixer (with paddle). You might need to use wet hands to get the last bit of flour to incorporate if you're not using a machine.

3. Cover (not airtight), and allow the dough to rest at room temperature until it rises and collapses (or flattens on top), approximately 2 hours.

4. The dough can be used immediately after its initial rise, though it is easier to handle when cold. Refrigerate it in a lidded (not airtight)

container and use over the next 7 days. The flavor will be best if you wait for at least 24 hours of refrigeration.

5. **On baking day,** dust the surface of the refrigerated dough with flour and cut off a 1-pound (grapefruit-size) piece. Dust the piece with more flour and quickly shape it into a ball by stretching the surface of the dough around to the bottom, rotating the ball a quarter turn as you go.

6. Elongate the ball into a narrow oval. Allow the loaf to rest, covered loosely with plastic wrap or an overturned bowl, on a pizza peel prepared with cornmeal or lined with parchment paper for 90 minutes (40 minutes if you're using fresh, unrefrigerated dough). Alternatively, you can rest the loaf on a silicone mat or a greased cookie sheet without using a pizza peel.

7. **Thirty minutes before baking time, preheat the oven to 400°F,** with a baking stone placed on the middle rack. Place an empty metal broiler tray on any other rack that won't interfere with the rising bread.

8. Just before baking, use a pastry brush to paint the top crust with water. Sprinkle with the seeds and slash the loaf diagonally with ½-inch-deep parallel cuts, using a serrated bread knife.

9. Slide the loaf directly onto the hot stone (or place the silicone mat or cookie sheet on the stone if you used one). Pour 1 cup of hot tap water into the broiler tray, and quickly close the oven door (see page 40 for steam alternatives). Bake for about 40 minutes, or until richly browned and firm. If you used parchment paper, a silicone mat, or a cookie sheet under the loaf, carefully remove it and bake the loaf directly on the stone or an oven rack two-thirds of the way through the baking time. Smaller or larger loaves will require adjustments in resting and baking time.

10. Allow the bread to cool on a rack before slicing.

7

BREADS WITH FRUITS AND VEGETABLES

There's been a lot written about sneaking healthy fruits and vegetables into cooked foods to boost nutrients in kids' meals (and in our own). In this chapter, we fortify our breads with vegetables and fruits rich in phytochemicals (beneficial plant chemicals), vitamins, and antioxidants. The United States Department of Agriculture now recommends that adults consume nine half-cup servings of fruits and vegetables every day. We have a friend who says that he cannot even name nine fruits and vegetables. He has a point. It's not easy to get that many fruits and vegetables every day, and it's especially challenging for children. Don't expect bread, or any single food, to meet all dietary requirements. Just remember that every little bit helps. This chapter has recipes that give you one extra chance to get kids to eat healthier foods. And don't forget pizzas with healthy ingredients like Oven-Baked Whole Grain Pizza with Roasted Red Peppers and Fontina (page 263), Zucchini Flatbread (page 267), or Pesto Pizza with Grilled Chicken on the Gas Grill (with a stone) (page 272). You can also try some unorthodox pizza crusts with some of the vegetable and fruit-enriched doughs in this chapter.

So make the most of the pretty colors, and let the kids help with their favorite recipes from this chapter. Who knows, in a few years, they may be the ones baking the daily bread. Your goal might be to get kids to eat their recommended nine servings, but often, the beautiful color will sell the kids on healthy food all by itself.

You can make these loaves without vital wheat gluten if you decrease total liquids by about ½ cup. But we recommend you use vital wheat in this chapter where we call for it—the fruit and vegetables tend to weigh down the loaves. And because there are lots of ingredients in these loaves other than whole wheat flour, we've found that it doesn't matter which kind of whole wheat flour you use, or whether you swap in spelt, Kamut, or sprouted whole wheat—no water adjustment is needed for that.

Tabbouleh Bread with Parsley, Garlic, and Bulgur

People don't usually think of parsley as a vegetable, because it's almost always used as a garnish. But the herb's bright flavor works beautifully with wheat; we got the idea by eating lots of Turkish tabbouleh salad one summer—the dominant flavors in tabbouleh are bulgur wheat, garlic, parsley, and lemon zest.

Makes enough dough for at least four 1-pound loaves. The recipe is easily doubled or halved.

Ingredient	Volume (U.S.)	Weight (U.S.)	Weight (Metric)
Olive oil	3 tablespoons	3 ounces	80 grams
2 medium garlic cloves, finely chopped			
1 bunch fresh flat-leaf parsley, tough stems removed, chopped (about 1½ cups loosely packed)			
All-purpose flour	5½ cups	1 pound, 11½ ounces	780 grams
Whole wheat flour	1 cup	4½ ounces	130 grams
Granulated yeast (can decrease to taste, see page 56)	1 tablespoon	0.35 ounce	10 grams
Kosher salt (can increase or decrease to taste, see page 56)	1 tablespoon	0.6 ounce	15 grams
½ cup whole grain bulgur, soaked at least 2 hours (or overnight) in 1 cup water (will make 2 cups of bulgur—do not drain if liquid isn't completely absorbed)			
2 teaspoons finely grated lemon zest (or more, to taste)			
Lukewarm water	3 cups	1 pound, 8 ounces	680 grams

1. Heat the olive oil over medium heat in a heavy skillet large enough to hold the parsley comfortably. Add the garlic and sauté until fragrant, and then add the parsley. Continue to sauté for approximately 5 minutes.

2. **Mixing and storing the dough:** Whisk together the flours, yeast, and salt in a 5-quart bowl, or a lidded (not airtight) food container.

3. Combine the sautéed parsley, bulgur, lemon zest, and water and mix them with the dry ingredients without kneading, using a spoon, a 14-cup food processor (with dough attachment), or a heavy-duty stand mixer (with paddle). You might need to use wet hands to get the last bit of flour to incorporate if you're not using a machine.

4. Cover (not airtight), and allow the dough to rest at room temperature until it rises and collapses (or flattens on top), approximately 2 hours.

5. The dough can be used immediately after its initial rise, though it is easier to handle when cold. Refrigerate it in a lidded (not airtight) container and use over the next 10 days. The flavor will be best if you wait for at least 24 hours of refrigeration.

6. **On baking day,** dust the surface of the refrigerated dough with flour and cut off a 1-pound (grapefruit-size) piece. Dust the piece with more flour and quickly shape it into a ball by stretching the surface of the dough around to the bottom, rotating the ball a quarter turn as you go.

7. Elongate the ball into a narrow oval. Allow the loaf to rest, loosely covered with plastic wrap or an overturned bowl, on a pizza peel prepared with cornmeal or lined with parchment paper for 90 minutes (40 minutes if you're using fresh, unrefrigerated dough). Alternatively, you can rest the loaf on a silicone mat or greased cookie sheet without using a pizza peel.

8. **Thirty minutes before baking time, preheat the oven to 450°F,** with a baking stone placed on the middle rack. Place an empty metal broiler tray on any other rack that won't interfere with the rising bread.

9. Just before baking, use a pastry brush to paint the top crust with water. Slash the loaf diagonally with ½-inch-deep parallel cuts, using a serrated bread knife.

10. Slide the loaf directly onto the hot stone (or place the silicone mat or cookie sheet on the stone if you used one). Pour 1 cup of hot tap water into the broiler tray, and quickly close the oven door (see page 40 for steam alternatives). Bake for about 30 minutes, or until richly browned and firm. If you used parchment paper, a silicone mat, or a cookie sheet under the loaf, carefully remove it and bake the loaf directly on the stone or an oven rack two-thirds of the way through the baking time. Smaller or larger loaves will require adjustments in resting and baking time.

11. Allow the bread to cool on a rack before slicing.

Garlic- or Tomato-Studded Baguette

"This is the grown-up, sophisticated version of the garlic bread from my child-hood, the one that came wrapped in foil and dripping with butter and garlic salt. Don't get me wrong, as a ten-year-old I could have eaten an entire loaf, but my tastes have changed and now I prefer the flavor of pure unadulterated roasted garlic. In this recipe we bake the raw garlic right on top of the loaf. Once the baguette is baked and crusty, the garlic will be mellow and soft enough to spread on the slices." —Zoë

This recipe also works beautifully with cherry tomatoes pressed into the top of the loaf. Their sweet roasted flesh is also wonderful on the warm sliced bread (see color photo). If you're a garlic fan you'll want to try our Roasted Garlic Bread on page 152 as well.

Makes one 16-inch baguette

Use any of these refrigerated pre-mixed doughs: Master Recipe (page 79), 100% Whole Wheat Bread with Olive Oil (page 119), or other non-enriched dough
½ pound (orange-size portion) of any pre-mixed dough listed above
4 garlic cloves, cut in half (or 6 cherry tomatoes)
Egg white wash (1 egg white beaten with 1 teaspoon water)

1. **Thirty minutes before baking time, preheat the oven to 450°F,** with a baking stone placed on the middle rack. Place an empty metal broiler tray on any other rack that won't interfere with the rising bread.

2. Dust the surface of the refrigerated dough with flour and quickly shape it into a ball by stretching the surface of the dough around to the bottom, rotating the ball a quarter turn as you go.

3. Gently stretch the dough into an oval. Fold the dough in thirds, like a letter. Bring in one side and gently press it into the center (see page 103).

4. Bring up the other side and pinch the seam closed. This will help you to get an evenly shaped baguette and a tapered end.

5. Stretch the dough very gently into a log, working the dough until you have a nice thin baguette. Don't compress the air out of the dough. If it resists pulling, let it rest for a moment to relax the gluten, then come back and continue to stretch. Don't fight the dough. The final width for a baguette should be about 1½ inches.

6. Allow the loaf to rest, loosely covered with plastic wrap or an over-turned bowl, on a pizza peel prepared with cornmeal or lined with parchment paper, for 40 minutes (or just 20 minutes if you're using fresh, unrefrigerated dough). Alternatively, you can rest the loaf on a silicone mat or a perforated baguette pan (see Equipment, pages 45–46) without using a pizza peel. Just before baking, use a pastry brush to paint the top crust with egg white wash. Then press the garlic (or cherry tomatoes) into the loaf, evenly spacing them along the baguette. Be sure to really press them in so they don't pop out when baking.

7. Slide the loaf directly onto the hot stone (or place the silicone mat or baguette pan on the stone if you used one). Pour 1 cup of hot tap water into the broiler tray, and quickly close the oven door (see page 40 for steam alternatives). Bake for about 25 minutes, or until richly browned and firm. If you used parchment paper, a silicone mat, or a baguette pan under the loaf, carefully remove it and bake the loaf directly on the stone or an oven rack two-thirds of the way through the baking time.

8. Allow the bread to cool on a rack before slicing. Spread the now-roasted garlic on the sliced bread.

Avocado-Guacamole Bread

Bite into our avocado bread for a unique, smoky sensation. Try it with a bowl of hot chili in the wintertime and you'll forget about the cold.

Makes enough dough for at least four 1-pound loaves. The recipe is easily doubled or halved.

Ingredient	Volume (U.S.)	Weight (U.S.)	Weight (Metric)
Whole wheat flour	4 cups	1 pound, 2 ounces	515 grams
All-purpose flour	3¼ cups	1 pound	460 grams
Granulated yeast (can decrease to taste, see page 56)	1 tablespoon	0.35 ounce	10 grams
Kosher salt (can increase or decrease to taste, see page 56)	1 tablespoon	0.6 ounce	15 grams
Vital wheat gluten	¼ cup	1⅜ ounces	40 grams
Lukewarm water	3½ cups	1 pound, 12 ounces	795 grams
1 garlic clove, finely minced			
1 ripe medium tomato, cubed, including liquid and seeds			
1 ripe avocado, pitted, peeled, and mashed			

1. **Mixing and storing the dough:** Whisk together the flours, yeast, salt, and vital wheat gluten in a 5-quart bowl, or a lidded (not airtight) food container.

2. Combine the water, garlic, tomato, and avocado and mix them with the dry ingredients without kneading, using a spoon, a 14-cup food processor (with dough attachment), or a heavy-duty stand mixer (with paddle).

❧

Avocado and tomato in bread: Though avocados are high in calories and fat, the fat is mostly monounsaturated and can improve your cholesterol profile. Just be sure to eat avocados in moderation.

Tomatoes are low in calories but rich in **lycopene**, which may offer some protection against certain cancers. Lycopene is a pigment responsible for the beautiful reddish color in tomatoes, guava, papaya, pink grapefruit, and watermelon. It's a potent antioxidant (see page 4). Tomatoes are also rich in iron.

You might need to use wet hands to get the last bit of flour to incorporate if you're not using a machine.

3. Cover (not airtight), and allow the dough to rest at room temperature until it rises and collapses (or flattens on top), approximately 2 hours.

4. The dough can be used immediately after its initial rise, though it is easier to handle when cold. Refrigerate it in a lidded (not airtight) container and use over the next 5 days.

5. **On baking day,** dust the surface of the refrigerated dough with flour and cut off a 1-pound (grapefruit-size) piece. Dust the piece with more flour and quickly shape it into a ball by stretching the surface of the dough around to the bottom, rotating the ball a quarter turn as you go.

6. Elongate the ball into a narrow oval. Allow the loaf to rest, loosely covered with plastic wrap or an overturned bowl, on a pizza peel prepared with cornmeal or lined with parchment paper for 90 minutes (40 minutes if you're using fresh, unrefrigerated dough). Alternatively, you can rest the loaf on a silicone mat or a greased cookie sheet without using a pizza peel.

7. **Thirty minutes before baking time, preheat the oven to 450°F,** with a baking stone placed on the middle rack. Place an empty metal broiler tray on any other rack that won't interfere with the rising bread.

8. Just before baking, use a pastry brush to paint the top crust with water. Slash the loaf diagonally with ½-inch-deep parallel cuts, using a serrated bread knife.

9. Slide the loaf directly onto the hot stone (or place the silicone mat or cookie sheet on the stone if you used one). Pour 1 cup of hot tap water into the broiler tray, and quickly close the oven door (see page 40 for steam alternatives). Bake for about 35 minutes, or until richly browned and firm. If you used parchment paper, a silicone mat, or a cookie sheet under the loaf, carefully remove it and bake the loaf directly on the stone or an oven rack two-thirds of the way through the baking time. Smaller or larger loaves will require adjustments in resting and baking time.

10. Allow the bread to cool on a rack before slicing.

Pain au Potiron (Peppery Pumpkin and Olive Oil Loaf)

Although pumpkin is generally thought of as quintessentially American (Native Americans were the first to cultivate it), there's actually a marvelous French Provençal tradition of bread spiked with peppered pumpkin. Dice the raw pumpkin small so that it will cook through during the baking time. You can substitute raw winter squash or sweet potato for the pumpkin (see color photo).

∽

Pumpkins are low in calories and high in fiber and Vitamin A.

Makes enough dough for at least four 1-pound loaves. The recipe is easily doubled or halved.

Ingredient	Volume (U.S.)	Weight (U.S.)	Weight (Metric)
Whole wheat flour	3¾ cups	17 ounces	485 grams
All-purpose flour	3½ cups	1 pound, 1½ ounces	495 grams
Granulated yeast (can decrease to taste, see page 56)	1 tablespoon	0.35 ounce	10 grams
Kosher salt (can increase or decrease to taste, see page 56)	1 tablespoon	0.6 ounce	15 grams
Vital wheat gluten	¼ cup	1⅜ ounces	40 grams
1¼ cups peeled, ¼-inch-dice raw pie pumpkin (sometimes called "sugar" pumpkin), or substitute squash or sweet potato			
Freshly ground black pepper			
Lukewarm water	3½ cups	1 pound, 12 ounces	795 grams
Olive oil	¼ cup	2 ounces	55 grams

1. **Mixing and storing the dough:** Whisk together the flours, yeast, salt, and vital wheat gluten in a 5-quart bowl, or a lidded (not airtight) food container.

2. Generously season the pumpkin, squash, or sweet potato to taste with the pepper.

3. Add the liquid ingredients and pumpkin to the dry ingredients and mix without kneading, using a spoon, a 14-cup food processor (with dough attachment), or a heavy-duty stand mixer (with paddle). You might need to use wet hands to get the last bit of flour to incorporate if you're not using a machine.

4. Cover (not airtight), and allow the dough to rest at room temperature until it rises and collapses (or flattens on top), approximately 2 hours.

5. The dough can be used immediately after its initial rise, though it is easier to handle when cold. Refrigerate it in a lidded (not airtight) container and use over the next 10 days. The flavor will be best if you wait for at least 24 hours of refrigeration.

6. **On baking day,** dust the surface of the refrigerated dough with flour and cut off a 1-pound (grapefruit-size) piece. Dust with more flour and quickly shape it into a ball by stretching the surface of the dough around to the bottom, rotating the ball a quarter turn as you go.

7. Elongate the ball into a narrow oval. Allow the loaf to rest, loosely covered with plastic wrap or an overturned bowl, on a pizza peel prepared with cornmeal or lined with parchment paper for 90 minutes (40 minutes if you're using fresh, unrefrigerated dough). Alternatively, you can rest the loaf on a silicone mat or a greased cookie sheet without using a pizza peel.

8. **Thirty minutes before baking time, preheat the oven to 450°F,** with a baking stone placed on the middle rack. Place an empty metal broiler tray on any other rack that won't interfere with the rising bread.

9. Just before baking, use a pastry brush to paint the top crust with water. Slash the loaf diagonally with ½-inch-deep parallel cuts, using a serrated bread knife.

10. Slide the loaf directly onto the hot stone (or place the silicone mat or cookie sheet on the stone if you used one). Pour 1 cup of hot tap water into the broiler tray, and quickly close the oven door (see page 40 for steam alternatives). Bake for about 30 minutes, or until richly browned and firm. If you used parchment paper, a silicone mat, or a cookie sheet under the loaf, carefully remove it and bake the loaf directly on the stone or an oven rack two-thirds of the way through the baking time. Smaller or larger loaves will require adjustments in resting and baking time.

11. Allow the bread to cool on a rack before slicing.

Provençal Fisherman's Bread (*Pain Bouillabaisse*)

Bouillabaisse is the delicious fish soup of Provence, France. There's an old Provençal tradition of taking the aromatic flavors from this soup (herbes de Provence, saffron, and fennel) and putting them into a bread (leave out the fish). Fresh fennel provides a subtle licorice flavor and sneaks in yet another vegetable. This bread is fantastic for serving with Provençal appetizers and condiments like aioli, Niçoise olives, and of course, bouillabaisse.

"Years ago, my wife, Laura, and I bicycled through Provence, the lush and hilly countryside of southern France bordering the Mediterranean. The weather can be extreme, and on one rainy and blustery day, we rode into the medieval town of Uzès, completely soaked, exhausted, and most important, starving. An old façade read Hostellerie Provençale Restaurant, so we parked our bicycles under an ancient embankment and walked inside for a well-deserved lunch in a charming, unassuming place where the warmth of the hostess made all the difference. Madame's bouillabaisse was fantastic, and warmed us to the core."—Jeff

Using authentic saffron threads: Our recipe calls for the widely available and affordable saffron powder, but authentic saffron threads produce a more delicate and delicious flavor. To use it, omit the powder, crumble enough threads to measure ⅛ teaspoon, and simmer gently in the 3½ cups of water for 10 minutes. Remove from heat, re-measure the liquid and add water (if needed) to bring back volume to 3½ cups. Cool to lukewarm before using in the recipe.

Makes enough dough for at least four 1-pound loaves. The recipe is easily doubled or halved.

Ingredient		Weight (U.S.)	Weight (Metric)
Whole wheat flour	3¾ cups	17 ounces	485 grams
All-purpose flour	3½ cups	1 pound, 1½ ounces	495 grams
1½ teaspoons herbes de Provence (use a prepared herb mix or make your own with an equal mixture of dried marjoram, thyme, rosemary, basil, and savory, plus a little lavender if it's available)			
Saffron powder	½ teaspoon		
Granulated yeast (can decrease to taste, see page 56)	1 tablespoon	0.35 ounce	10 grams
Kosher salt (can increase or decrease to taste, see page 56)	1 tablespoon	0.6 ounce	15 grams
Vital wheat gluten	¼ cup	1⅜ ounces	40 grams
2 to 4 garlic cloves, minced			
1 cup thinly sliced fennel bulb, cut into 1-inch pieces, white parts only			
Lukewarm water	3½ cups	1 pound, 12 ounces	795 grams
Olive oil (see page 28 for substitutions)	½ cup	3¾ ounces	105 grams

1. **Mixing and storing the dough:** Whisk together the flours, herbes de Provence, saffron powder, yeast, salt, and vital wheat gluten in a 5-quart bowl, or a lidded (not airtight) food container.

2. Add the garlic to taste, the fennel, and the liquid ingredients and mix without kneading, using a spoon, a 14-cup food processor (with dough

attachment), or a heavy-duty stand mixer (with paddle). You might need to use wet hands to get the last bit of flour to incorporate if you're not using a machine.

3. Cover (not airtight), and allow the dough to rest at room temperature until it rises and collapses (or flattens on top), approximately 2 hours.

4. The dough can be used immediately after its initial rise, though it is easier to handle when cold. Refrigerate it in a lidded (not airtight) container and use over the next 10 days. The flavor will be best if you wait for at least 24 hours of refrigeration.

5. **On baking day,** dust the surface of the refrigerated dough with flour and cut off a 1-pound (grapefruit-size) piece. Dust with more flour and quickly shape it into a ball by stretching the surface of the dough around to the bottom, rotating the ball a quarter turn as you go.

6. Elongate the ball into a narrow oval. Allow the loaf to rest, loosely covered with plastic wrap or an overturned bowl, on a pizza peel prepared with cornmeal or lined with parchment paper for 90 minutes (40 minutes if you're using fresh, unrefrigerated dough). Alternatively, you can rest the loaf on a silicone mat or a greased cookie sheet without using a pizza peel.

7. **Thirty minutes before baking time, preheat the oven to 450°F,** with a baking stone placed on the middle rack. Place an empty metal broiler tray on any other rack that won't interfere with the rising bread.

8. Just before baking, use a pastry brush to paint the top crust with water. Slash the loaf diagonally with ½-inch-deep parallel cuts, using a serrated bread knife.

9. Slide the loaf directly onto the hot stone (or place the silicone mat or cookie sheet on the stone if you used one). Pour 1 cup of hot tap water

into the broiler tray, and quickly close the oven door (see page 40 for steam alternatives). Bake for about 30 minutes, or until richly browned and firm. If you used parchment paper, a silicone mat, or a cookie sheet under the loaf, carefully remove it and bake the loaf directly on the stone or an oven rack two-thirds of the way through the baking time. Smaller or larger loaves will require adjustments in resting and baking time.

10. Allow the bread to cool on a rack before slicing.

Lentil Curry Bread

Lentils are a great source of fiber and vitamins, but some kids won't eat curried lentil soup. Here's a great way to get them to try the flavor—we haven't found a kid yet who won't eat this. It's one of our all-time favorites, and lentils are loaded with protein, folic acid, and B vitamins.

Makes enough dough for at least four 1-pound loaves. The recipe is easily doubled or halved.

The Lentils

Ingredient	Volume (U.S.)	Weight (U.S.)	Weight (Metric)
Water	4¼ cups	2 pounds, 2 ounces	965 grams
Lentils, dried	1 cup	7 ounces	200 grams
Curry powder	1 tablespoon	¼ ounce	7 grams

The Dough

Ingredient	Volume (U.S.)	Weight (U.S.)	Weight (Metric)
Whole wheat flour	2 cups	9 ounces	260 grams
All-purpose flour	5½ cups	1 pound, 11½ ounces	780 grams
Granulated yeast (can decrease to taste, see page 56)	1 tablespoon	0.35 ounce	10 grams
Kosher salt (can increase or decrease to taste, see page 56)	1 tablespoon	0.6 ounce	15 grams
Vital wheat gluten	3 tablespoons	1 ounce	30 grams

(continued)

Ingredient	Volume (U.S.)	Weight (U.S.)	Weight (Metric)
Lukewarm water	2 cups	1 pound	455 grams
Vegetable oil, olive oil, or melted unsalted butter or coconut oil (see page 28 for options)	¼ cup	2 ounces	55 grams

1. **Preparing the lentils:** Put the water and lentils in a medium saucepan and bring to a boil. Cover, reduce to a low simmer, and cook for 30 to 60 minutes, or until the lentils are soft. Add small amounts of water to the lentils to keep them just covered during cooking as needed. Remove from heat and allow to cool slightly.

2. Without draining the liquid, pour the mixture into a blender, add the curry powder, and process until smooth.

3. **Mixing and storing the dough:** Whisk together the flours, yeast, salt, and vital wheat gluten in a 5-quart bowl, or a lidded (not airtight) food container.

4. Add the liquid ingredients and the lentils and mix without kneading, using a spoon, a 14-cup food processor (with dough attachment), or a heavy-duty stand mixer (with paddle). You might need to use wet hands to get the last bit of flour to incorporate if you're not using a machine.

5. Cover (not airtight), and allow the dough to rest at room temperature until it rises and collapses (or flattens on top), approximately 2 hours.

6. The dough can be used immediately after its initial rise, though it is easier to handle when cold. Refrigerate it in a lidded (not airtight) container and use over the next 7 days. As the dough ages, its surface might develop a yellow-green color from the curried lentils. This is normal.

7. **On baking day,** dust the surface of the refrigerated dough with flour and cut off a 1-pound (grapefruit-size) piece. Dust the piece with more flour and quickly shape it into a ball by stretching the surface of the dough around to the bottom, rotating the ball a quarter turn as you go.

8. Elongate the ball into a narrow oval. Allow the loaf to rest, loosely covered with plastic wrap or an overturned bowl, on a pizza peel prepared with cornmeal or lined with parchment paper for 90 minutes (40 minutes if you're using fresh, unrefrigerated dough). Alternatively, you can rest the loaf on a silicone mat or a greased cookie sheet without using a pizza peel.

9. **Thirty minutes before baking time, preheat the oven to 450°F,** with a baking stone placed on the middle rack. Place an empty metal broiler tray on any other rack that won't interfere with the rising bread.

10. Just before baking, use a pastry brush to paint the top crust with water. Slash the loaf diagonally with ½-inch-deep parallel cuts, using a serrated bread knife.

11. Slide the loaf directly onto the hot stone (or place the silicone mat or cookie sheet on the stone if you used one). Pour 1 cup of hot tap water into the broiler tray, and quickly close the oven door (see page 40 for steam alternatives). Bake for about 30 minutes, or until richly browned and firm. If you used parchment paper, a silicone mat, or a cookie sheet under the loaf, carefully remove it and bake the loaf directly on the stone or an oven rack two-thirds of the way through the baking time. Smaller or larger loaves will require adjustments in resting and baking time.

12. Allow the bread to cool on a rack before slicing.

Mesquite Bread

"Zoë and I have been privileged to teach at Barbara Fenzl's Les Gourmettes Cooking School in Phoenix. The school is in her lovely home, and we were captivated by the photographs on her kitchen wall. The first ones our eyes fell on were of Julia Child and Jacques Pépin teaching in her kitchen—a bit intimidating, but Barbara immediately put us at ease by digging in and helping us with the prep work.

"As we left, Barbara pressed a sample of mesquite flour into my hands, and suggested that I might like it in bread. I enhanced the mesquite flavor with a few other Southwestern and Mexican ingredients: agave syrup, hot serrano peppers, masa flour, and cilantro. Flavor aside, hot peppers may have potent health effects, and corn masa is a rich nutrient source (see below). For a great Southwestern flatbread, try this dough in Southwestern Flatbread with Roasted Corn and Goat Cheese (page 280)."—Jeff

Hot peppers contain capsaicin, a potent phytochemical (beneficial plant chemical): Capsaicin is what makes spicy peppers hot and it also may decrease the likelihood of blood clots, heart attack, and stroke.

Corn masa, also called *masa harina,* is a Latin American corn product treated with alkali, which produces the distinctive flavor in Latin American dishes like tamales and tortillas; it also releases niacin from undigestible parts of the corn. Corn, whether alkali-treated or not, is an excellent source of lutein, an antioxidant that may prevent some cancers and some vision problems. If you use mesquite dough for the Southwestern Flatbread with Roasted Corn and Goat Cheese (page 280) you'll be getting a good helping of both kinds of corn.

Makes enough dough for at least four 1-pound loaves. The recipe is easily doubled or halved.

Ingredient	Volume (U.S.)	Weight (U.S.)	Weight (Metric)
Mesquite flour (sometimes sold as mesquite powder or meal)	1 cup	7 ounces	200 grams
All-purpose flour	3½ cups	1 pound, 1½ ounces	495 grams
Whole wheat flour	2¼ cups	10 ounces	285 grams
Corn masa (masa harina)	½ cup	2 ounces	55 grams
Granulated yeast (can decrease to taste, see page 56)	1 tablespoon	0.35 ounce	10 grams
Kosher salt (can increase or decrease to taste, see page 56)	1 tablespoon	0.6 ounce	15 grams
Vital wheat gluten	¼ cup	1⅜ ounces	40 grams
Lukewarm water	3½ cups	1 pound, 12 ounces	795 grams
Agave syrup	¼ cup	2 ounces	55 grams
2 serrano peppers, seeded, then finely minced (use rubber gloves for handling cut hot peppers and substitute jalapeños if you want less heat)			
½ cup chopped fresh cilantro			

1. **Mixing and storing the dough:** Whisk together the flours, corn masa, yeast, salt, and vital wheat gluten in a 5-quart bowl, or a lidded (not airtight) food container.

2. Add the liquid ingredients, peppers, and cilantro and mix without kneading, using a spoon, 14-cup food processor (with dough attachment),

or a heavy-duty stand mixer (with paddle). You might need to use wet hands to get the last bit of flour to incorporate if you're not using a machine.

3. Cover (not airtight), and allow the dough to rest at room temperature until it rises and collapses (or flattens on top), approximately 2 hours.

4. The dough can be used immediately after its initial rise, though it is easier to handle when cold. Refrigerate it in a lidded (not airtight) container and use over the next 7 days. The flavor will be best if you wait for at least 24 hours of refrigeration.

5. **On baking day,** dust the surface of the refrigerated dough with flour and cut off a 1-pound (grapefruit-size) piece. Dust with more flour and quickly shape it into a ball by stretching the surface of the dough around to the bottom, rotating the ball a quarter turn as you go.

6. Elongate the ball into a narrow oval. Allow the loaf to rest, loosely covered with plastic wrap or an overturned bowl, on a pizza peel prepared with corn masa or lined with parchment paper for 90 minutes (40 minutes if you're using fresh, unrefrigerated dough). Alternatively, you can rest the loaf on a silicone mat or a greased cookie sheet without using a pizza peel.

7. **Thirty minutes before baking time, preheat the oven to 400°F,** with a baking stone placed on the middle rack. Place an empty metal broiler tray on any other rack that won't interfere with the rising bread.

8. Just before baking, use a pastry brush to paint the top crust with water. Slash the loaf diagonally with ½-inch-deep parallel cuts, using a serrated bread knife.

9. Slide the loaf directly onto the hot stone (or place the silicone mat or cookie sheet on the stone if you used one). Pour 1 cup of hot tap water

into the broiler tray, and quickly close the oven door (see page 40 for steam alternatives). Bake for 35 to 40 minutes, or until richly browned and firm. If you used parchment paper, a silicone mat, or a cookie sheet under the loaf, carefully remove it and bake the loaf directly on the stone or an oven rack two-thirds of the way through the baking time. Smaller or larger loaves will require adjustments in resting and baking time.

10. Allow the bread to cool on a rack before slicing.

Four-Leaf Clover Broccoli and Cheddar Buns

Broccoli contains vitamins like A, C, and K, not to mention all the fiber. It is good for your eyes, bones, and immune system and even helps to prevent some forms of cancer. These cute green buns in the shape of four-leaf clovers are packed with broccoli, sprinkled with cheddar cheese, and are a great way to serve veggies even to the picky eaters in your house. Try the kale variation, too.

Makes at least 3 batches of 8 buns (24 total)

Ingredient	Volume (U.S.)	Weight (U.S.)	Weight (Metric)
Broccoli florets, raw	5 cups	15 ounces	425 grams
1½ cups water for cooking the broccoli	1½ cups	12 ounces	340 grams
Whole wheat flour	3 cups	13½ ounces	385 grams
All-purpose flour	4 cups	1 pound, 4 ounces	565 grams
Granulated yeast (can decrease to taste, see page 56)	1 tablespoon	0.35 ounce	10 grams
Kosher salt (can increase or decrease to taste, see page 56)	1 tablespoon	0.6 ounce	15 grams
Vital wheat gluten	¼ cup	1⅜ ounces	40 grams
Lukewarm water	1¾ cups	14 ounces	400 grams
Neutral-flavored oil for greasing the muffin pan			
1 cup shredded cheddar cheese for sprinkling on the buns, per batch			

1. **Cooking the broccoli**: In a medium saucepan, bring the water to a boil, add the broccoli, and cook on medium-high heat, covered, for 3 to 4 minutes. It is very important not to overcook the broccoli or it will taste bitter. It should be bright green. Remove from the stove and place the broccoli and the cooking water into a blender. Puree as finely as you can, but don't expect it to be perfectly smooth. This will yield 3 cups of broccoli puree. Set aside to cool slightly.

2. **Mixing and storing the dough:** Whisk together the flours, yeast, salt, and vital wheat gluten in a 5-quart bowl, or in a lidded (not airtight) food container.

3. Add the 1¾ cups lukewarm water and broccoli puree and mix without kneading, using a spoon, a 14-cup food processor (with dough attachment), or a heavy-duty stand mixer (with paddle). You might need to use wet hands to get the last bit of flour to incorporate if you're not using a machine.

4. Cover (not airtight), and allow the dough to rest at room temperature until it rises and collapses (or flattens on top), approximately 2 hours.

5. The dough can be used immediately after its initial rise, although it is easier to handle when cold. Refrigerate it in a non-airtight lidded container and use over the next 7 days.

6. **On baking day,** grease a muffin pan. Dust the surface of the refrigerated dough with flour and cut off a 1½-pound (cantaloupe-size) piece. Dust the piece with more flour and quickly shape it into a loose ball by stretching the surface of the dough around to the bottom, rotating the ball a quarter turn as you go.

7. **To form the rolls,** divide the ball into 8 roughly equal portions (each about the size of a plum). Cut each of the plum-size pieces into 4 smaller pieces. Shape each one into a smooth small ball. Put the

4 balls together to form the clover leaf and place in the cups of the muffin pan. Allow to rest, loosely covered with plastic wrap, for 40 minutes (20 minutes if you're using fresh, unrefrigerated dough).

8. **Thirty minutes before baking time, preheat the oven to 450°F**, with a baking stone placed on the middle rack. Place an empty metal broiler tray on any other rack that won't interfere with the rising buns.

9. Just before baking, sprinkle the buns with the cheddar cheese, being careful not to get it on the pan.

10. Slide the muffin pan directly onto the hot stone. Pour 1 cup of hot tap water into the broiler tray, and quickly close the oven door (see page 40 for steam alternatives). Bake for 20 to 25 minutes, or until richly browned and firm. The cheese will be melted and a bit caramelized.

11. Remove the buns from the pan and allow them to cool slightly before eating.

VARIATION WITH KALE

Replace the broccoli with kale. The amounts are the same, but the kale has to be well packed if measuring by cups.

Georgian Cheesy-Egg Boats (*Khachapuri*)

In the former Soviet Republic of Georgia (now an independent country nestled against the Black Sea), there's a wonderful egg, bread, and butter dish that sticks to your ribs in this cold mountainous place, and it's beautiful to look at as well (see color photo). The country has many versions of enriched bread that go by this name, but this beautiful open boat-shaped one comes from the coastal southeastern Adjara region. Traditional recipes call for the sour/salty *sulguni* cheese but we used feta cheese as a handy substitute (please come to the website and let us know if you find the authentic stuff).

Makes 4 boats

1 tablespoon oil or butter, plus additional butter to finish, if desired
1 garlic clove, minced
4 cups loosely packed fresh spinach leaves, washed and stemmed
2 tablespoons finely chopped fresh flat-leaf parsley
2 large eggs
4 ounces crumbled feta cheese
6 ounces Master Recipe (page 79), Soft Whole Wheat Sandwich Bread
    (page 132), 100% Whole Wheat Bread with Olive Oil (page 119), or other
    non-enriched dough
Salt and freshly ground black pepper

1. **Preheat the oven to 400°F.**

2. Warm the oil or butter in a skillet, add the garlic, spinach, and parsley, and sauté until most of the water has evaporated. Allow to cool slightly. Mix one of the eggs with the cheese in a separate bowl.

3. Dust the surface of the refrigerated dough with flour and cut off a 6-ounce (small orange-size) piece. Dust with more flour and quickly

shape it into a ball by stretching the surface of the dough around to the bottom, rotating the ball a quarter turn as you go.

4. Flatten the dough with your hands and a rolling pin on a work surface, to produce a ⅛-inch-thick oval, about 12 inches long and 5 inches wide). Dust with flour to keep the dough from adhering to the surface. Use a dough scraper to unstick the dough as needed, and transfer to a rimmed baking sheet lined with parchment paper or a silicone mat (this will prevent egg from running everywhere if it slips off).

5. Place the filling in the middle of the dough. Starting with the long side, fold the dough up over the filling; the dough will come halfway into the middle. Fold the other side over to form a boat shape. Pinch the overlapping ends together to make a good seal.

6. Brush the dough with oil or butter and bake for 15 minutes near the center of the oven.

7. Remove the boat from the oven. Using a large spoon make an indentation in the cheese mixture to keep the egg from running out, and crack the remaining egg into the space.

8. **Place the baking sheet back in the oven,** and bake, checking for doneness in 12 to 15 minutes, or until the egg is cooked to your liking. Turn the boat around in the oven if one side is browning faster than the other.

9. Remove from the oven, allow to cool slightly, and brush the dough with more butter or oil. The tradition in Adjara is to place a large pat of butter on the egg (your move). Season with salt and pepper to taste.

Red Beet Buns

These are beautiful bright buns, with a crimson crust and a crumb flecked with red. The sweetness of beets adds a wonderful flavor, and the color is glorious (see color photo).

Makes enough dough for five batches of 8 buns (40 total)

Ingredient	Volume (U.S.)	Weight (U.S.)	Weight (Metric)
Whole wheat flour	2 cups	9 ounces	260 grams
All-purpose flour	2 cups	10 ounces	285 grams
Spelt flour	3 cups	15½ ounces	435 grams
Granulated yeast (can decrease to taste, see page 56)	1 tablespoon	0.35 ounce	10 grams
Kosher salt (can increase or decrease to taste, see page 56)	1 tablespoon	0.6 ounce	15 grams
Vital wheat gluten	¼ cup	1⅜ ounces	40 grams
Lukewarm water	3¼ cups	1 pound, 10 ounces	735 grams
3 cups finely shredded peeled raw beets			
½ white onion, finely chopped			

〜

Beets: The root's deep red color comes from beta-cyanin, but this is more than a pretty face. The pigment may help prevent cell mutations that can cause cancer. Beets are also a rich source of folic acid.

1. **Mixing and storing the dough:** Whisk together the flours, yeast, salt, and vital wheat gluten in a 5-quart bowl, or a lidded (not airtight) food container.

2. Add the water, beets, and onion and mix without kneading, using a spoon, a 14-cup food processor (with dough attachment), or a heavy-duty stand mixer (with paddle). You might need to use wet hands to get the last bit of flour to incorporate if you're not using a machine.

3. Cover (not airtight), and allow the dough to rest at room temperature until it rises and collapses (or flattens on top), approximately 2 hours.

4. The dough can be used immediately after its initial rise, though it is easier to handle when cold. Refrigerate it in a lidded (not airtight) container and use over the next 5 days. The flavor will be best if you wait for at least 24 hours of refrigeration.

5. **On baking day,** dust the surface of the refrigerated dough with flour and cut off a 1-pound (grapefruit-size) piece. Dust the piece with more flour and quickly shape it into a ball by stretching the surface of the dough around to the bottom, rotating the ball a quarter turn as you go.

6. **To form the buns:** Divide the ball into 8 roughly equal portions (each about the size of a golf ball). Shape each one into a smooth ball. Allow

them to rest, loosely covered with plastic wrap or an overturned bowl, on a baking sheet lined with parchment paper for 40 minutes (20 minutes if you're using fresh, unrefrigerated dough). Alternatively, you can rest the buns on a silicone mat–lined baking sheet or a greased baking sheet.

7. **Thirty minutes before baking time, preheat the oven to 450°F,** with a baking stone placed on the middle rack. Place an empty metal broiler tray on any other shelf that won't interfere with the rising buns.

8. Just before baking, use a pastry brush to paint the top crusts with water.

9. Slide the cookie sheet directly onto the hot stone. Pour 1 cup of hot tap water into the broiler tray, and quickly close the oven door (see page 40 for steam alternatives). Bake for about 20 minutes, or until richly browned and firm.

10. Allow the buns to cool on a rack before eating.

Stuffed "Sandwich" Loaf

In our constant attempt to find things for children to bring to school for lunch, we developed a bread with the filling rolled right into the dough. Here are three of our favorite combinations—you should let your imagination run wild and come up with your own versions, to suit your taste.

Makes one 2-pound loaf

Use any lean or enriched dough to your liking

1 pound (grapefruit-size portion) of any pre-mixed dough listed above

The Roasted Vegetable and Chèvre Filling

1 bell pepper or 1 jarred roasted pepper
2 tablespoons olive oil
6 ounces portobello mushrooms, sliced ⅛ inch thick
Salt and freshly ground black pepper
4 marinated artichoke hearts, canned or jarred, thinly sliced
6 ounces chèvre (goat cheese)

1. **Preparing the vegetables**: If grilling your own bell pepper, cut the pepper into quarters and then flatten the pieces, making additional cuts as needed to make the pieces flat. Grill the pepper pieces on a gas or charcoal grill, with the skin side closest to the heat source, or place them under the broiler. Check often and remove when the skins have blackened, about 10 minutes or more, depending on the heat source.

2. Drop the roasted pieces into a bowl or pot and cover. The skin will loosen by steaming in its own heat and moisture for 10 minutes.

3. Gently hand-peel the pepper pieces and discard the blackened skins; it's fine if some dark bits adhere to the pepper's flesh.

4. Heat the olive oil in a skillet over medium heat. Add the portobello mushrooms and sauté until wilted. Season with salt and pepper to taste. Set aside.

5. Lightly grease an 8½×4½-inch nonstick loaf pan. Dust the surface of the refrigerated dough with flour and cut off a 1-pound (grapefruit-size) piece. Dust the piece with more flour and quickly shape it into a ball by stretching the surface of the dough around to the bottom, rotating the ball a quarter turn as you go.

6. With a rolling pin, roll the dough out until it is a ¼-inch-thick rectangle. As you roll out the dough, use enough flour to prevent it from sticking to the work surface but not so much as to make the dough dry.

7. Spread the roasted pepper, sautéed mushroom mixture, artichoke hearts, and chèvre over the rolled-out dough. Leave a border all around the edge. Roll the dough into a log, starting at the short end. Using wet hands, crimp the ends shut and tuck them under. Place the log in the loaf pan and allow it to rest, loosely covered with plastic wrap, for 90 minutes (40 minutes if you're using fresh unrefrigerated dough).

8. **Thirty minutes before baking time, preheat the oven to 350°F,** with a baking stone placed on the middle rack. If you're not using a stone in the oven, a 5-minute preheat is adequate.

9. Just before baking, use a pastry brush to paint the top crust with water.

10. Slide the loaf directly onto the hot stone or on a rack near the middle of the oven. Bake for 50 to 60 minutes, or until deeply browned and firm. Smaller or larger loaves will require adjustments in resting and baking time.

11. Remove the bread from the pan and allow it to cool before slicing.

VARIATIONS

Spinach, Feta, and Turkey Filling

2 cups fresh whole spinach leaves, loosely packed
4 ounces crumbled feta cheese
4 to 6 slices thinly sliced cooked turkey breast

Ham, Emmental Cheese, and Sautéed Cabbage Filling

2 tablespoons olive oil
2 cups cabbage, shredded
4 to 6 slices thinly sliced ham
6 ounces grated Emmental cheese
Salt and freshly ground black pepper
2 tablespoons grainy Dijon mustard

To prepare the cabbage: Heat the olive oil in a skillet over medium heat. Add the cabbage and sauté until wilted. Season with salt and pepper to taste. Allow to cool slightly before rolling into the dough with the ham, cheese, and mustard.

Turkish Pear Coffee Bread

This is a very unusual bread with some unlikely ingredients: pear puree and ground coffee (which turns out to have plenty of antioxidants, see the Chocolate Espresso Bread box on page 378). We were dubious about ground coffee in a bread, but its slightly bitter and delicious flavor, combined with the juicy pears, sweet spices, and brown sugar, add up to a winner. There's not much caffeine in each slice—the entire four-loaf batch has the equivalent of two cups of coffee, but it can also be made with decaf.

Turkish Pear Coffee Bread has a tendency to spread sideways, so don't be surprised if your bread looks more flat than tall.

Makes enough dough for at least four 1-pound loaves. The recipe is easily doubled or halved.

Ingredient	Volume (U.S.)	Weight (U.S.)	Weight (Metric)
Whole wheat flour	¼ cup	1 ounce	30 grams
All-purpose flour	6 cups	1 pound, 14 ounces	850 grams
Ground coffee (regular grind)	4 teaspoons	⅓ ounce	10 grams
½ teaspoon ground cardamom			
Brown sugar, packed	¼ cup	2 ounces	55 grams
Granulated yeast (can decrease to taste, see page 56)	1 tablespoon	0.35 ounce	10 grams
Kosher salt (can increase or decrease to taste, see page 56)	1 tablespoon	0.6 ounce	15 grams
Vital wheat gluten*	¼ cup	1⅜ ounces	40 grams
3 ripe pears, cored and pureed with skin, or 6 canned pear halves, pureed			

*Don't try to omit the vital wheat gluten or the results will be dense.

Ingredient	Volume (U.S.)	Weight (U.S.)	Weight (Metric)
Lukewarm water	1 cup	8 ounces	225 grams
2 large eggs, lightly beaten			
Vegetable oil, olive oil, or melted unsalted butter or coconut oil (see page 28 for options)	¼ cup	2 ounces	55 grams
½ teaspoon pure vanilla extract			
Plain nonfat (or whole milk) yogurt	¼ cup	2 ounces	55 grams
Egg wash (1 egg beaten with 1 tablespoon water) for painting the top crust			
Raw sugar for sprinkling on top crust			
Cornmeal or parchment paper for the pizza peel			

1. **Mixing and storing the dough:** Whisk together the flours, coffee, cardamom, brown sugar, yeast, salt, and vital wheat gluten in a 5-quart bowl, or a lidded (not airtight) food container.

2. Combine the pears with all the liquid ingredients and mix them with the dry ingredients without kneading, using a spoon, a 14-cup food processor (with dough attachment), or a heavy-duty stand mixer (with paddle). You might need to use wet hands to get the last bit of flour to incorporate if you're not using a machine.

3. Cover (not airtight), and allow the dough to rest at room temperature until it rises and collapses (or flattens on top), approximately 2 hours.

4. The dough can be used immediately after its initial rise, though it is easier to handle when cold. Refrigerate it in a lidded (not airtight)

container and use over the next 5 days. The dough can be frozen in single-loaf portions and defrosted overnight in the refrigerator.

5. **On baking day,** dust the surface of the refrigerated dough with flour and cut off a 1-pound (grapefruit-size) piece. Dust the piece with more flour and quickly shape it into a ball by stretching the surface of the dough around to the bottom, rotating the ball a quarter turn as you go.

6. Elongate the ball into a narrow oval. Allow the dough to rest, loosely covered with plastic wrap or an overturned bowl, on a pizza peel prepared with cornmeal or lined with parchment paper for 90 minutes (40 minutes if you're using fresh, unrefrigerated dough). Alternatively, you can rest the loaf on a silicone mat or a greased cookie sheet without using a pizza peel.

7. **Thirty minutes before baking time, preheat the oven to 350°F,** with a baking stone placed on the middle rack.

8. Just before baking, use a pastry brush to paint the top crust with egg wash, then sprinkle it with raw sugar. Slash the loaf diagonally with ½-inch-deep parallel cuts, using a serrated bread knife.

9. Slide the loaf directly onto the hot stone (or place the silicone mat or cookie sheet on the stone if you used one). Bake for 35 to 40 minutes, or until richly browned and firm. If you used parchment paper, a silicone mat, or a cookie sheet under the loaf, carefully remove it and bake the loaf directly on the stone or an oven rack two-thirds of the way through the baking time. Smaller or larger loaves will require adjustments in resting and baking time.

10. Allow the bread to cool on a rack before slicing.

Brown Rice and Prune Bread (... Try It, You'll Like It)

We know, we know, these two ingredients don't sound like the most obvious pairing. But you simply have to try it; they are fantastic together. The sweet prune juice caramelizes the crust and helps it to crisp, countering the tendency of whole grain doughs to produce a soft crust. You'll need to turn down the heat a bit to prevent the crust from burning—to 425°F. Pomegranate juice and açai are much more fashionable than prune juice these days, so try the variations below if they strike your fancy.

Makes enough dough for at least five 1-pound loaves. The recipe is easily doubled or halved.

Ingredient	Volume (U.S.)	Weight (U.S.)	Weight (Metric)
Whole wheat flour	5 cups	1 pound, 6½ ounces	640 grams
All-purpose flour	3 cups	15 ounces	425 grams
Granulated yeast (can decrease to taste, see page 56)	1 tablespoon	0.35 ounce	10 grams
Kosher salt (can increase or decrease to taste, see page 56)	1 tablespoon	0.6 ounce	15 grams
Vital wheat gluten	¼ cup	1⅜ ounces	40 grams
Lukewarm water	1 cup	8 ounces	225 grams
Lukewarm prune juice	3 cups	1 pound, 8 ounces	680 grams
Brown rice, cooked	1 cup	6½ ounces	185 grams
Prunes, finely chopped	¾ cup	5 ounces	140 grams

Pomegranate juice appears to have a variety of terrific health benefits. It's chock-full of vitamin C, calcium, potassium, and iron, plus three kinds of antioxidants. If you find the juice too sour to drink by itself, this bread is a great way to get the health benefits in a delicious and mellower form.

Açai juice is another fruit juice that has been touted as a super-food, even richer in antioxidants than pomegranate. The juice comes from a Brazilian berry that's just starting to be imported to the U.S. Most of the açai products available to us are made from a blend of fruits, with only modest contributions from açai; 100% açai juice is available through the Web or by mail order, but it's quite expensive—we didn't test with it.

1. **Mixing and storing the dough:** Whisk together the flours, yeast, salt, and vital wheat gluten in a 5-quart bowl, or a lidded (not airtight) food container.

2. Add the liquid ingredients, brown rice, and prunes, and mix without kneading, using a spoon, a 14-cup food processor (with dough attachment), or a heavy-duty stand mixer (with paddle). You might need to use wet hands to get the last bit of flour to incorporate if you're not using a machine.

3. Cover (not airtight), and allow the dough to rest at room temperature until it rises and collapses (or flattens on top), approximately 2 hours.

4. The dough can be used immediately after its initial rise, though it is easier to handle when cold. Refrigerate it in a lidded (not airtight) container and use over the next 10 days. The flavor will be best if you wait for at least 24 hours of refrigeration.

5. **On baking day,** dust the surface of the refrigerated dough with flour and cut off a 1-pound (grapefruit-size) piece. Dust the piece with more flour and quickly shape it into a ball by stretching the surface of

the dough around to the bottom, rotating the ball a quarter turn as you go.

6. Elongate the ball into a narrow oval. Allow the loaf to rest, loosely covered with plastic wrap or an overturned bowl, on a pizza peel prepared with cornmeal or lined with parchment paper for 90 minutes (40 minutes if you're using fresh, unrefrigerated dough). Alternatively, you can rest the loaf on a silicone mat or a greased cookie sheet without using a pizza peel.

7. **Thirty minutes before baking time, preheat the oven to 425°F,** with a baking stone placed on the middle rack. Place an empty metal broiler tray on any other rack that won't interfere with the rising bread.

8. Just before baking, use a pastry brush to paint the top crust with water. Slash the loaf diagonally with ½-inch-deep parallel cuts, using a serrated bread knife.

9. Slide the loaf directly onto the hot stone (or place the silicone mat or cookie sheet on the stone if you used one). Pour 1 cup of hot tap water into the broiler tray, and quickly close the oven door (see page 40 for steam alternatives). Bake for about 30 minutes, or until richly browned and firm. If you used parchment paper, a silicone mat, or a cookie sheet under the loaf, carefully remove it and bake the loaf directly on the stone or an oven rack two-thirds of the way through the baking time. Smaller or larger loaves will require adjustments in resting and baking time.

10. Allow the bread to cool on a rack before slicing.

VARIATION: Brown Rice and Pomegranate (or Açai) Bread

Simply substitute an equal volume of pomegranate or açai juice in place of the prune juice in the recipe above. You'll get the same caramelization but a more tart flavor. If prunes border on the cloyingly sweet, then pomegranate juice borders on the bracingly sour. A 50:50 blend of prune juice with pomegranate or açai juice also works nicely and plays the opposing sweet and tart off each other. Try varying the fruit as well—raisins or dried cranberries work beautifully instead of prunes.

Oatmeal Date Bread

You'll make this loaf over and over, not for the high fiber and nutrition of the steel-cut oats and dates, but because it is absolutely delicious. Steel-cut oats are often sold as "Scottish" or "Irish" oats. Ignore our rule of waiting until the bread is perfectly cool—slice into this one when it is still a touch warm.

Makes enough dough for at least two 2-pound loaves. The recipe is easily doubled or halved.

Ingredient	Volume (U.S.)	Weight (U.S.)	Weight (Metric)
Whole wheat flour*	3 cups	13½ ounces	385 grams
All-purpose flour	2 cups	10 ounces	285 grams
Steel-cut oats	2 cups	6 ounces	170 grams
Granulated yeast (can decrease to taste, see page 56)	1 tablespoon	0.35 ounce	10 grams
Kosher salt (can increase or decrease to taste, see page 56)	1 tablespoon	0.6 ounce	15 grams
Vital wheat gluten*	¼ cup	1⅜ ounces	40 grams
Lukewarm water	3 cups	1 pound, 8 ounces	680 grams
Maple syrup	⅓ cup	2⅔ ounces	75 grams
Vegetable oil, olive oil, or melted unsalted butter or coconut oil (see page 28 for options)	¼ cup	2 ounces	55 grams
1½ cups dates, finely chopped (about 15 large dates)			

*For whole wheat flours other than Gold Medal or Pillsbury, or for omitting vital wheat gluten, see page 82 for guidelines on adjustment.

(continued)

Visit BreadIn5.com, where you'll find recipes, photos, videos, and instructional material.

Ingredient	Volume (U.S.)	Weight (U.S.)	Weight (Metric)
1½ cups walnuts, finely chopped (optional, for walnut variation)			
Egg wash (1 egg beaten with 1 tablespoon water) for brushing on the top crust			
Raw sugar for sprinkling on top			

1. **Mixing and storing the dough:** Whisk together the flours, oats, yeast, salt, and vital wheat gluten in a 5-quart bowl, or a lidded (not airtight) food container.

2. Combine the liquid ingredients and dates and mix them with the dry ingredients without kneading, using a spoon, a 14-cup food processor (with dough attachment), or a heavy-duty stand mixer (with paddle). You might need to use wet hands to get the last bit of flour to incorporate if you're not using a machine.

3. Cover (not airtight), and allow the dough to rest at room temperature until it rises and collapses (or flattens on top), approximately 2 hours.

4. The dough can be used immediately after its initial rise, though it is easier to handle when cold. Refrigerate it in a lidded (not airtight) container and use over the next 7 days.

5. **On baking day,** lightly grease an 8½×4½-inch nonstick loaf pan. Dust the surface of the refrigerated dough with flour and cut off a 2-pound (cantaloupe-size) piece. Dust the piece with more flour and quickly shape it into a ball by stretching the surface of the dough around to the bottom, rotating the ball a quarter turn as you go.

6. Elongate the ball into an oval and place it into the loaf pan; your goal is to fill the pan about three-quarters full. Cover loosely with plastic wrap. Allow the loaf to rest and rise for 1 hour 45 minutes (60 minutes if you're using fresh, unrefrigerated dough).

7. **Thirty minutes before baking time, preheat the oven to 375°F,** with a baking stone placed on the middle rack. The baking stone is not essential for loaf-pan breads; if you omit it, the preheat can be as short as 5 minutes.

8. Just before baking, use a pastry brush to paint the top crust with egg wash, then sprinkle it with raw sugar.

9. Place the loaf on the stone or on a rack near the center of the oven. Bake for 45 to 50 minutes, or until richly browned and firm.

10. Remove the bread from the pan and allow it to cool slightly on a rack before slicing.

VARIATION: Oatmeal-Date-Walnut Bread

After taking the dough from the bucket, flatten the dough with wet hands to a thickness of ½ inch and sprinkle with the walnuts. Roll up the dough from the short end, like a jelly roll, to form a log. Using wet hands, crimp the ends shut and tuck them under to form an oval loaf. Place it into the loaf pan, as in step 6, and follow the baking instructions starting at step 7.

Apple-Barley Bread

This bread is all about fall, when apples are at their peak. Combined with the warm, comforting taste of barley flour they make a great marriage. Barley is a much underused flour for baking; it not only has great flavor but also is incredibly high in fiber. This bread is sweetened with barley malt, normally associated with the taste of beer. It jump-starts the development of yeasty flavors, giving the dough more character quickly. They say an apple a day keeps the doctor away, and it's true that apples contain plenty of fiber and antioxidants, but what's more important is that they're irresistible. Use a combination of tart, sweet, soft, and firm apples for the best flavor, like the McIntosh and Granny Smith. We've combined the freshly grated fruit with dried apples and cider to give a nice chew and an even more intense flavor.

Makes enough dough for at least two 2-pound loaves. The recipe is easily doubled or halved.

Ingredient	Volume (U.S.)	Weight (U.S.)	Weight (Metric)
Barley flour	2¾ cups	11¾ ounces	330 grams
All-purpose flour	3½ cups	1 pound, 1½ ounces	495 grams
Rye flour	½ cup	2 ounces	55 grams
Granulated yeast (can decrease to taste, see page 56)	1 tablespoon	0.35 ounce	10 grams
Kosher salt (can increase or decrease to taste, see page 56)	1 tablespoon	0.6 ounce	15 grams
Vital wheat gluten	¼ cup	1⅜ ounces	40 grams
Lukewarm apple cider	2½ cups	1 pound, 4 ounces	565 grams

Ingredient	Volume (U.S.)	Weight (U.S.)	Weight (Metric)
Honey	¼ cup	3 ounces	85 grams
Barley malt syrup	½ cup	5¾ ounces	165 grams
Vegetable oil, olive oil, or melted unsalted butter or coconut oil (see page 28 for options)	¼ cup	2 ounces	55 grams
2 medium apples, cored and grated (include the skin)			
4 ounces dried apples, chopped			
Egg wash (1 egg beaten with 1 tablespoon water) for painting the top crust			
Raw sugar for sprinkling on top			

1. **Mixing and storing the dough:** Whisk together the flours, yeast, salt, and vital wheat gluten in a 5-quart bowl, or a lidded (not airtight) food container.

2. Add the liquid ingredients and the apples and mix them with the dry ingredients without kneading, using a spoon, a 14-cup food processor (with dough attachment), or a heavy-duty stand mixer (with paddle). You might need to use wet hands to get the last bit of flour to incorporate if you're not using a machine.

3. Cover (not airtight), and allow the dough to rest at room temperature until it rises and collapses (or flattens on top), approximately 2 hours.

4. The dough can be used immediately after its initial rise, though it is easier to handle when cold. Refrigerate it in a lidded (not airtight) container and use over the next 7 days.

5. **On baking day,** lightly grease an 8½×4½-inch nonstick loaf pan. Dust the surface of the refrigerated dough with flour and cut off a 2-pound

(cantaloupe-size) piece. Dust the piece with more flour and quickly shape it into a ball by stretching the surface of the dough around to the bottom, rotating the ball a quarter turn as you go.

6. Elongate the ball into an oval and place it in the loaf pan; your goal is to fill the pan about three-quarters full. Allow the loaf to rest and rise for 1 hour 45 minutes (60 minutes if you're using fresh, unrefrigerated dough).

7. **Thirty minutes before baking time, preheat the oven to 375°F,** with a baking stone placed on the middle rack. The baking stone is not essential for loaf-pan breads; if you omit it, the preheat can be as short as 5 minutes.

8. Just before baking, use a pastry brush to paint the top crust with egg wash, then sprinkle it with raw sugar.

9. Place the loaf on the stone or on a rack near the center of the oven. Bake for 45 to 50 minutes, or until richly browned and firm.

10. Remove the bread from the pan and allow it to cool on a rack before slicing.

8

FLATBREADS AND PIZZA

When we teach bread classes, busy people tell us that our flatbreads and pizza recipes are the ones they come back to the most often. That's because dough turns into flatbread in record time. Whether whole grain or not, thin breads need little or no resting time, and take short baking times. And people keep telling us that speed is the name of the game. But it's not the only game—it turns out that **pizza is the easiest hiding place for whole grains.** Because of the toppings, even the most finicky kids don't seem to notice whole grains in pizza dough. The stronger the topping flavors, the easier it will be to get kids to sample whole grains and vegetables. And they'll say that this pizza is superior to any from a chain restaurant.

We bake pizza three ways:

- **Old-fashioned high-temperature oven baking:** This will be the most familiar to you. No steam is needed; just bake it without steam in the bottom third of the oven.
- **Directly over the grates on an outdoor gas grill:** This gives the crunchiest, most rustic result, adding some smoky notes to the pizza.
- **On top of a baking stone on the outdoor gas grill:** The pizza will be pretty close to what you get inside an oven, but check with your stone's manufacturer and consider cast iron or steel if durability is a concern.

⌒⌒

In 2007, University of Maryland researchers showed that **pizza has more antioxidants when the crust is whole grain baked at high temperature.** How do we get on that research team? Pizza's antioxidant activity was highest when the crust was whole grain, and the baking temperature was high, resulting in rich browning. Works for us—we've always favored high-heat pizza, in the Neapolitan style. The research fits well with other studies that showed that there are more antioxidants in the browned crust of white bread than in the white crumb. Maybe that's why Mom always told us to finish our crusts.

With any pizza method, have all your toppings prepared and measured in advance so that the dough doesn't sit on the board waiting once it's rolled out (which would give it time to stick).

Oven-Baked Whole Grain Pizza with Roasted Red Peppers and Fontina

This is the traditional indoor method for baking pizza; you can do any of our other pizzas this way. For this recipe, we decided to pair a traditional crust with somewhat nontraditional toppings. Of course, you can put whatever you like on this pizza, including the standard thick tomato sauce and mozzarella cheese. In this recipe, leaving out tomatoes really lets you savor the unique smoky flavor of roasted red peppers. Chop them into a coarse dice and make sure to use the juices that run out of the peppers to infuse the whole pie with the flavor of the roasted pepper. It's a perfect blend with lovely fontina cheese.

Makes one 12- to 14-inch pizza; serves 2 to 4

Use any of these refrigerated pre-mixed doughs: Master Recipe (page 79), Soft Whole Wheat Sandwich Bread (page 132), 100% Whole Wheat Bread with Olive Oil (page 119), or other non-enriched dough
½ pound (orange-size portion) of any pre-mixed dough listed above
1 red bell pepper
¼ pound coarsely grated fontina cheese
Olive oil for drizzling
Extra flour for dusting the pizza peel

1. **Roasting the pepper:** Grill the pepper on a gas or charcoal grill, with the skin side closest to the heat source, or place it under the broiler. Check often and remove the pepper when the skin has blackened, about 10 minutes or more, depending on the heat source.

2. Drop the roasted pepper into a bowl or pot and cover. The skin will loosen by steaming in its own heat and moisture for 10 minutes.

---

3. Gently hand peel the bell pepper and discard the blackened skin. Some dark bits will adhere to the pepper's flesh—this is fine.

4. Cut the pepper into a coarse dice, reserving any liquid.

5. **Thirty minutes before baking time, preheat the oven to 550°F (or 500°F if that's your oven's maximum)** with a baking stone placed near the bottom third of the oven. You won't be using steam, so you can omit the broiler tray.

ᏩᎧ

Turn on your exhaust fan if you have one: This recipe calls for an exhaust fan because there can be a lot of smoke from stray flour on such a hot stone. Make sure the stone is scraped clean before preheating. If you don't have an exhaust fan, choose a lower oven temperature (450°F), and bake 15 to 20 percent longer.

---

6. Prepare and measure all the toppings in advance. The key to a pizza that slides right off the peel is to work quickly—don't let the dough sit on the peel any longer than necessary.

7. Dust the surface of the refrigerated dough with flour and cut off a ½-pound (orange-size) piece. Dust the piece with more flour and quickly shape it into a ball by stretching the surface of the dough around to the bottom, rotating the ball a quarter turn as you go. You don't need to be careful about shaping a perfect ball because it won't be your final shape anyway.

8. Directly on a wooden pizza peel, flatten the dough with your hands and a rolling pin to produce a ⅛-inch-thick round. Dust with flour to keep the dough from adhering to the board. A little sticking to the board can be helpful in overcoming the dough's resistance to stretch. Use a dough scraper to unstick the dough as needed. When you're done, the dough round should have enough flour under it to move easily when you shake the peel.

With experience, you'll learn just how much flour to use so you don't end up with too much on the bottom of your pizza and on the stone.

9. Scatter the fontina cheese over the surface of the dough, then distribute the diced bell pepper and reserved liquid. No further resting is needed prior to baking. Drizzle with olive oil.

10. If you have an exhaust fan, turn it on now, because some of the flour on the pizza peel will smoke at this temperature (see sidebar). Slide the pizza directly onto the stone (it may take a number of back-and-forth shakes to dislodge). Check for doneness in 8 to 10 minutes; at this time, turn the pizza around in the oven if one side is browning faster than the other. It may take up to 5 minutes more in the oven.

11. Allow the pizza to cool slightly on a cooling rack before serving, to allow the cheese to set.

VARIATION: Pizza Margherita

This is a world-famous Italian specialty—instead of bell pepper and fontina, top lightly with thick tomato sauce (we prefer plain canned tomatoes, broken up or pureed, and then reduced until thick on the stovetop), then fresh mozzarella, cut into large cubes—3 or 4 ounces for a pie this size. Fresh basil leaves are traditional on pizza margherita, and if you want eye-popping color, you can wait until your pie's out of the oven before using it, whole-leaf or hand torn. Or, bake the basil on the pizza with the rest of the toppings (see color photo).

Zucchini Flatbread

Seems that everyone who *doesn't* have a green thumb grows zucchini—they grow like weeds. The problem is that you end up with bushels of zucchini and no one could possibly eat them all. If you have stored dough, some Parmigiano-Reggiano or other grating cheese, and parsley, you can create this very fast zucchini flatbread—it's absolutely scrumptious (see color photo).

Makes one 12- to 14-inch flatbread; serves 2 to 4

Use any of these refrigerated pre-mixed doughs: Master Recipe (page 79), 100% Whole Wheat Master Recipe (page 91), 100% Whole Wheat Bread with Olive Oil (page 119), other non-enriched dough, or Gluten-Free Olive Oil Bread (page 302)

½ pound (orange-size portion) of any pre-mixed dough listed above

¼ cup (2 ounces/55 grams) olive oil

2 scallions, sliced thinly into rounds

½ bunch fresh flat-leaf parsley, tough stems removed, chopped (about ¾ loosely packed cup)

2 small or 1 large zucchini, coarsely grated

½ teaspoon kosher salt, plus additional for sprinkling

Freshly ground black pepper

½ cup grated Parmigiano-Reggiano cheese

Extra flour for dusting the pizza peel

Additional zucchini, sliced very thinly with a knife or on a mandoline

2 to 4 tablespoons pine nuts, toasted in a hot dry pan until lightly browned

1. **Thirty minutes before baking time, preheat the oven to 450°F,** with a baking stone placed in the bottom third of the oven. You won't be using steam, so you can omit the broiler tray.

2. **Prepare the topping:** Heat the olive oil over medium heat in a skillet. Add the scallions and sauté until softened and fragrant, then add the

parsley, grated zucchini, salt, and pepper to taste. Continue to sauté until the vegetables are wilted and the liquid has mostly evaporated, about 10 minutes. Remove from heat and set aside for 10 minutes, then stir in the grated cheese.

3. Dust the surface of the refrigerated dough with flour and cut off a ½-pound (orange-size) piece. Dust the piece with more flour and quickly shape it into a rough ball by stretching the surface of the dough around to the bottom, rotating the ball a quarter turn as you go. You don't need to be as careful about shaping a perfect ball because it won't be your final shape anyway.

4. Flatten the dough with your hands and a rolling pin directly onto a wooden pizza peel to produce a ⅛-inch-thick round, dusting with flour to keep the dough from sticking to the board. A little sticking to the board can be helpful in overcoming the dough's resistance. Use a dough scraper to unstick the dough when it sticks to the board. When you're done, the dough should have enough flour under it to move easily when you shake the peel.

5. Working quickly, cover the surface of the dough with about a ¼-inch coating of the sautéed vegetables (you may have more than you need). Top with the sliced zucchini.

6. Slide the pizza directly onto the stone (it may take a number of back-and-forth shakes to dislodge the pizza). Check for doneness in 12 to 15 minutes; at this time, turn the pizza around in the oven if one side is browning faster than the other. Continue baking until nicely browned. Finish with the pine nuts and a fresh grinding of pepper and additional kosher salt if desired.

7. Allow the pizza to cool slightly on a rack before serving.

Whole Grain Pizza on the Gas Grill (Right on the Grates)

Baking pizza outside on the gas grill answers one of the age-old problems that face home bakers: Who wants to bake inside in the summer? We sure don't. We wondered whether dough this wet would stick to the grates, fall into the flames, or otherwise cause mayhem. It didn't. As long as your grates are in good shape and you keep the dough well dusted before sliding it onto the grill, it's no problem at all. Just remember to first bake the crust "blind" (without toppings), flipping when the bottom browns. Otherwise it's hard to get pizza to bake through without burning unless you use a stone (see page 272).

"This pizza has been the source of many happy summer lawn parties in my backyard, where it is served with lots of cold semi-sparkling Italian wine. Have your guests make their own pizza by having a variety of toppings all ready to go—see who can throw their dough into the air the highest. Visit our YouTube

∽

You say you don't like anchovies? We made anchovies optional in this pizza because, well, they're not for everyone. Kids, in particular, can be a little closed-minded about these salty, oily little guys. But if you don't like anchovies, maybe you should reconsider. They're extraordinarily rich in omega-3 fatty acids, pretty much the healthiest fat you can eat. If your kids simply won't eat them . . . send them off to sleepovers, chop up some anchovies, throw them on your pizza, and serve with a big glass of red wine.

channel (YouTube.com/BreadIn5) and search on 'pizza throwing' for instruc-tions on how to throw and twirl the dough."—Jeff

Makes one 12- to 14-inch pizza; serves 2 to 4

Use any of these refrigerated pre-mixed doughs: Master Recipe (page 79), 100% Whole Wheat Master Recipe (page 91), 100% Whole Wheat Bread with Olive Oil (page 119), or other non-enriched dough

½ pound (orange-size portion) of any pre-mixed dough listed above

Extra flour for dusting the pizza peel

½ cup canned Italian-style chopped tomatoes, strained and pressed of liquid (or substitute canned tomato sauce)

¼ pound sliced fresh mozzarella cheese

10 fresh basil leaves, cut into thin strips

2 to 4 anchovy fillets, chopped (optional) (see sidebar)

Olive oil for drizzling

Additional olive oil for oiling the grates (may not be needed if grates are clean and in good condition)

1. Preheat your gas grill with medium flame on all burners. Prepare and measure all the toppings in advance.

2. Dust the surface of the refrigerated dough with flour and cut off a ½-pound (orange-size) piece. Dust the piece with more flour and quickly shape it into a rough ball by stretching the surface of the dough around to the bottom, rotating the ball a quarter turn as you go. You don't need to be as careful about shaping a perfect ball because it won't be your final shape anyway.

3. Directly on a wooden pizza peel, flatten the dough with your hands and a rolling pin to produce a ⅛-inch-thick round, dusting with flour to keep the dough from adhering to the board. A little sticking to the board can be helpful in overcoming the dough's resistance to stretch. Use a dough scraper to unstick the dough as needed. When you're done,

the dough round should have enough flour under it to move easily when you shake the peel. Dock (puncture) the dough all over with a fork.

4. Bake the crust "blind." Bring the dough round and all the ingredients to the outdoor gas grill. Slide the dough onto the grates, directly over the lit burners, and close the lid. Keep the lid closed except for the occasional peek, or it's going to be difficult to get the dough to bake through. You may have to rotate the dough, or adjust the heat, in order to get an even doneness. If the dough puffs too much, poke it with a fork. Flip the dough with a spatula when the top surface looks puffy and the bottom surface is nicely browned (it may char a bit in places), 2 to 3 minutes.

5. Distribute the tomato, cheese and other toppings; be relatively sparing with them. Drizzle the pizza with olive oil and close the grill lid. It's difficult to get the cheese to brown, but the crust will caramelize so beautifully that you won't be disappointed. It will take another 3 to 5 minutes, depending on how much heat your grill delivers. Watch carefully and remove before the bottom burns. Keep the lid closed as much as possible to trap the heat, which will help to bake the toppings. Use your nose to detect when the bottom crust is just beginning to char.

6. Allow to cool slightly on a rack before eating.

Pesto Pizza with Grilled Chicken on the Gas Grill (with a Stone)

Many recipes specify boneless skinless chicken breasts, but we use boneless skinless chicken thighs in this kind of preparation; they're much less likely to become dry and overcooked. When you use a stone on the grill, you don't have to bake the crust "blind" (see page 269) because the stone will allow longer baking time without burning. Check with your stone's manufacturer and consider cast iron or steel if durability is a concern.

There's plenty of basil in this pizza, one of the vegetable world's richest sources of vitamin K (essential for normal blood clotting).

Makes one 12- to 14-inch pizza; serves 2 to 4

Use any of these refrigerated pre-mixed doughs: Master Recipe (page 79), 100% Whole Wheat Master Recipe (page 91), 100% Whole Wheat Bread with Olive Oil (page 119), other non-enriched dough, or Gluten-Free Olive Oil Bread (page 302)

½ pound (orange-size portion) of any pre-mixed dough listed above

4 garlic cloves

2 cups fresh basil leaves, loosely packed

½ cup (½ ounces/70 grams) pine nuts

2 ounces grated Parmigiano-Reggiano cheese

1 cup (7 ounces/200 grams) olive oil

½ teaspoon kosher salt

¼ teaspoon freshly ground black pepper

3 or 4 boneless skinless chicken thighs, brushed with olive oil and seasoned with salt and freshly ground black pepper

Extra flour for dusting the pizza peel

Pain au Potiron (Peppery Pumpkin and Olive Oil Loaf), page 222

Georgian Cheesy-Egg Boats (*Khachapuri*), page 239

Pizza Margherita, page 265 and Zucchini Flatbread, page 267

Cherry Black Pepper Focaccia, page 278

Turkish-Style Pita Bread with Black Sesame Seeds, page 283, and Seed-Encrusted Pita Bread, page 285

Aloo Paratha (Potato and Pea-Stuffed Flatbread), page 287

Msemmen (Algerian Flatbread), page 290

Grissini (Olive Oil Bread Sticks), page 293

Seeded Crackers, page 296

Gluten-Free Crusty Boule, page 299

Braided Challah with Whole Wheat and Wheat Germ, page 324

Apples and Honey Whole Grain Challah, page 331

Braided Raisin Buns, page 339

Whole Wheat Brioche, page 343

Apple Strudel Bread, page 346

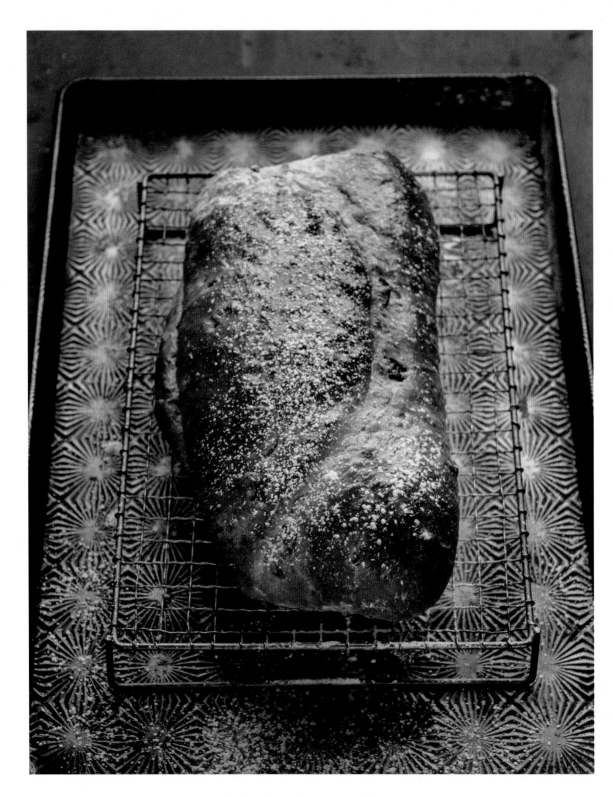

100% Whole Wheat Christmas Stollen, page 348

1. Process the garlic, basil, pine nuts, cheese, olive oil, salt, and pepper in a food processor until smooth.

2. Grill the chicken over medium heat on an outdoor grill until just cooked through. Cool briefly, then chop coarsely.

3. **Thirty minutes before grilling time, preheat a baking stone on an outdoor gas grill over medium flame on all burners;** try to achieve a constant temperature of about 500°F. **We recommend a stone that is made to withstand direct flame.** We've found that the cast-iron and steel baking surfaces get too hot with direct flame and can burn the pizza crust before the toppings are cooked, so be careful if using them on the grill.

4. Dust the surface of the refrigerated dough with flour and cut off a ½-pound (orange-size) piece. Dust the piece with more flour and quickly shape it into a rough ball by stretching the surface of the dough around to the bottom, rotating the ball a quarter turn as you go. You don't need to be as careful about shaping a perfect ball because it won't be your final shape anyway.

5. Directly on a wooden pizza peel, flatten the dough with your hands and a rolling pin to produce a ⅛-inch-thick round, dusting with flour to keep the dough from adhering to the board. A little sticking to the board can be helpful in overcoming the dough's resistance to stretch. Use a dough scraper to unstick the dough as needed. When you're done, the dough round should have enough flour under it to move easily when you shake the peel.

6. Thinly coat the dough with the pesto and top with the chicken (you might have enough pesto left over to use as pasta sauce, or on another small pizza).

7. Slide the pizza directly onto the stone (it may take a number of back-and-forth shakes to dislodge the pizza), and close the grill lid. Check

> **The gas grill makes great loaf breads, too:** The gas grill with a baking stone can be used to bake loaf breads (free-form or pan). Preheat the stone to the desired temperature for 30 minutes and place the loaf (or pan) onto it. Then cover it with a roomy aluminum roasting pan and bake for the usual time (with the grill's lid closed).

for doneness in 8 to 10 minutes; at this time, turn the pizza around if one side is browning faster than the other.

8. Bake for another 3 to 5 minutes, depending on the heat your grill delivers. Watch carefully and remove from the heat before the bottom burns. Keep the lid closed as much as possible, and use your nose to detect when the bottom crust is just beginning to char in places.

9. Allow to cool slightly on a rack before eating.

Focaccia with Artichokes, Garlic Shards, and Rosemary

For a simple but elegant twist on focaccia, we used artichokes in place of onions. Some people just can't abide the onions that are so traditional in this classic Italian flatbread. So we developed this one specifically for them, because no one should be left out of the focaccia party. For the standard onion and rosemary focaccia, see the variation below.

We bake the focaccia in a large pie tin, because it is the perfect shape and it will keep the olive oil close to the dough while it bakes.

Makes 6 appetizer portions

Use any of these refrigerated pre-mixed doughs: 100% Whole Wheat Bread with Olive Oil is our first choice (page 119), but you can also use the Master Recipe (page 79), any other non-enriched dough, or Gluten-Free Olive Oil Bread (page 302)

1 pound (grapefruit-size portion) of any pre-mixed dough listed above

2 large garlic cloves, sliced as thinly as possible with a very sharp knife

2 tablespoons extra-virgin olive oil, plus additional for drizzling

¼ to ½ cup canned or jarred marinated artichokes, drained well and sliced thinly (you can use both the "hearts" and the leafy layers)

¾ teaspoon dried rosemary leaves (or 1½ teaspoons fresh)

Coarse salt and freshly ground black pepper for sprinkling on the top crust

1. **Thirty minutes before baking time, preheat the oven to 425°F,** with an empty metal broiler tray placed on any rack that won't interfere with the focaccia. The baking stone is not essential when using a cookie sheet; if you omit the stone the preheat can be as short as 5 minutes.

2. In a skillet over medium heat, sauté the garlic slices in the 2 tablespoons of olive oil until softened but not browned; if you brown them

they'll burn in the oven. Set aside while preparing the dough, making sure to reserve the oil.

3. Grease a 10-inch pie tin with olive oil. Dust the surface of the refrigerated dough with flour and cut off a 1-pound (grapefruit-size) piece. Dust the piece with more flour and quickly shape it into a ball by stretching the surface of the dough around to the bottom, rotating the ball a quarter turn as you go.

4. Flatten it into a ½- to ¾-inch-thick round, using your hands and/or a rolling pin and a minimal amount of flour. Place the round in the prepared pie tin. Using your fingertips, deeply "dimple" the surface of the dough to hold the olive oil.

5. Scatter the garlic sparingly over the surface of the dough, leaving a ½-inch border at the edge, then do the same with the artichoke slices. Allow some of the dough surface to show through as bare dough. You may have leftover garlic and artichoke at the end. Sprinkle the loaf with rosemary, coarse salt, and freshly ground pepper. Finish with a drizzle of the reserved olive oil in the sauté pan. You can drizzle with additional olive oil, but not so much that it starts dripping off the sides.

6. Allow the focaccia to rest for 20 minutes.

7. Place the pie tin on the stone or on a rack near the center of the oven. Pour 1 cup of hot tap water into the broiler tray, and quickly close the oven door (see page 40 for steam alternatives). Bake for 20 to 25 minutes, or until the crust is medium brown. Be careful not to burn the garlic. The baking time will vary according to the focaccia's thickness. Focaccia will not develop a crackling crust, because of the olive oil.

8. Cut into wedges and serve warm.

VARIATION: Onion-Rosemary Focaccia

Omit the garlic and artichoke. Thinly slice about a quarter of a medium onion and sauté with ¾ teaspoon dried rosemary (or 1½ teaspoons chopped fresh rosemary) over medium heat in the olive oil until softened but not browned; if you brown them they'll burn in the oven. Season the onions with salt and pepper, and scatter them over the surface of the prepared dough, leaving a ½-inch border at the edge. Bake as above.

Cherry–Black Pepper Focaccia

This is a great balance between sweet and savory. The sweet dried cherries are soaked in wine, black pepper, and shallots as the dough rises. When the dough is ready to go into the oven, it is sprinkled with the plumped cherries and drizzled with olive oil. Soaking the cherries first prevents them from drying out and burning in the hot oven. This delightful bread can be paired with pastas, cheeses, or just the red wine you used to poach the cherries. (see color photo)

Makes 6 appetizer portions

Use any of these refrigerated pre-mixed doughs: Master Recipe (page 79), 100% Whole Wheat Master Recipe (page 91), 100% Whole Wheat Bread with Olive Oil (page 119), any other non-enriched dough, or Gluten-Free Olive Oil Bread (page 302)

1 pound (grapefruit-size portion) of any pre-mixed dough listed above)

½ cup (3½ ounces/95 grams) dried cherries

¼ cup red wine

¼ cup water

½ teaspoon freshly ground black pepper

Pinch of salt

¼ cup finely minced shallots

2 tablespoons olive oil for drizzling

Coarse sea salt and freshly ground black pepper for sprinkling on top crust

⌒⌒

Cherries are a healthy winner because they contain three fantastic phytochemicals (beneficial plant chemicals): the antioxidant quercetin, in addition to anthocyanins and cyanidin. They're also rich in vitamins C and E (which work together as a dynamic duo of antioxidant effect; see page 5), and the essential mineral potassium, which can lower blood pressure, especially in people eating lots of sodium.

"There's some evidence that cherries may also help prevent jet lag, though it's too early to tell if that's going to hold up. But they were a much healthier snack for kids than that weird box the airline was selling on my family's recent transatlantic flight."—Jeff

1. **Thirty minutes before baking time, preheat the oven to 425°F,** with an empty metal broiler tray placed on any rack that won't interfere with the focaccia. The baking stone is not essential when using a cookie sheet; if you omit the stone the preheat can be as short as 5 minutes.

2. In a small bowl combine the cherries, wine, water, pepper, salt, and shallots. Allow to sit while your dough is resting.

3. Grease a 10-inch pie tin with olive oil. Dust the surface of the refrigerated dough with flour and cut off a 1-pound (grapefruit-size) piece. Dust with more flour and quickly shape it into a ball by stretching the surface of the dough around to the bottom, rotating the ball a quarter turn as you go.

4. Flatten it into a ½- to ¾-inch-thick round, using your hands and/or a rolling pin and a minimal amount of flour. Place the round in the prepared pie tin. Using your fingertips, deeply "dimple" the surface of the dough to hold olive oil. Allow the focaccia to rest for 20 minutes.

5. After the focaccia has rested, strain the cherries and spread them over the surface of the dough. Press them into the dough so that they won't pop off while baking. Drizzle with olive oil and sprinkle with sea salt and pepper.

6. Place the pie tin on the stone or on a rack near the center of the oven. Pour 1 cup of hot tap water into the broiler tray, and quickly close the oven door (see page 40 for steam alternatives). Bake for approximately 25 minutes, but check for browning at 20 minutes. Continue baking until medium brown and without burning the cherries; baking time will depend on the focaccia's thickness. Focaccia does not develop a crackling crust because of the olive oil.

7. Cut into wedges and serve warm.

Southwestern Flatbread with Roasted Corn and Goat Cheese

When Minnesotans spend time in Arizona during March, they come back and want to cook every Southwestern specialty there is; every roasted pepper and roasted corn tidbit. Maybe it brings on spring a little faster. So after returning from a Phoenix TV appearance one winter, we wanted to find other ways to enjoy our mesquite dough (page 232).

The poblano peppers in this recipe are becoming more and more available in U.S. supermarkets, but if yours doesn't have them you can find them in your local Mexican market. They're milder than jalapeños, but hotter than American green bell peppers, so they add some heat to this focaccia. If you don't like hot peppers at all, substitute sweet green or red ones. This recipe is designed to be vegetarian, but it works quite nicely with the same grilled chicken we used in the Pesto Pizza with Grilled Chicken on the Gas Grill (with a Stone) (see page 272).

We like to roast the corn on a gas grill with the silks mostly removed but just a thin layer of husk left on the ear; that allows for a little charring. Wrapping husked corn in aluminum foil works, too, but it tends to eliminate the charring.

Makes one 10- to 12-inch flatbread; 6 appetizer portions

Use any of these refrigerated pre-mixed doughs: Mesquite Bread (page 232), Master Recipe (page 79), 100% Whole Wheat Master Recipe (page 91), 100% Whole Wheat Bread with Olive Oil (page 119), or other non-enriched dough

1 pound (grapefruit-size portion) of any pre-mixed dough listed above

1 ear fresh corn (can substitute ¼ cup frozen corn niblets, especially the roasted variety)

1 dried chile pepper (New Mexico red, guajillo, or ancho variety), or substitute 1½ teaspoons of your favorite chili powder

1 tablespoon olive oil for the sauté pan

1 medium onion, chopped

1 fresh poblano pepper, seeded, stemmed, and diced

1 teaspoon ground cumin

One 14-ounce can pureed or diced tomatoes

1 teaspoon kosher salt

Corn masa or cornmeal for dusting the pizza peel

2 ounces semisoft goat cheese

1 or 2 grilled chicken thighs (optional) (see page 272)

1 tablespoon chopped fresh cilantro leaves

Additional kosher salt for sprinkling on the finished focaccia

1. **Roasting the corn:** Peel off most of the corn husk layers but leave some of the inner layers in place; try to pull out the silks without disrupting the inner layers of corn husk. This allows for a little charring of the kernels, but protects against burning. If you prefer, you can peel the ear of corn completely and wrap it in aluminum foil. Preheat a gas grill with burners set to medium for 5 minutes. Roast the corn over direct heat for about 15 minutes, turning every 5 minutes, but otherwise keeping the cover closed. Check frequently to be sure that the corn isn't burning. When done, cool slightly, remove the husk if needed, and then use a sharp knife to slice the kernels from the cob.

2. **If you're grinding your own chili powder,** briefly toast the dried pepper in a 400°F oven until fragrant but not burned, 1 to 2 minutes (it will remain flexible but will firm up when cool). Break up the cooled pepper and discard the stems and seeds. Grind the pepper in a spice grinder (or a coffee grinder used just for spices).

3. **Sauté the onion and pepper:** Heat the olive oil over medium heat in a skillet. Add the onion and sauté until beginning to brown, then add the poblano pepper and continue cooking until softened. Add the cumin and chili powder to the skillet and sauté until fragrant, about 2 minutes.

4. Add the tomatoes and salt, bring to a simmer for 2 minutes, then remove from the heat.

5. **Thirty minutes before baking time, preheat the oven to 425°F,** with a baking stone placed on the middle rack. Place an empty metal broiler tray on any other rack that won't interfere with the flatbread.

6. Dust the surface of the refrigerated dough with flour and cut off a 1-pound (grapefruit-size) piece. Dust the piece with more flour and quickly shape it into a rough ball by stretching the surface of the dough around to the bottom, rotating the ball a quarter turn as you go.

7. Flatten it into a ½- to ¾-inch-thick round, using your hands and/or a rolling pin and a minimal amount of flour. Place the round on a pizza peel prepared with corn masa, cornmeal, parchment paper, or a silicone mat, and allow it to rest, loosely covered with plastic wrap or an overturned bowl, for 20 minutes.

8. Cover the surface of the dough with the sauce, leaving a narrow border at the edge—don't layer it too thickly; you might have some left over for next time. Make sure you use the pepper and onion chunks in the sauce. Dot the surface with pieces of goat cheese, and finish with the roasted corn kernels. If you're using the chicken, roughly chop it and sprinkle it over the dough round.

9. Slide the flatbread onto the stone. Pour 1 cup of hot tap water into the broiler tray, and quickly close the oven door (see page 40 for steam alternatives). Bake for about 25 minutes, or until the crust has browned. The baking time will vary according to the flatbread's thickness.

10. Remove the flatbread from the oven and sprinkle it with the chopped cilantro and salt to taste.

11. Cut into wedges and serve warm.

Turkish-Style Pita Bread with Black Sesame Seeds

Turkish and Greek pita bread differ from Israeli/Palestinian pita in two very important ways: First, it doesn't puff, and second, it's enriched, either by mixing butter or oil into the dough, or by brushing it on after the loaves are formed (see color photo). We avoid puffing here by rolling it a little thicker, "docking" (perforating) the surface with a fork, and baking it at a lower temperature. We've topped the pita with the traditional black sesame seeds, which you can buy at most Asian groceries, or through mail order at Penzeys Spices (see Sources for Bread-Baking Products page 398). The seeds create a great flavor combination with the olive oil or butter. Somehow, it both crunches *and* melts in your mouth. You'll see. Serve it with Turkish or Greek dips and appetizers, like *taramasalata* (fish roe spread), feta cheese, and olives.

If you want classically puffed Middle Eastern pita, try the Seed-Encrusted Pita on page 285. Turkish-style pita also works beautifully when baked on a gas grill outdoors (see Whole Grain Pizza on the Gas Grill, page 269).

Makes 1 pita

Use any of these refrigerated pre-mixed doughs: Master Recipe (page 79), 100% Whole Wheat Master Recipe (page 91), 100% Whole Wheat Bread with Olive Oil (page 119), or other non-enriched dough
1 pound (grapefruit-size portion) of any pre-mixed dough listed above
1 tablespoon olive oil or melted unsalted butter
2 teaspoons black sesame seeds for sprinkling

1. **Thirty minutes before baking time, preheat the oven to 450°F,** with a baking stone placed on the middle rack. Place an empty metal broiler tray on any other rack that won't interfere with the bread.

2. Just before baking, dust the surface of the refrigerated dough with flour and cut off a 1-pound (grapefruit-size) piece. Dust the piece with more flour and quickly shape it into a ball by stretching the surface of

the dough around to the bottom, rotating the ball a quarter turn as you go. Place the ball on a flour-dusted pizza peel.

3. Use your hands to stretch the dough into a round, then roll out to a uniform thickness of ¼ inch. Sprinkle with more flour as needed to prevent sticking.

4. Brush the surface with oil or melted unsalted butter, dock (puncture) the dough all over with the tines of a fork, and sprinkle it with sesame seeds.

5. Slide the loaf directly onto the hot stone. Pour 1 cup of hot tap water into the broiler tray, and quickly close the oven door. Bake for 15 to 20 minutes, or until golden brown. Use the fork to dock (puncture) again if large bubbles form or if puffing begins.

6. Cut into wedges with kitchen shears or a serrated bread knife. Serve warm or at room temperature.

Seed-Encrusted Pita Bread

Traditional Middle Eastern puffed pita works just as beautifully with our whole grain dough as it does with the traditional white flour dough. One way to boost the fiber and vitamins in pita (or any bread) is to top the loaf with a generous mixture of seeds. It's not a traditional pita, but it's delicious (see color photo).

"In my house, we use little round or rectangular pita as a lazy-man's hamburger or hot dog bun. Just cut rolled-out pita dough into the shapes and sizes that you need and bake while you're grilling the meat. The burgers and hot dogs go into the pocket. For American-style hamburger and hot dog buns, see page 144."—Jeff

Makes 1 pita

Use any of these refrigerated pre-mixed doughs: Master Recipe (page 79), 100% Whole Wheat Master Recipe (page 91), 100% Whole Wheat Bread with Olive Oil (page 119), or other non-enriched dough
½ pound (orange-size portion) of any pre-mixed dough listed above
Seed mixture for sprinkling to your taste, 1 to 2 tablespoons: sesame, flaxseed, caraway, raw sunflower, poppy, and/or anise seeds

1. **Thirty minutes before baking time, preheat the oven to 500°F,** with a baking stone. You don't need a broiler tray, and rack placement of the stone is not critical.

2. Just before baking, dust the surface of the refrigerated dough with flour and cut off a ½-pound (orange-size) piece. Dust the piece with more flour and quickly shape it into a ball by stretching the surface of the dough around to the bottom, rotating the ball a quarter turn as you go. Place the dough on a flour-dusted pizza peel.

3. Using your hands and a rolling pin, roll the dough out into a round (or several rounds) with a uniform thickness of ⅛ inch throughout. This is crucial because if it's too thick, it may not puff. You'll need to sprinkle the peel lightly with flour as you work, occasionally flipping to prevent sticking to the rolling pin or to the board. Use a dough scraper to remove the round of dough from the peel if it sticks. Do not slash the pita, or it will not puff. No rest/rise time is needed. If you are making smaller individual-size pitas, form, roll, and shape the rest. Before trying to slide the pita onto the baking stone, be sure it's moving well on the board and not sticking anywhere.

4. Brush the top of the dough with water and sprinkle seeds over the surface.

5. Slide the pita directly onto the hot stone (it may take a number of back-and-forth shakes to dislodge the pita). Bake for 5 to 7 minutes, or until very lightly browned and puffed. Don't overbake whole grain pitas.

6. For the most authentic, soft-crusted result, wrap the pita in a clean cotton dish towel and set on a cooling rack when baking is complete. The pita will deflate slightly as it cools. The space between the crusts will still be there, but may have to be nudged apart with a fork. Pitas made from 100% whole grain dough may puff only a little.

7. Once the pita is cool, store it in a plastic bag. Unlike hard-crusted breads, pita is not harmed by airtight storage.

Aloo Paratha (Potato and Pea–Stuffed Flatbread)

In our first book, we included a recipe for naan, an Indian flatbread that we pan-fried in ghee (Indian-style clarified butter). In truth, naan isn't intended for pan-frying; it traditionally gets its enrichment from ghee that's brushed on after baking in an enormous *tandoor* (traditional stone oven). It's really *paratha* that's fried in India, but for our healthy-ingredients book, we decided to include a stuffed (*aloo*) paratha as an oven-baked bread. We're filling

it with a mixture of potato, peas, and curry, and it works beautifully as an appetizer before just about anything, or as the first course of an Indian or vegetarian dinner. Use a thin-skinned potato and leave the skin on for more fiber; with the protein and vegetable benefits of peas in the mix, you can consider this a full and balanced vegetarian meal (see color photo).

Makes 1 aloo paratha; serves 6 as an appetizer

Use any of these refrigerated pre-mixed doughs: Master Recipe (page 79), 100% Whole Wheat Master Recipe (page 91), 100% Whole Wheat Bread with Olive Oil (page 119), or other non-enriched dough

1 pound (grapefruit-size portion) of any pre-mixed dough listed above

Partake of peas as the perfect food?

Peas are readily available as a high-quality frozen product, and we really should be eating lots of them. Interestingly, we find that frozen peas generally are sweeter and fresher tasting than some fresh green peas. The explanation is that fresh peas become stale and starchy tasting within 24 hours of being picked; their nutrient content also declines. Frozen peas are usually frozen immediately after harvest, and that preserves their flavor and nutrition.

Like all legumes, peas are great sources of B vitamins, zinc, potassium, magnesium, calcium, and iron.

2 medium thin-skinned potatoes, such as Yukon Gold

1½ tablespoons ghee gently melted in the microwave or on the stovetop, plus
   additional for brushing on top of the assembled aloo paratha (see page 30
   to make your own)

1½ tablespoons vegetable oil

1 teaspoon curry powder, plus additional for sprinkling on top

½ teaspoon kosher salt

½ cup frozen or fresh peas (no need to defrost or pre-cook)

1. **Thirty minutes before baking time, preheat the oven to 450°F,** with a
   baking stone placed on the middle rack. Place an empty metal broiler
   tray on any other rack that won't interfere with the aloo paratha as it
   rises (rise will be modest).

2. Boil the unpeeled potatoes whole in water for 30 minutes, or until
   tender. Drain and mash with a fork or potato-masher; use everything,
   including the skin.

3. Add the ghee, oil, curry powder, and salt to the potatoes and vigor-
   ously blend with a fork to distribute evenly. Gently fold in the peas so
   as not to mash them.

4. Dust the surface of the refrigerated dough with flour and cut off a
   1-pound (grapefruit-size) piece. Dust the piece with more flour and
   quickly shape it into a ball by stretching the surface of the dough
   around to the bottom, rotating the ball a quarter turn as you go.

5. Flatten the dough with your hands and a rolling pin directly onto a
   wooden pizza peel to produce a, large, ⅛-inch-thick round, dusting
   with flour to keep the dough from adhering to the board. A little
   sticking to the board can be helpful in overcoming the dough's resistance. Use a dough scraper to unstick the dough as needed. Transfer
   the dough round to a baking sheet prepared with ghee, butter, oil, or
   parchment paper.

6. Cover half the dough round with the potato mixture, leaving a ½-inch border at the edge. Using a pastry brush, wet the border with water. Fold the bare side of the dough over the potato mixture and seal the border by pinching it closed with your fingers.

7. Brush the top surface with some additional ghee, and dust with additional curry powder. Cut three slits in the top crust, all the way through the top layer of dough, using a serrated knife. No resting time is needed.

8. Place the baking sheet near the center of the oven. Pour 1 cup of hot tap water into the broiler tray, and quickly close the oven door (see page 40 for steam alternatives). Bake for about 25 minutes, or until golden brown.

9. Allow the aloo paratha to cool slightly before serving.

∽

Turmeric: a modern-day fountain of youth? The filling for our *msemmen* is flavored with turmeric, among other delicious spices. Turmeric's health effects (as an anticancer agent) hit the news in 2000, when it was touted as a marinade ingredient to counter the effects of carcinogens (cancer-causing chemicals) that form in grilled meat. Researchers cite the low rate of cancer in India (where turmeric consumption is high), and even lower rates of cancer in southern India, where more turmeric is consumed than in the north. The active ingredient is curcumin, which makes up 2 to 3 percent of the weight of turmeric.

In addition to finding anti-cancer properties, some researchers have suggested that turmeric may have anti-inflammatory properties in general, which means it may be useful in countering arthritis, heart disease, and other degenerative conditions. The jury's out on definitive health effects, but the flavor's definitively delicious.

Msemmen (Algerian Flatbread)

This is one of the most fascinating breads we've ever made. The flavor is haunting: an otherworldly combination of richness, salt, and spice. Its color and spiral make it one of our most visually intriguing breads as well. Serve it with North African lamb dishes and other hearty fare (see color photo).

Makes one 12-inch flatbread

Use any of these refrigerated pre-mixed doughs: 100% Whole Wheat Bread with Olive Oil (page 119), Master Recipe (page 79), 100% Whole Wheat Master Recipe (page 91), or other non-enriched dough

½ pound (orange-size portion) of any pre-mixed dough listed above

3 tablespoons olive oil, plus 2 tablespoons for the skillet

1 teaspoon ground cumin

1 teaspoon paprika

1 teaspoon ground turmeric

½ teaspoon cayenne pepper

¼ teaspoon kosher salt, plus additional for sprinkling on the top crust

1. Mix the 3 tablespoons olive oil with the spices and ¼ teaspoon salt.

2. Dust the surface of the refrigerated dough with flour and cut off a ½-pound (orange-size) piece. Dust the piece with more flour and quickly shape it into a ball by stretching the surface of the dough around to the bottom, rotating the ball a quarter turn as you go. Flatten the ball with your fingers and then with a rolling pin to about ⅛ inch thick.

3. Evenly spread the spice-oil mixture over the surface of the dough, leaving a ½-inch border, and roll it up into a log. Coil the rope tightly around itself. Place it on a work surface lightly greased with olive oil and allow it to rest, loosely covered with plastic wrap or an overturned bowl, for 20 minutes.

4. Once the dough has rested, roll the coil out until you have a ⅛-inch-thick circle.

5. Heat a heavy 12-inch skillet over medium-high heat on the stovetop, until water droplets flicked into the pan skitter across the surface and evaporate quickly. Add the 2 tablespoons olive oil, and allow to heat until hot *but not smoking.*

6. Drop the rolled-out dough into the skillet, reduce the heat to medium, and cover the skillet to trap steam and heat.

7. Check for doneness with a spatula in 2 to 5 minutes, or sooner if you're smelling overly quick browning. Adjust the heat as needed. Flip the msemmen when the underside is richly browned.

8. Continue cooking another 2 to 5 minutes, or until the msemmen feels firm, even at the edges, and the second side is browned. You'll need more pan time if you've rolled a thicker msemmen.

9. Allow to cool slightly on a rack and sprinkle with coarse salt if desired. Break apart with your fingers before eating.

VARIATION: Baked Msemmen

If you want to skip the frying step, msemmen works great baked in the oven just like a pita (page 285). After step 4, just bake on a preheated stone in the oven (500°F) for 5 to 7 minutes. Drizzle with oil before serving warm, and sprinkle with coarse salt if desired.

Grissini (Olive Oil Bread Sticks)

Grissini are Italian bread sticks infused with olive oil. Since the oil will infuse whether you drizzle it over the unbaked sticks or mix it into the dough, you have a variety of pre-mixed doughs to choose from—you don't have to use an olive oil dough (and even our olive oil dough benefits from additional oil).

Immediately after being photographed (see color photo), the grissini met a delicious fate—wrapped up with strips of prosciutto and consumed with Italian white wine.

Makes twenty-four 12-inch grissini

Use any of these pre-mixed doughs: Master Recipe (page 79), 100% Whole
  Wheat Bread Master Recipe (page 91), 100% Whole Wheat Bread with Olive
  Oil (page 119), any other non-enriched dough, or any gluten-free dough
½ pound (orange-size portion) of any pre-mixed dough listed above
Olive oil for brushing on top, preferably extra virgin
Kosher salt for sprinkling
Rosemary for sprinkling (fresh or dried—some chopped, some whole leaves)
Prosciutto, cut into 1-inch strips (optional for serving)

1. **Preheat the oven to 400°F,** with a rack placed in the middle of the oven.
    A baking stone is optional, but if you're using one,
    allow for a 30-minute preheat, otherwise 5 minutes
    is adequate.

2. Line a cookie sheet with parchment paper or a
    silicone mat, or simply grease it well with olive oil.

3. Roll the dough into an 8×12-inch rectangle, ⅛
    inch thick. Then cut ⅛-inch-wide strips with a
    pizza cutter or sharp knife.

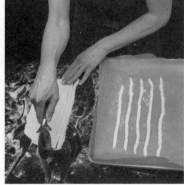

4. Lay the strips out on the prepared cookie sheet with ½ inch or so between each strip. Generously daub olive oil over each strip with a pastry brush. Sprinkle with salt and rosemary.

5. Bake near the center of the oven for 10 to 16 minutes, depending on the thickness and width. The grissini are done when they are nicely browned and beginning to crisp (they will firm up when they cool). Serve plain as an hors d'oeuvre or with one half of the bread stick wrapped in a prosciutto strip.

Spicy Chili Whole Grain Snack Crackers

Crackers were developed long ago as a baked product that could be stored for a long time yet wouldn't go stale—they were hard and dry in the first place. If you make your own crackers, you won't need to store them long because they won't last—they taste too good. These colorful little squares are bursting with the flavors of grain and chili. Just make small quantities, use a healthy oil like canola or olive, and salt them to your taste. Top them with a bit of cheese and you're ready to watch the game. These crackers are just as tasty with a smattering of seeds baked on the top if you're not one for spicy flavors (see color photo).

Makes about 50 small crackers

Use any of these refrigerated pre-mixed doughs: Master Recipe (page 79), 100% Whole Wheat Master Recipe (page 91), 100% Whole Wheat Bread with Olive Oil (page 119), or any gluten-free dough
½ pound (orange-size portion) of any pre-mixed dough listed above
3 teaspoons chili powder (or make your own, see Southwestern Flatbread with Roasted Corn and Goat Cheese, page 280)
½ teaspoon kosher salt
Olive or canola oil for brushing the crackers
Coarse salt for sprinkling on the top

1. Mix the chili powder and salt in a small bowl until uniform.

2. **Thirty minutes before baking time, preheat the oven to 400°F**, with a baking stone placed on the middle rack. Place an empty metal broiler tray on any other rack. The baking stone is optional and if you omit it, the preheat can be as short as 5 minutes.

3. Dust the surface of the refrigerated dough with flour and cut off a ½-pound (orange-size) piece. Dust the piece with more flour and

quickly shape it into a ball by stretching the surface of the dough around to the bottom, rotating the ball a quarter turn as you go.

4. Dust the dough with flour and flatten it with your hands and a rolling pin to get it as thin as possible without tearing. Paper thin is the goal—no thicker than ⅟₁₆ inch or it won't be like a cracker. Use as much flour as is needed to prevent sticking. It's easiest to get it super-thin by cutting the dough into smaller balls first.

5. Use a pastry brush to paint the rolled-out dough generously with oil, then sprinkle it with spice mixture (you may have some of the spice mixture left over; it can be stored for the next batch). Dock (puncture) the dough all over with the tines of a fork to prevent the crackers from puffing.

6. Cut the dough into 1½-inch squares with a pizza wheel. Using a spatula, transfer them to a greased cookie sheet or one prepared with parchment paper or a silicone mat. Don't let the crackers touch or overlap.

7. Place the cookie sheet in the preheated oven and pour 1 cup of hot tap water into the broiler tray, and quickly close the oven door (see page 40 for steam alternatives). Bake for about 15 minutes, or until browned and beginning to firm up. Don't overbake or you'll get a scorched flavor. You'll need less time if you successfully rolled them very thin. They will be a bit soft when they first come out of the oven, but they will become crisper when they cool completely.

8. Serve with robust cheeses, with beer, or all by themselves.

VARIATION: Seeded Crackers

Omit the spice mixture and sprinkle with your favorite seeds.

9

GLUTEN-FREE BREADS AND PASTRIES

On our website, many people asked us for gluten-free versions of our stored doughs, but only a few of them can't eat gluten themselves. The rest were people entertaining guests with celiac disease who can't tolerate this particular wheat protein. It quickly became obvious to us that many of our readers wanted a few delicious gluten-free recipes, even if gluten wasn't a problem for them. If you're ever unsure whether an ingredient is a problem for people who can't eat gluten, a great resource is the University of Chicago's Celiac Disease Center. Their website has a free e-book, listing foods that do (and do not) contain gluten (CureCeliacDisease.org/ebook). The University of Chicago website is aimed at people with celiac disease, an autoimmune digestive condition. People with celiac absolutely cannot eat gluten at all.

We really wanted to create recipes that emulate both the taste and texture of traditional breads. Many of the existing gluten-free recipes tasted odd to us, had a dry texture or were overly gummy—often they didn't taste much like bread. Creating recipes that met our standards and were able to be stored posed a challenge, but we are quite pleased with the results. Beyond what you'll find in this chapter you should check out the bagels (see page 139) and our Flatbreads and Pizza chapter; many of those recipes work beautifully with gluten-free doughs.

There are a few ingredients in gluten-free breads that you may not be familiar with (xanthan gum, tapioca starch, and others), so we covered them in some detail in Ingredients (chapter 2, page 9). **One important note about measuring gluten-free flours:** if you measure gluten-free flours by volume, be sure to pack them firmly into the measuring cup (as if you were measuring brown sugar). Otherwise, you'll get inconsistent results.

If you choose to use psyllium husk in place of the xanthan gum, you will have a looser dough when you first mix it, but as it sits, the dough will firm up. Finally: we strongly recommend using a heavy-duty stand mixer to get the best consistency in these doughs—the mixer does a much better job of emulsifying gluten-free ingredients and getting a smooth, higher-rising result.

Gluten-Free Crusty Boule

Shauna and Danny of the Gluten-Free Girl website generously shared a wealth of knowledge with us as we developed this fabulous crusty loaf. The dough is incredibly versatile; we bake it as a classic boule or in a loaf pan for sandwiches (follow the baking instructions on page 308). It also makes a wonderful pizza crust with your favorite toppings or great crackers if it is rolled thin.

Makes enough dough for at least four 1-pound loaves. The recipe is easily doubled or halved.

Ingredient	Volume (U.S.)	Weight (U.S.)	Weight (Metric)
Brown rice flour	2 cups	10¾ ounces	305 grams
Sorghum flour	1½ cups	7½ ounces	210 grams
Tapioca flour (tapioca starch)	3 cups	13½ ounces	385 grams
Granulated yeast	2 tablespoons	0.7 ounce	20 grams
Kosher salt*	1 tablespoon	0.6 ounce	15 grams
Xanthan gum or ground psyllium husk**	2 tablespoons	¾ ounce	20 grams
Lukewarm water	2⅔ cups	1 pound, 5⅓ ounces	605 grams
Eggs, large	4	8 ounces	225 grams
Vegetable oil, olive oil, or melted unsalted butter or coconut oil (see page 28 for options)	⅓ cup	2½ ounces	70 grams
Honey	2 tablespoons	1½ ounces	45 grams

*Can increase or decrease to taste (see page 56)
**Double quantity if using psyllium.

1. **Mixing and storing the dough:** Whisk together the flours, yeast, salt, and xanthan gum in a 5-quart bowl, or a lidded (not airtight) food container.

2. Combine the liquid ingredients and gradually mix them with the dry ingredients, using a spoon or a heavy-duty stand mixer (with paddle), until all of the dry ingredients are well incorporated. You might have to use wet hands to get the last bit of flour to incorporate if you're not using a machine. *We highly recommend the mixer for gluten-free doughs.*

3. Cover (not airtight), and allow the dough to rest at room temperature until it rises, approximately 2 hours.

4. The dough can be used immediately after the initial rise. Refrigerate in a lidded (not airtight) container and use over the next 7 days. The flavor will be best if you wait for at least 24 hours of refrigeration.

5. **On baking day,** use wet hands to take out a 1-pound (grapefruit-size) piece of the refrigerated dough. Quickly shape it into a ball; this dough isn't stretched because there is no gluten in it—just gently press it into the shape. You might need to wet your hands a little to prevent the dough from sticking and to create a smooth surface, but don't use so much water as to make the dough soggy.

6. Allow the dough to rest, loosely covered with plastic wrap or an overturned bowl, on a pizza peel prepared with cornmeal or lined with parchment paper for 90 minutes (40 minutes if you're using fresh, unrefrigerated dough). Alternatively, you can rest the loaf on a silicone mat or a greased cookie sheet.

7. **Thirty minutes before baking time, preheat the oven to 450°F, with a baking stone placed on the middle rack.** Place an empty metal broiler tray on any other rack that won't interfere with the rising bread.

8. Just before baking, slash the loaf with ½-inch-deep parallel cuts, using a serrated bread knife.

9. Slide the loaf directly onto the hot stone (or place the silicone mat or cookie sheet on the stone if you used one). Pour 1 cup of hot tap water into the broiler tray, and quickly close the oven door (see page 40 for steam alternatives). Bake for about 35 minutes, or until lightly browned and firm. If you used parchment paper, a silicone mat, or a cookie sheet under the loaf, carefully remove it two-thirds of the way through the baking time and bake the loaf directly on the stone or an oven rack. Smaller or larger loaves will require adjustments in resting and baking time.

10. Allow to cool completely on a rack before slicing.

Gluten-Free Olive Oil Bread

This dough is enriched with delicious olive oil, and is a great fit for pizza and other Mediterranean-style specialties. It is also lovely as a free-form loaf with a crispy crust.

Makes enough dough for at least four 1-pound loaves. The recipe is easily doubled or halved.

Ingredient	Volume (U.S.)	Weight (U.S.)	Weight (Metric)
Brown rice flour	1 cup	5⅓ ounces	150 grams
Soy, garbanzo, or sorghum flour	½ cup	2 ounces	55 grams
Tapioca flour (tapioca starch)	1 cup	4½ ounces	130 grams
Cornstarch	3½ cups	1 pound, 1½ ounces	500 grams
Granulated yeast	2 tablespoons	0.7 ounce	20 grams
Kosher salt*	1 tablespoon	0.6 ounce	15 grams
Xanthan gum or ground psyllium husk**	2 tablespoons	¾ ounce	20 grams
Lukewarm water	2½ cups	1 pound, 4 ounces	565 grams
Eggs, large	4	8 ounces	225 grams
Olive oil	⅔ cup	5 ounces	140 grams
White or cider vinegar	2 teaspoons	⅓ ounce	10 grams

*Can increase or decrease to taste (see page 56).

**Double quantity if using psyllium.

1. **Mixing and storing the dough:** Whisk together the flours, tapioca starch, cornstarch, yeast, salt, and xanthan gum in a 5-quart bowl, or a lidded (not airtight) food container.

2. Combine the liquid ingredients and gradually mix them into the dry ingredients without kneading, using a spoon, or a heavy-duty stand mixer (with paddle). *We highly recommend the mixer for gluten-free doughs.*

3. Cover (not airtight), and allow the dough to rest at room temperature for approximately 2 hours.

4. The dough can be used immediately after its initial rise, or you can refrigerate it in a lidded (not airtight) container and use it over the next 7 days. The flavor will be best if you wait for at least 24 hours of refrigeration.

5. **On baking day**, use wet hands to take out a 1-pound (grapefruit-size) piece of the refrigerated dough. Quickly shape it into a ball; this dough isn't stretched because there is no gluten in it—just gently press it into the shape. You might need to wet your hands a little to prevent the dough from sticking and to create a smooth surface, but don't use so much water as to make the dough soggy.

6. Pat the ball into a narrow oval. Allow the loaf to rest and rise, loosely covered with plastic wrap or an overturned bowl, on a pizza peel prepared with cornmeal or lined with parchment paper, for 90 minutes (40 minutes if you're using fresh, unrefrigerated dough). Alternatively, you can rest the loaf on a silicone mat or a greased cookie sheet without using a pizza peel.

7. **Thirty minutes before baking time, preheat the oven to 450°F,** with a baking stone placed on the middle rack. Place an empty metal broiler tray on any other rack that won't interfere with the rising bread.

8. Slide the loaf directly onto the hot stone (or place the silicone mat or cookie sheet on the stone if you used one). Pour 1 cup of hot tap water into the broiler tray, and quickly close the oven door (see page 40 for

steam alternatives). Bake for about 30 minutes, or until lightly browned and firm. If you used parchment paper, a silicone mat, or a cookie sheet under the loaf, carefully remove it and bake the loaf directly on the stone or an oven rack two-thirds of the way through the baking time. Smaller or larger loaves will require adjustments in resting and baking time.

9. Allow the bread to cool completely on a rack before slicing.

Gluten-Free Pizza with Fresh Mozzarella, Olives, Basil, and Anaheim Peppers

The secret to making really good gluten-free pizza is a thin crust. The Gluten-Free Olive Oil Bread dough (page 302) is our favorite, and makes the toppings shine. Our testers thought they were eating traditional pizza crust. Try any of the flatbreads and pizzas from chapter 8.

Makes one 12- to 16-inch pizza; serves 4 to 6

½ pound (orange-size portion) Gluten-Free Olive Oil Bread
   (page 302), or Gluten-Free Crusty Boule (page 299)
White or brown rice flour for dusting
½ cup canned Italian-style chopped tomatoes, well drained through a strainer,
   or use any prepared tomato sauce you like
¼ pound sliced mozzarella cheese, fresh buffalo-milk variety if available
6 fresh basil leaves, roughly torn
⅛ cup sliced Mediterranean-style black or green olives
½ Anaheim pepper, thinly sliced crosswise
1 tablespoon grated Parmigiano-Reggiano cheese (optional)
Olive oil for drizzling on top of the pizza

1. **Thirty minutes before baking time, preheat the oven to 550°F,** with a baking stone placed on the middle rack. You won't be using steam, so you can omit the broiler tray.

2. Prepare and measure all toppings in advance. The key to a pizza that slides right off the peel is to work quickly—don't let the dough sit on the peel any longer than necessary.

3. Dust the surface of the refrigerated dough with rice flour and cut off a ½-pound (orange-size) piece. Dust the piece with more rice flour and

quickly shape it into a ball; this dough isn't stretched because there is no gluten in it—just press it into the shape of a ball. You will need to use lots of rice flour to prevent the dough from sticking to your hands or the work surface, but avoid working lumps of flour into the dough.

4. Flatten the dough with your hands and a rolling pin directly on a wooden pizza peel to produce a ¹⁄₁₆ to ¹⁄₈-inch-thick round, dusting with lots of rice flour to keep the dough from sticking to the rolling pin and board (see sidebar). A metal dough scraper is very helpful here; use it to scrape the expanding dough round off the work surface when it sticks. Be sure that the dough is still movable before adding the toppings; if it isn't, sprinkle more rice flour under the dough.

5. Distribute a thin layer of tomatoes over the surface of the dough.

6. Scatter the mozzarella over the surface of the dough, then the basil, olives, pepper, and Parmigiano-Reggiano, if desired. Drizzle the pizza with about a teaspoon of olive oil. No further resting is needed prior to baking.

Gluten-Free Baking Tip: Roll your pizza out between a piece of lightly oiled parchment paper and plastic wrap. Peel up the oiled plastic wrap, top the dough, and bake right on the parchment paper. If the bottom isn't crisping enough, just pull the paper out from under the dough after about 10 minutes.

7. Slide the pizza directly onto the stone (it may take a number of back-and-forth shakes to dislodge the pizza—use the dough scraper to help). Check for doneness in 10 to 12 minutes; turn the pizza around in the oven if one side is browning faster than the other. It may need 5 more minutes in the oven, or until the cheese and crust are nicely browned.

8. Allow the pizza to cool slightly on a rack before serving, or until the cheese is set.

Gluten-Free Cheddar and Sesame Bread

The sharpness of the cheddar and the nuttiness of the sesame make this a fantastic loaf to be served with sandwich meats, or toasted and served with marmalade. The addition of soy flour, eggs, and cheese makes this loaf particularly high in protein. It is also excellent baked as crackers in the recipe on page 312.

Makes enough dough for at least three 1½-pound loaves.
The recipe is easily doubled or halved.

Ingredient	Volume (U.S.)	Weight (U.S.)	Weight (Metric)
Sorghum flour	3 cups	14¾ ounces	420 grams
Soy flour	½ cup	2 ounces	55 grams
Tapioca flour (tapioca starch)	2 cup	9 ounces	255 grams
Cornstarch	½ cup	2½ ounces	70 grams
Sesame seeds, plus additional for sprinkling on top	½ cup	2½ ounces	70 grams
Granulated yeast	2 tablespoons	0.7 ounce	20 grams
Kosher salt*	1 tablespoon	0.6 ounce	15 grams
Xanthan gum or ground psyllium husk**	2 tablespoons	¾ ounce	20 grams
Lukewarm water	3 cups	1 pound, 8 ounces	680 grams
Eggs, large	4	8 ounces	225 grams
Vegetable oil, olive oil, or melted unsalted butter or coconut oil (see page 28 for options)	½ cup	3¾ ounces	105 grams
Honey	2 tablespoons	1½ ounces	45 grams
Cheddar cheese, shredded	1½ cups	6 ounces	230 grams

*Can increase or decrease to taste (see page 56).
**Double quantity if using psyllium.

---

1. **Mixing and storing the dough:** Mix the flours, tapioca starch, cornstarch, ½ cup sesame seeds, yeast, salt, and xanthan gum in a 5-quart bowl, or a lidded (not airtight) food container. Whisk the dry ingredients to be sure that the xanthan gum is thoroughly incorporated.

2. Combine the remaining ingredients and gradually mix them with the dry ingredients without kneading, using a spoon or a heavy-duty stand mixer (with paddle). You might need to use wet hands to get the last bit of flour to incorporate if you're not using a machine. *We highly recommend the mixer for gluten-free doughs.*

3. Cover (not airtight), and allow the dough to rest at room temperature for approximately 2 hours.

4. The dough can be used immediately after its initial rise, or you can refrigerate it in a lidded (not airtight) container and use it over the next 7 days.

5. **On baking day,** heavily grease an 8½×4½-inch nonstick loaf pan. Use wet hands to break off a 1½-pound (cantaloupe-size) piece of the refrigerated dough. Quickly shape it into a ball; this dough isn't stretched because there is no gluten in it—just gently press it into the shape. You might need to wet your hands a little more to prevent the dough from sticking and to create a smooth surface, but don't use so much water as to make the dough soggy.

6. Pat the ball into a narrow oval and put it in the loaf pan. Allow the loaf to rest, loosely covered with plastic wrap, for 90 minutes (40 minutes if you're using fresh, unrefrigerated dough).

7. **Thirty minutes before baking time, preheat the oven to 425°F.** Place an empty metal broiler tray on any other rack that won't interfere with the rising bread.

8. Just before baking, use a pastry brush to paint the top with water, then sprinkle it with sesame seeds.

9. Place the pan on a rack near the center of the oven. Pour 1 cup of hot tap water into the broiler tray, and quickly close the oven door (see page 40 for steam alternatives). Bake for about 40 minutes, or until richly browned and firm. Smaller or larger loaves will require adjustments in resting and baking time.

10. Remove the bread from the pan and allow it to cool on a rack before slicing.

Gluten-Free Sesame Baguette

It's not traditionally French to put sesame seeds on top of a baguette, but who cares? It's delicious and really adds another dimension to this bread. These loaves look beautiful, too, with the slashes alternating with curving rows of sesame seeds.

Makes 1 large or 2 small baguettes

1 pound (grapefruit-size portion) Gluten-Free Olive Oil Bread dough
    (page 302), Gluten-Free Crusty Boule dough (page 299), or Gluten-Free
    Cheddar and Sesame Bread dough (page 307)
Sesame seeds for sprinkling on top crust

1. **On baking day,** use wet hands to break off a 1-pound (grapefruit-size) piece of the refrigerated dough. Quickly pat it into a cylinder; this dough isn't stretched because there is no gluten in it—just gently press it into the shape. You might need to wet your hands a little to prevent the dough from sticking and to create a smooth surface, but don't use so much water as to make the dough soggy.

2. Allow the loaf to rest, loosely covered with plastic wrap or an over-turned bowl, on a pizza peel prepared with rice flour or lined with parchment paper for 60 minutes (40 minutes if you're using fresh, unrefrigerated dough). Alternatively, you can rest the loaf on a silicone mat or a greased cookie sheet without using a pizza peel.

3. **Thirty minutes before baking time, preheat the oven to 450°F,** with a baking stone placed on the middle rack. Place an empty metal broiler tray on any other rack that won't interfere with the rising bread.

4. Just before baking, use a pastry brush to paint the top crust with water, then sprinkle it with sesame seeds. Slash the loaf diagonally with longitudinal cuts, using a serrated bread knife.

5. Slide the loaf directly onto the hot stone (or place the silicone mat or cookie sheet on the stone if you used one). Pour 1 cup of hot tap water into the broiler tray, and quickly close the oven door (see page 40 for steam alternatives). Bake for about 25 minutes, or until richly browned and firm. If you used parchment paper, a silicone mat, or a cookie sheet under the loaf, carefully remove it and bake the loaf directly on the stone or an oven rack two-thirds of the way through the baking time. Smaller or larger loaves will require adjustments in resting and baking time.

6. Allow the bread to cool completely on a rack before slicing.

Gluten-Free Cheddar and Sesame Crackers

These crackers are fantastic with just about everything from cheese to dips. You will need to use parchment paper or a silicone mat and plastic wrap to roll out this dough.

Makes enough dough for at least twelve 2-inch crackers

½ pound Gluten-Free Cheddar and Sesame Bread dough (page 307), Gluten-Free Crusty Boule dough (page 299), Gluten-Free Olive Oil Bread dough (page 302), or Not Rye (But So Very Close), and Gluten-Free dough (page 315)
2 tablespoons sesame seeds for sprinkling on top

1. **Thirty minutes before baking time,** preheat the oven to 400°F, with a baking stone placed on the middle rack.

2. Dust the surface of the refrigerated dough with rice flour and cut off a ½-pound (orange-size) piece of dough from the container. Place the dough on a sheet of lightly oiled parchment paper or a silicone mat and cover the dough with a piece of plastic wrap. Using a rolling pin, roll the dough between the plastic wrap and the silicone mat until you have a ⅟₁₆-inch-thick rectangle. Peel off the plastic wrap, and transfer the silicone mat to a baking sheet.

3. Using a pizza cutter, very gently score the dough into crackers in the shape and size you desire. **Warning: It is important not to cut through the dough with too much pressure or you may damage your silicone mat.**

4. Just before baking, use a pastry brush to paint the surface with water, then sprinkle the surface of the dough with sesame seeds. Bake for 15 minutes, or until the crackers just start to turn golden brown. The crackers on the edges may turn brown first; use a spatula to take them off the baking sheet and continue baking the rest.

5. Allow the crackers to cool on a rack before eating.

Gluten-Free Parmesan Bread Sticks

If gluten-free dough can make a crusty baguette (page 310), it should be a natural as a bread stick—it's just skinnier. A little olive oil, salt, and Parmesan cheese perk up the flavor. Serve them plain or as an hors d'oeuvre with dips.

Makes a generous handful of bread sticks

Use any of these refrigerated, pre-mixed doughs: Gluten-Free Crusty Boule (page 299), Gluten-Free Olive Oil Bread (page 302), Gluten-Free Cheddar and Sesame Bread (page 307), or Not Rye (But so Very Close), and Gluten-Free (page 315)
½ pound (orange-size portion) of any pre-mixed dough above
Rice flour for dusting
Olive oil for drizzling, preferably extra virgin
1 to 2 tablespoons finely grated Parmigiano-Reggiano cheese
Kosher salt for sprinkling

1. **Thirty minutes before baking time, preheat the oven to 425°F.** A baking stone is optional, but if you're using one, allow for a 30-minute preheat, otherwise 5 minutes is adequate.

2. Line a cookie sheet with parchment paper or a silicone mat, or simply grease it well with olive oil.

3. Dust the surface of the refrigerated dough with rice flour and cut off a ½-pound (orange-size) piece. Press it out with your hands or a rolling pin on a wooden board, using lots of rice flour, until you have a rectangle ⅛ inch thick. Then cut ⅛-inch-wide strips with a pizza cutter or sharp knife.

4. Carefully pick up the strips (a long spatula can be helpful) and lay them out on the prepared cookie sheet with ½ inch or so between

each one. Drizzle olive oil over the strips, and sprinkle with the Parmigiano-Reggiano and a light sprinkling of salt to taste.

5. Bake for about 15 minutes. The bread sticks are done when they are nicely browned but not scorched. Smaller bread sticks might turn brown first; use a spatula to take them off the baking sheet and continue baking the rest. They may still feel soft when done but will firm up when they cool.

6. Cool the bread sticks on a rack before eating.

Not Rye (But So Very Close), and Gluten-Free

We both grew up eating rye bread; it was the bread that was the muse for our first book. When we decided to add a chapter on gluten-free breads, we made a list of all the essentials to be included, and rye was at the top of our lists. But rye has some gluten in it—so nothing doing.

In place of rye we have used teff flour, which is completely gluten-free. It has a sweet-sour molasses flavor, which lends itself perfectly to a mock rye bread. Add the caraway seeds and we're very close to childhood memories.

∞

Teff is high in protein, calcium, and iron. Its iron is particularly easily absorbed by humans (often a difficult trick for plant-based iron sources). It's a major source of nutrition worldwide, especially in northeast Africa, where it is made into Ethiopia's national flatbread, *injera*.

Makes enough dough for at least four 1-pound loaves. The recipe is easily doubled or halved.

Ingredient	Volume (U.S.)	Weight (U.S.)	Weight (Metric)
Brown rice flour	2 cups	10⅔ ounces	305 grams
Teff flour	1½ cups	8 ounces	225 grams
Tapioca flour (tapioca starch)	3 cups	13½ ounces	385 grams
Granulated yeast	2 tablespoons	0.7 ounce	20 grams
Kosher salt*	1 tablespoon	0.6 ounce	15 grams

*Can increase or decrease to taste (see page 56).

(continued)

Ingredient	Volume (U.S.)	Weight (U.S.)	Weight (Metric)
Xanthan gum or ground psyllium husk**	2 tablespoons	¾ ounce	20 grams
Caraway seeds	¼ cup	1¼ ounces	35 grams
Lukewarm water	2⅔ cups	1 pound, 5⅓ ounces	605 grams
Eggs, large	4	8 ounces	225 grams
Vegetable oil, olive oil, or melted unsalted butter or coconut oil (see page 28 for options)	⅓ cup	2½ ounces	70 grams
Honey	2 tablespoons	1½ ounces	45 grams
Molasses	2 tablespoons	1¼ ounces	35 grams

**Double quantity if using psyllium.

1. **Mixing and storing the dough:** Whisk together the flours, yeast, salt, xanthan gum, and caraway seeds in a 5-quart bowl, or a lidded (not airtight) food container.

2. Combine the liquid ingredients and gradually mix them with the dry ingredients without kneading, using a spoon or a heavy-duty stand mixer (with paddle), until all the dry ingredients are well incorporated. *We highly recommend the mixer for gluten-free doughs.*

3. Cover (not airtight), and allow the dough to rest at room temperature for approximately 2 hours.

4. The dough can be used immediately after its initial rise, or you can refrigerate it in a lidded (not airtight) container and use it over the next 7 days. The flavor will be best if you wait for at least 24 hours of refrigeration.

5. **On baking day**, use wet hands to take out a 1-pound (grapefruit-size) piece of the refrigerated dough. Quickly shape it into a ball; this dough isn't stretched because there is no gluten in it—just gently press it into the shape. You might need to wet your hands a little more to prevent the dough from sticking and to create a smooth surface, but don't use so much water as to make the dough soggy.

6. Pat the ball into a narrow oval. Allow the loaf to rest, loosely covered with plastic wrap or an overturned bowl, on a pizza peel prepared with cornmeal or lined with parchment paper for 90 minutes (40 minutes if you're using fresh, unrefrigerated dough). Alternatively, you can rest the loaf on a silicone mat or a greased cookie sheet without using a pizza peel.

7. **Thirty minutes before baking time, preheat the oven to 450°F,** with a baking stone placed on the middle rack. Place an empty metal broiler tray on any other rack that won't interfere with the rising bread.

8. Just before baking, use a pastry brush to paint the loaf's top crust with water and sprinkle it with caraway seeds. Slash the dough with ½-inch-deep parallel cuts, using a serrated bread knife.

9. Slide the loaf directly onto the hot stone (or place the silicone mat or cookie sheet on the stone if you used one). Pour 1 cup of hot tap water into the broiler tray, and quickly close the oven door (see page 40 for steam alternatives). Bake for about 30 minutes, or until richly browned and firm. If you used parchment paper, a silicone mat, or a cookie sheet under the loaf, carefully remove it and bake the loaf directly on the stone two-thirds of the way through the baking time. Smaller or larger loaves will require adjustments in resting and baking time.

10. Allow the bread to cool on a rack before slicing.

Gluten-Free Brioche

This recipe is dynamite baked as a traditionally shaped brioche or as a sandwich loaf for your kids' lunches, and is also perfect in the "Super Sam" Gluten-Free Cinnamon Buns on page 321. It has a soft texture with a light sweetness from the honey and vanilla that is pure comfort food. It can also be used in place of the brioche dough in chapter 10 for many of the pastries in that chapter. A word about coconut oil in this recipe: if you use it, be aware that the dough will seem a little drier, but it bakes up beautifully and the flavor is fantastic.

Makes enough dough for at least three 1½-pound loaves. The recipe is easily doubled or halved.

Ingredient	Volume (U.S.)	Weight (U.S.)	Weight (Metric)
Brown rice flour	1 cup	5⅓ ounces	150 grams
Tapioca flour (tapioca starch)	1 cup	4½ ounces	130 grams
Cornstarch	3¾ cups	1 pound, 3 ounces	535 grams
Granulated yeast	2 tablespoons	0.7 ounce	20 grams
Kosher salt*	1 tablespoon	0.6 ounce	15 grams
Xanthan gum or ground psyllium husk**	2 tablespoons	¾ ounce	20 grams
Milk	2½ cups	1 pound, 4 ounces	565 grams
Honey	1 cup	12 ounces	340 grams
Eggs, large	4	8 ounces	225 grams

*Can increase or decrease to taste (see page 56).
**Double quantity if using psyllium.

(continued)

Ingredient	Volume (U.S.)	Weight (U.S.)	Weight (Metric)
Vegetable oil, olive oil, or melted unsalted butter or coconut oil (see page 28 for options)	1 cup	7½ ounces	215 grams
Vanilla, pure extract	1 tablespoon	½ ounce	15 grams
Egg wash (1 egg beaten with 1 tablespoon water) for brushing on the loaf			
Raw sugar for sprinkling on top crust			

1. **Mixing and storing the dough:** Whisk together the flour, tapioca starch, cornstarch, yeast, salt, and xanthan gum in a 5-quart bowl, or a lidded (not airtight) food container.

2. Combine the liquid ingredients and gradually mix them into the dry ingredients, using a spoon or a heavy-duty stand mixer (with paddle), until all the dry ingredients are well incorporated. *We highly recommend the mixer for gluten-free doughs.*

3. Cover (not airtight), and allow the dough to rest at room temperature for approximately 2 hours.

4. The dough can be used immediately after its initial rise. Refrigerate it in a lidded (not airtight) container and use over the next 5 days.

5. **On baking day,** grease a brioche pan or an 8½×4½-inch nonstick loaf pan. Use wet hands to break off a 1½-pound (small cantaloupe-size) piece of the refrigerated dough. Quickly pat it into a ball; this dough isn't stretched because there is no gluten in it—just gently press it into the shape. You might need to wet your hands a little more to prevent the dough from sticking and to create a smooth surface, but don't use so much water as to make the dough soggy.

6. Pat the ball into a narrow oval and put it in the brioche or loaf pan. Allow the loaf to rest, loosely covered with plastic wrap, for 90 minutes (40 minutes if you're using fresh, unrefrigerated dough).

7. **Preheat the oven to 350°F.** If you're not using a stone in the oven, a 5-minute preheat is adequate.

8. Just before baking, use a pastry brush to paint the loaf's top crust with egg wash and sprinkle it with raw sugar.

9. Bake near the center of the oven for 40 to 45 minutes. The loaf is done when caramel brown and firm. Smaller or larger loaves will require adjustments in resting and baking time.

10. Remove the brioche from the pan and allow it to cool on a rack before slicing.

"Super Sam" Gluten-Free Cinnamon Buns

*"This recipe was inspired by my friend's young nephew, who has celiac disease. 'Super Sam,' as his family calls him, had been flipping through **The New Artisan Bread in Five Minutes a Day** and said he really wished he could eat the pecan sticky buns. His aunt Jenny called me and asked what we could come up with. I created these buns and then tested the recipe on a group of four- to nine-year-olds—they all ate them, came back for seconds, and had no idea that the buns were gluten-free. Now 'Super Sam' can have sticky buns, too!"—Zoë*

Makes 12 buns

1½ pounds (small cantaloupe-size portion) of Gluten-Free Brioche dough (page 318)

The Filling

⅔ cup (6 ounces/170 grams) packed brown sugar
1½ teaspoons ground cinnamon
⅔ cup chopped nuts (optional)

The Glaze

1 cup (4 ounces/115 grams) confectioners' sugar
1 teaspoon pure vanilla extract
2 tablespoons milk (add 1 tablespoon at a time)
1 tablespoon unsalted butter, at room temperature, or zero trans fat, zero hydrogenated oil margarine, at room temperature
½ teaspoon finely grated orange zest

1. **On baking day:** Grease a 9-inch cake pan. Using wet hands, take a 1½-pound (small cantaloupe-size) piece of dough from the bucket.

Visit BreadIn5.com, where you'll find recipes, photos, videos, and instructional material.

2. Sprinkle sugar on a silicone mat and place the dough on top of the sugar. Cover the dough with a piece of plastic wrap. Using your hands and a rolling pin, roll the dough between the plastic wrap and silicone mat until you have a ¼-inch-thick rectangle. Peel off the plastic wrap.

3. **Make the filling:** Combine the filling ingredients. Sprinkle the filling over the surface of the dough. Roll the dough, starting at the long end, into a log, lifting the silicone mat to help ease the dough from its surface.

4. Remove the dough from the silicone mat and, with a very sharp knife or kitchen shears, cut the log into 12 equal pieces and arrange them in the pan, with the "swirled" edge visible to you. Cover loosely with plastic wrap and allow to rest about 1 hour.

5. **Preheat the oven to 350°F,** with a rack placed in the center of the oven.

6. Bake the buns for 20 to 25 minutes, or until the tops are lightly brown and the dough feels set when touched.

7. Allow the buns to cool on a rack for a few minutes, and then invert onto a serving plate.

8. **Make the glaze:** Mix together the glaze ingredients and spread the glaze over the tops of the warm buns. These are best eaten while slightly warm.

10

ENRICHED BREADS AND PASTRIES FROM HEALTHY INGREDIENTS

∽

Even though we try to maintain a healthy diet, we still need a bit of decadence in our lives. We've re-created some of our favorite enriched breads from the traditional palette, using our usual fast method, but with a healthier philosophy. You can have challah, Christmas stollen, pumpkin brioche, and many more sweet breads and pastries without feeling as though you are breaking your commitment to eating well—just eat enriched breads and pastries in moderation.

In this chapter we have tried to give you alternatives to using white flours, white sugar, and butter. Not that they can't be used in small amounts in a healthy diet, but there are so many other wonderful flavors that lend themselves well to our breads. We used whole grains, natural sweeteners, and unsaturated oils as much as possible, and in all cases we've cut way back. If you eat these breads in moderation you will continue on a healthy path that is just a bit more enjoyable.

Braided Challah with Whole Wheat and Wheat Germ

Here's a delicious and nutritious braided loaf, with all the classic flavors of challah: eggs, poppy seeds, and honey with a little nutty flavor from wheat germ, which also adds vitamin E and other nutrients. The eggy dough for this traditional Jewish bread is very similar to doughs used in some spectacular Scandinavian holiday treats, so don't forget to try the variations at the end of this recipe. If you're avoiding butter, then vegetable oil (including coconut oil), makes a great challah. If you go with coconut oil or butter, you'll need to melt it in the microwave or on the stovetop first.

If you're an old hand at baking challah with traditional dough, you'll notice that our version creates a gorgeous loaf, but the strands sometimes separate near the center, and this is more of a problem with larger loaves (see color photo). This is normal.

Makes enough dough for at least five 1-pound loaves. The recipe is easily doubled or halved.

Ingredient	Volume (U.S.)	Weight (U.S.)	Weight (Metric)
Whole wheat flour*	5 cups	1 pound, 6½ ounces	640 grams
All-purpose flour	3 cups	15 ounces	425 grams
Wheat germ	¼ cup	1 ounce	30 grams
Granulated yeast (can decrease to taste, see page 56)	1 tablespoon	0.35 ounce	10 grams
Kosher salt (can increase or decrease to taste, see page 56)	1 tablespoon	0.6 ounce	15 grams
Vital wheat gluten*	¼ cup	1⅜ ounces	40 grams

*For whole wheat flours other than Gold Medal or Pillsbury, or for omitting vital wheat gluten, see page 82 for guidelines on adjustment.

(continued)

Ingredient	Volume (U.S.)	Weight (U.S.)	Weight (Metric)
Lukewarm water	3 cups	1 pound, 8 ounces	680 grams
Vegetable oil, olive oil, or melted unsalted butter or coconut oil (see page 28 for options)	¼ cup	2 ounces	55 grams
Honey	½ cup	6 ounces	170 grams
Eggs, large, at room temperature	3	6 ounces	170 grams
Vanilla extract, pure	1 teaspoon		
Egg wash (1 egg beaten with 1 tablespoon water) for brushing on the loaf			
Poppy seeds for sprinkling on top			

1. **Mixing and storing the dough:** Whisk together the flours, wheat germ, yeast, salt, and vital wheat gluten in a 5-quart bowl, or a lidded (not airtight) food container.

2. Combine the liquid ingredients and mix them with the dry ingredients without kneading, using a spoon, a 14-cup food processor (with dough attachment), or a heavy-duty stand mixer (with paddle). You might need to use wet hands to get the last bit of flour to incorporate if you're not using a machine.

3. Cover (not airtight), and allow the dough to rest at room temperature until it rises and collapses (or flattens on top), approximately 2 hours.

4. The dough can be used immediately after its initial rise, though it is easier to handle when cold. Refrigerate it in a lidded (not airtight) container and use over the next 5 days. Or store the dough for up to 2 weeks in the freezer in 1-pound portions. When using frozen dough, thaw it in the refrigerator for 24 hours before use, then allow the usual rest/rise time.

5. **On baking day,** dust the surface of the refrigerated dough with flour and cut off a 1-pound (grapefruit-size) piece. Dust the piece with more flour and quickly shape it into a ball by stretching the surface of the dough around to the bottom, rotating the ball a quarter turn as you go.

6. Gently roll and stretch the dough, dusting with flour so your hands don't stick to it, until you have a long rope about ¾ inch thick. You may need to let the dough relax for 5 minutes so it won't resist your efforts. Using a dough scraper or knife, make angled cuts to divide the rope into 3 equal-length strands with tapering ends.

7. **Braiding the challah:** Starting from one end of the loaf, pull the left strand over the center strand and lay it down; always pull the outer strands into the middle, never moving what becomes the center strand.

8. Now pull the right strand over the center strand. Continue, alternating outer strands but always pulling into the center. When you get to the end, pinch the strands together.

9. If the braid is oddly shaped, fix it by nudging and stretching. Place the braid on a greased cookie sheet or one prepared with parchment paper or a silicone mat, and allow it to rest, loosely covered with plastic wrap or an overturned bowl, for 90 minutes (or 40 minutes if you're using fresh, unrefrigerated dough).

10. **Preheat the oven to 350°F,** with a rack placed in the center of the oven. If you're not using a stone in the oven, a 5-minute preheat is adequate.

11. Just before baking, use a pastry brush to paint the top crust with egg wash (see sidebar), and then sprinkle the crust with poppy seeds.

12. Place the cookie sheet in the oven and bake the bread for 30 to 35 minutes, or until browned and firm. Smaller or larger loaves will require adjustments in resting and baking time.

13. Allow the challah to cool on a rack before slicing

◌◟◞

Getting a super-shine on challah: If you follow our egg wash-painting directions exactly, you'll get a lovely loaf and the seeds will stick securely, but it won't be that shiny. If you want a shiny result, paint the top crust with egg wash twice. First, apply a coat and let it dry for 15 minutes. Then, just before baking, paint it again and *then* sprinkle on the seeds.

VARIATIONS: Scandinavian Christmas Breads

Our basic lightly enriched dough above can be used in two terrific Scandinavian Christmas favorites: *pulla* (from Finland) and *julekage* (from Norway, Sweden, and Denmark). You can make them with a brioche base (pages 318, 343, and 354) but traditional recipes favor a more lightly enriched and sweetened dough. The secret's in the spices.

Pulla

Simply add 1 teaspoon ground cardamom and ½ teaspoon ground anise seeds to the dry ingredients in the challah recipe. Braid the loaf as for challah and paint it with egg wash, but sprinkle it with raw sugar instead of poppy seeds before resting and baking at 350°F as above.

Julekage

Base your julekage on the same spiced enriched dough variation that you used for pulla, but add ¾ cup dried fruits such as raisins, currants, cranberries, apricots, cherries, candied citron, candied lemon peel, or candied orange peel to the liquid ingredients. Shape the loaf as a flattened round. After resting, bake at 350°F as above. When slightly cooled but still warm, paint it with the icing below, then sprinkle it with toasted slivered or sliced almonds.

Icing for Julekage

1½ teaspoons milk
¼ cup (1 ounce/30 grams) confectioners' sugar
¼ teaspoon pure almond extract

Mix all the ingredient together in a small bowl.

100% Whole Wheat Challah with No Added Gluten

The reason so many 100% whole grain challah recipes fail is that eggs have a surprising effect on baked bread dough. Everyone thinks that they'll add moisture, but in fact, eggs can have the opposite effect if you're not careful. Biochemists tell us that when egg doughs bake, the long protein strands in egg (albumen) actually curl, tighten, and contract, squeezing water out of the matrix. So one important word of advice when making this challah: bake it fully, but don't *overbake* it. This might take a bit of practice with your particular oven, so be sure yours runs accurately by using an oven thermometer (see page 42).

Butter in challah is delicious, but the vegetable oils work nicely, including coconut oil, which also lends wonderful flavor. If you go with coconut oil, you'll need to melt it in the microwave or on the stovetop first (just like butter), and be aware that dough made with coconut oil will seem firmer than doughs made with the other fats. Don't worry—it bakes up beautifully.

And if you decide you'd like a higher rise, you can experiment with adding ¼ cup of vital wheat gluten, and increase the water ¼ to ½ cup.

Makes enough dough for at least four 1-pound loaves.
The recipe is easily doubled or halved.

Ingredient	Volume (U.S.)	Weight (U.S.)	Weight (Metric)
Whole wheat flour*	7⅔ cups	2 pounds, 3 ounces	1,000 grams
Granulated yeast (can decrease to taste, see page 56)	1 tablespoon	0.35 ounce	10 grams

*For whole wheat flours other than Gold Medal or Pillsbury, or for omitting vital wheat gluten, see page 92 for guidelines on adjustment.

(continued)

Visit BreadIn5.com, where you'll find recipes, photos, videos, and instructional material.

Ingredient	Volume (U.S.)	Weight (U.S.)	Weight (Metric)
Kosher salt (can increase or decrease to taste, see page 56)	1 tablespoon	0.6 ounce	15 grams
Lukewarm water	2¼ cups	1 pound, 2 ounces	515 grams
Honey	¾ cup	9 ounces	255 grams
Vegetable oil, olive oil, or melted unsalted butter or coconut oil (see page 28 for options)	½ cup	3¾ ounces	105 grams
Eggs, large, at room temperature	4	8 ounces	225 grams
Egg wash (1 egg beaten with 1 tablespoon of water)			
Poppy or sesame seeds for sprinkling on top crust			
Oil, butter, or parchment paper for the baking sheet			

Follow the directions for Braided Challah with Whole Wheat and Wheat Germ on page 324.

VARIATIONS: You use this dough to make any of the Scandanavian Christmas Breads on page 328.

Apples and Honey Whole Grain Challah

Apples and honey are the traditional culinary welcome to Jewish New Year, and though they don't usually make their way into the turban-shaped holiday challah, their combination is absolutely irresistible any time of the year. Use Braeburn or another firm variety so that the apples maintain their shape, and leave the skin on—it adds wonderful color and flavor (see color photo).

Makes enough dough for at least five 1-pound loaves. The recipe is easily doubled or halved.

Ingredient	Volume (U.S.)	Weight (U.S.)	Weight (Metric)
Whole wheat flour	5 cups	1 pound, 6½ ounces	640 grams
All-purpose flour	3 cups	15 ounces	425 grams
Wheat germ	¼ cup	1 ounce	30 grams
Granulated yeast (can decrease to taste, see page 56)	1 tablespoon	0.35 ounce	10 grams
Kosher salt (can increase or decrease to taste, see page 56)	1 tablespoon	0.6 ounce	15 grams
Vital wheat gluten*	¼ cup	1⅜ ounces	40 grams
Lukewarm water	3 cups	1 pound, 8 ounces	680 grams
Vegetable oil, olive oil, or melted unsalted butter or coconut oil (see page 28 for options)	½ cup	3¾ ounces	105 grams
Honey	½ cup	6 ounces	170 grams

*For whole wheat flours other than Gold Medal or Pillsbury, or for omitting vital wheat gluten, see page 82 for guidelines on adjustment

(continued)

Visit BreadIn5.com, where you'll find recipes, photos, videos, and instructional material.

Ingredient	Volume (U.S.)	Weight (U.S.)	Weight (Metric)
Eggs, large, at room temperature	3	6 ounces	170 grams
4 large baking apples, Braeburn or other firm variety, cored, and cut into ½-inch dice (leave skin on)			
Egg wash (1 egg beaten with 1 tablespoon water) for brushing on the loaf			
Sesame seeds for sprinkling on top			

1. **Mixing and storing the dough:** Whisk together the flours, wheat germ, yeast, salt, and vital wheat gluten in a 5-quart bowl, or a lidded (not airtight) food container.

2. Combine the liquid ingredients and the apples and mix with the dry ingredients without kneading, using a spoon, a 14-cup food processor (with dough attachment), or a heavy-duty stand mixer (with paddle). You might need to use wet hands to get the last bit of flour to incorporate if you're not using a machine.

3. Cover (not airtight), and allow the dough to rest at room temperature until it rises and collapses (or flattens on top), approximately 2 hours.

4. The dough can be used immediately after its initial rise, though it is easier to handle when cold. Refrigerate it in a lidded (not airtight) container and use over the next 5 days. Or store the dough for up to 2 weeks in the freezer in 1-pound portions. When using frozen dough, thaw it in the refrigerator for 24 hours before use, then allow the usual rest/rise time.

5. **On baking day,** dust the surface of the refrigerated dough with flour and cut off a 1-pound (grapefruit-size) piece. Dust with more flour and quickly shape it into a ball by stretching the surface of the dough

around to the bottom, rotating the ball a quarter turn as you go.

6. Gently roll and stretch the dough, dusting with flour so that your hands don't stick to it, until you have a cylinder. Thin out one end so you end up with a tapered rope. You might need to let the dough relax for 5 minutes so that it won't resist your efforts.

7. **Winding the turban:** Keeping the thick end stationary, wind the thinner end around it and, finally, tuck it underneath to seal.

8. Place the turban on a greased cookie sheet, or one prepared with parchment paper or a silicone mat, and allow it to rest, loosely covered with plastic wrap or an overturned bowl, for 90 minutes (40 minutes if you're using fresh, unrefrigerated dough).

9. **Preheat the oven to 350°F,** with a rack placed in the center of the oven. If you're not using a stone in the oven, a 5-minute preheat is adequate.

10. Just before baking, use a pastry brush to paint the top crust with egg wash, and then sprinkle the crust with sesame seeds.

11. Place the cookie sheet in the oven and bake the bread for about 35 minutes, until browned and firm. Smaller or larger loaves will require adjustments in resting and baking time.

12. Allow the challah to cool on a rack before slicing.

Il Bollo (Italian Yom Kippur Challah with Anise and Olive Oil)

Il bollo, which literally means nothing more than "the ball," is justly famous for its flavor, spiked with olive oil, anise, vanilla, and lemon. It's eaten to break the fast of Yom Kippur, a Jewish holy day, but it's great anytime. We left this loaf mostly white, but you can increase the whole grain and liquids if you like, and make a version based on the Braided Challah with Whole Wheat and Wheat Germ dough (page 324).

Makes enough dough for at least four 1-pound loaves. The recipe is easily doubled or halved.

Ingredient	Volume (U.S.)	Weight (U.S.)	Weight (Metric)
Whole wheat flour	1½ cups	6¾ ounces	195 grams
All-purpose flour	7 cups	2 pounds, 3 ounces	990 grams
Granulated yeast (can decrease to taste, see page 56)	1 tablespoon	0.35 ounce	10 grams
Kosher salt (can increase or decrease to taste, see page 56)	1 tablespoon	0.6 ounce	15 grams
Anise seeds, whole, plus additional for sprinkling	2 tablespoons	0.35 ounce	10 grams
Vital wheat gluten	2 tablespoons	¾ ounce	20 grams
Lukewarm water	2 cups	1 pound	455 grams
Honey	¾ cup	9 ounces	255 grams

*If omitting vital wheat gluten, decrease water to 1¾ cups.

Ingredient	Volume (U.S.)	Weight (U.S.)	Weight (Metric)
Olive oil	½ cup	3¾ ounces	105 grams
2 teaspoons pure vanilla extract			
Eggs, large, at room temperature	4	8 ounces	225 grams
½ teaspoon finely grated lemon zest			
Egg wash (1 egg beaten with 1 tablespoon water) for brushing on the loaf			

1. **Mixing and storing the dough:** Whisk together the flours, yeast, salt, anise seeds, and vital wheat gluten in a 5-quart bowl, or a lidded (not airtight) food container.

2. Add the liquid ingredients and lemon zest and mix without kneading, using a spoon, a 14-cup food processor (with dough attachment), or a heavy-duty stand mixer (with paddle). You might need to use wet hands to get the last bit of flour to incorporate if you're not using a machine.

3. Cover (not airtight), and allow the dough to rest at room temperature until it rises and collapses (or flattens on top), approximately 2 hours.

4. The dough can be used immediately after its initial rise, though it is easier to handle when cold. Refrigerate it in a lidded (not airtight) container and use over the next 5 days. Or store the dough for up to 2 weeks in the freezer in 1-pound portions. When using frozen dough, thaw it in the refrigerator for 24 hours before use, then allow the usual rest/rise time.

5. **On baking day,** prepare a cookie sheet with olive oil, parchment paper, or a silicone mat. Dust the surface of the refrigerated dough with flour and cut off a 1-pound (grapefruit-size) piece. Dust the piece with

more flour and quickly shape it into a ball by stretching the surface of the dough around to the bottom, rotating the ball a quarter turn as you go.

6. Allow the loaf to rest, loosely covered with plastic wrap or an overturned bowl, on the prepared cookie sheet for 90 minutes (or 40 minutes if you're using fresh, unrefrigerated dough).

7. **Preheat the oven to 350°F,** with a rack placed in the center of the oven. If you're not using a stone in the oven, a 5-minute preheat is adequate.

8. Just before baking, use a pastry brush to paint the loaf with egg wash, and then sprinkle the crust lightly with additional anise seeds. Slash the loaf with a ½-inch-deep slash into the top, using a serrated bread knife.

9. Place the cookie sheet on the stone or on a rack in the center of oven and bake for about 35 minutes, or until browned and firm. Smaller or larger loaves will require adjustments in resting and baking time.

10. Allow the bollo to cool on a rack before slicing.

Indian Spiced Whole Grain Doughnuts, page 357

Pear Tarte Tatin with Whole Wheat Brioche, page 360

Honey Caramel Sticky Nut Buns, page 363

Rosemary Crescent Rolls, page 367

Pistachio Twist, page 374

Chocolate Espresso Whole Wheat Bread, page 378

Sourdough Starter, page 385

100% Whole Grain Levain-Risen Bread, page 389

Milk and Honey Raisin Bread

Milk and honey both tenderize wheat breads, so for people who are looking for a soft whole grain bread, this is the one. The raisins are a perfect fit for the sweet, tender crumb. An added bonus is that these flavors are universally loved by children.

Makes enough dough for at least two 2-pound loaves. The recipe is easily doubled or halved.

Ingredient	Volume (U.S.)	Weight (U.S.)	Weight (Metric)
Whole wheat flour	4¾ cups	1 pound, 5½ ounces	605 grams
All-purpose flour	4½ cups	1 pound, 6½ ounces	640 grams
Granulated yeast (can decrease to taste, see page 56)	1 tablespoon	0.35 ounce	10 grams
Kosher salt (can increase or decrease to taste, see page 56)	1 tablespoon	0.6 ounce	15 grams
Vital wheat gluten*	¼ cup	1⅜ ounces	40 grams
Milk	2 cups	1 pound	455 grams
Lukewarm water	2 cups	1 pound	455 grams
Honey or agave syrup	⅓ cup	4 ounces	115 grams
Eggs, large, at room temperature	2	4 ounces	115 grams
Raisins	¾ cup	4½ ounces	130 grams
Egg wash (1 egg beaten with 1 tablespoon water) for brushing on the loaf			
Raw sugar for sprinkling on top			

*If omitting vital wheat gluten, decrease water to ½ cup.

Milk is one of the best ways to get calcium and vitamin D into your diet: There's some evidence that children in particular may not be meeting their recommended daily allowance for calcium. Since milk makes a nice liquid base for bread, this loaf is a great way to get more calcium and vitamin D into your kids' diets. Most adults will also benefit as well. Milk is also rich in the mineral zinc.

1. **Mixing and storing the dough:** Whisk together the flours, yeast, salt, and vital wheat gluten.

2. Combine the remaining ingredients and mix them with the dry ingredients without kneading, using a spoon, a food processor (with dough attachment), or a heavy-duty stand mixer (with paddle). You might need to use wet hands to get the last bit of flour to incorporate if you're not using a machine.

3. Cover (not airtight), and allow the dough to rest at room temperature until it rises and collapses (or flattens on top), approximately 2 hours.

4. The dough can be used immediately after its initial rise, though it is easier to handle when cold. Refrigerate it in a lidded (not airtight) container and use over the next 5 days, or store the dough for up to 2 weeks in the freezer in loaf-size portions.

5. **On baking day**, grease an 8½×4½-inch nonstick loaf pan. Dust the surface of the refrigerated dough with flour and cut off a 2-pound (cantaloupe-size) piece. Dust the piece with more flour and quickly shape it into a ball by stretching the surface of the dough around to the bottom, rotating the ball a quarter turn as you go.

6. Elongate the ball into an oval and place it in the loaf pan; your goal is to fill the pan about three-quarters full. Allow the loaf to rest, loosely covered with plastic wrap or an overturned bowl, for 90 minutes (or 40 minutes if you're using fresh, unrefrigerated dough).

7. **Preheat the oven to 375°F,** with a rack placed in the center of the oven. A stone is not needed for loaf-pan breads; if you omit it, the preheat time can be as short as 5 minutes.

8. Just before baking, use a pastry brush to paint the top crust with egg wash, and then sprinkle with raw sugar.

9. Bake for about 45 minutes, or until richly browned and firm. Smaller or larger loaves will require adjustments in resting and baking time.

10. Remove the bread from the pan and allow to cool on a rack before slicing.

VARIATION: Raisin Buns

These make an incredible and easy same-morning treat. When you wake up, preheat the oven to 375°F. You can use the milk and honey dough in this recipe, or use plain whole grain dough and fold some raisins into each bun as you shape it. Dust with flour and pat out flattened, elongated ovals, using 2 or 3 ounces of dough for each (peach-size). Set on a baking sheet prepared with parchment paper, a silicone mat, butter, or oil, rest for 20 minutes, brush with egg wash (1 egg beaten with 1 tablespoon water), and bake for about 25 minutes. Serve slightly warm with butter, cheese, or jam.

Braided raisin buns are easy too—just cut each bun portion into thirds, stretch into thin ropes, and braid as would for challah (page 326), but when you're done, tuck the ends under and pinch them together (see color photo).

Bran Muffin Bread

This unusual yeasted bread has the flavors of American-style bran muffins, with lots of bran and spice. It's a breakfast favorite!

Makes enough dough for at least four 1-pound loaves. The recipe is easily doubled or halved.

Ingredient	Volume (U.S.)	Weight (U.S.)	Weight (Metric)
Wheat bran	1½ cups	4½ ounces	130 grams
Whole wheat flour	1 cup	4½ ounces	130 grams
All-purpose flour	4¼ cups	1 pound, 5¼ ounces	600 grams
Granulated yeast (can decrease to taste, see page 56)	1 tablespoon	0.35 ounce	10 grams
Kosher salt (can increase or decrease to taste, see page 56)	1 tablespoon	0.6 ounce	15 grams
Cinnamon, ground	1 teaspoon		
Nutmeg, ground	¼ teaspoon		
Vital wheat gluten*	¼ cup	1⅜ ounces	40 grams
Lukewarm water	2¼ cups	1 pound, 2 ounces	510 grams
Maple syrup	¾ cup	6 ounces	170 grams
Molasses	1 tablespoon	⅔ ounce	20 grams
Vegetable oil, olive oil, or melted unsalted butter or coconut oil (see page 28 for options)	½ cup	3¾ ounces	105 grams

*If omitting vital wheat gluten, decrease water to 1¾ cups.

Ingredient	Volume (U.S.)	Weight (U.S.)	Weight (Metric)
Vanilla extract, pure	½ teaspoon		
Eggs, large, at room temperature	2	4 ounces	115 grams
Raisins	¾ cup	4½ ounces	130 grams

1. **Mixing and storing the dough:** Whisk together the wheat bran, flours, yeast, salt, cinnamon, nutmeg, and vital wheat gluten in a 5-quart bowl, or a lidded (not airtight) food container.

2. Combine the liquid ingredients and raisins and mix them with the dry ingredients without kneading, using a spoon, a 14-cup food processor (with dough attachment), or a heavy-duty stand mixer (with paddle). You might need to use wet hands to get the last bit of flour to incorporate if you're not using a machine.

3. Cover (not airtight), and allow the dough to rest at room temperature until it rises and collapses (or flattens on top), approximately 2 hours.

4. The dough can be used immediately after its initial rise, though it is easier to handle when cold. Refrigerate it in a lidded (not airtight) container and use over the next 5 days. The dough can be frozen in single-loaf portions and defrosted overnight in the refrigerator.

5. **On baking day,** dust the surface of the refrigerated dough with flour and cut off a 1-pound (grapefruit-size) piece. Dust the piece with more flour and quickly shape it into a ball by stretching the surface of the dough around to the bottom, rotating the ball a quarter turn as you go.

6. Elongate the ball into a narrow oval. Allow the loaf to rest, loosely covered with plastic wrap or an overturned bowl, on a pizza peel

prepared with cornmeal or lined with parchment paper for 90 minutes (40 minutes if you're using fresh, unrefrigerated dough). Alternatively, you can rest the loaf on a silicone mat or a greased cookie sheet without using a pizza peel.

7. **Preheat the oven to 350°F,** with a baking stone placed on the middle rack. Place an empty metal broiler tray on any other rack that won't interfere with the rising bread.

8. Just before baking, use a pastry brush to paint the top crust with water. Slash the loaf diagonally with deep parallel cuts, using a serrated bread knife.

9. Slide the loaf directly onto the hot stone (or place the silicone mat or cookie sheet on the stone if you used one). Pour 1 cup of hot tap water into the broiler tray, and quickly close the oven door (see page 40 for steam alternatives). Bake for about 40 minutes, or until richly browned and firm. If you used parchment paper, a silicone mat, or a cookie sheet under the loaf, carefully remove it and bake the loaf directly on the stone or an oven rack two-thirds of the way through the baking time. Smaller or larger loaves will require adjustments in resting and baking time.

10. Allow the bread to cool on a rack before slicing.

Whole Wheat Brioche

"Considering my pastry chef roots it would make sense that I consider sweets to be an important part of the diet. It would have been my preference to put the sweets chapter at the beginning of the book, but perhaps I am alone in thinking that we should eat dessert first. Even though this is a book about eating healthier breads, we didn't want to eliminate the sweets, we just wanted them to fit into our healthier diets. We've used natural sweeteners and made use of nutritious whole grains. The recipes we have based on this lovely dough are both delicious and satisfying, and while brioche is usually made with butter, you can consider substituting other fats if you like."—Zoë

Makes enough dough for at least two 2-pound loaves. The recipe is easily doubled or halved.

Ingredient	Volume (U.S.)	Weight (U.S.)	Weight (Metric)
Whole wheat flour	4 cups	1 pound, 2 ounces	515 grams
All-purpose flour	3 cups	15 ounces	425 grams
Granulated yeast (can decrease to taste, see page 56)	1 tablespoon	0.35 ounce	10 grams
Kosher salt (can increase or decrease to taste, see page 56)	1 tablespoon	0.6 ounce	15 grams
Vital wheat gluten*	¼ cup	1⅜ ounces	40 grams
Lukewarm water	2¼ cups	1 pound, 2 ounces	510 grams

*If omitting vital wheat gluten, decrease water to 1¾ cups.

(continued)

Ingredient	Volume (U.S.)	Weight (U.S.)	Weight (Metric)
Unsalted butter, melted (can substitute vegetable oil options on page 28)	¾ cup (1½ sticks)	6 ounces	170 grams
Honey	¾ cup	9 ounces	255 grams
Eggs, large, at room temperature	5	10 ounces	285 grams
Egg wash (1 egg beaten with 1 tablespoon water) for brushing on the top crust			

1. **Mixing and storing the dough:** Whisk together the flours, yeast, salt, and vital wheat gluten in a 5-quart bowl, or a lidded (not airtight) food container.

2. Combine the liquid ingredients and mix them with the dry ingredients without kneading, using a spoon, a 14-cup food processor (with dough attachment), or a heavy-duty stand mixer (with paddle).

3. The dough will be loose, but it will firm up when chilled. *Don't try to use it without chilling* for at least 2 hours. You may notice lumps in the dough, but they will disappear in your finished products.

4. Cover (not airtight), and allow the dough to rest at room temperature until it rises and collapses (or flattens on top), approximately 2 hours.

5. Refrigerate the dough in a lidded (not airtight) container and use over the next 5 days, or store in the freezer for up to 2 weeks in an airtight container. Freeze it in 2-pound portions. When using frozen dough, thaw it in the refrigerator for 24 hours before use, then allow the usual rest/rise time.

6. **On baking day,** grease a brioche pan, or an 8½×4½-inch nonstick loaf pan. Dust the surface of the refrigerated dough with flour and cut off a 2-pound (cantaloupe-size) piece of dough. Dust the piece with more flour and quickly shape it into a ball. Place the ball in the prepared pan and allow to rest, loosely covered with plastic wrap, for 1 hour 45 minutes.

7. **Preheat the oven to 350°F,** with a rack placed in the center of the oven. If you're not using a stone in the oven, a 5-minute preheat is adequate. Steam is not needed.

8. Just before baking, use a pastry brush to brush the loaf's top crust with egg wash.

9. Bake the loaf near the center of the oven for 40 to 45 minutes. Brioche will not form a hard, crackling crust. The loaf is done when it is medium brown and firm. Smaller or larger loaves will require adjustments in resting and baking time.

10. Remove the brioche from the pan and allow to cool on a rack before slicing.

Apple Strudel Bread

This bread is perfect for breakfast or a Sunday brunch. Inspired by the classic Austrian pastry, the loaf is made from brioche dough that is rolled thin and layered with tons of apples, raisins, and nuts. A sprinkle of cinnamon and raw sugar is the crowning touch. This makes a large loaf, but trust us—there will be none left over (see color photo).

Makes one 2-pound loaf

Use any of these refrigerated pre-mixed doughs: Braided Challah with Whole Wheat and Wheat Germ (page 324), Whole Wheat Brioche (page 343), 100% Whole Grain Butterfat- and Yolk-Free Brioche (page 351), Pumpkin Pie Brioche (page 354), Soft Whole Wheat Sandwich Bread (page 132), or any other enriched dough

1½ pounds (small cantaloupe-size portion) of any pre-mixed dough listed above, defrosted overnight in the refrigerator if frozen

2 medium apples, skin on, thinly sliced, then finely chopped

½ cup (3 ounces/85 grams) raisins

¾ cup (3 ounces/85 grams) finely chopped walnuts (optional)

¼ cup (2 ounces/55 grams) raw sugar

½ teaspoon ground cinnamon

Egg wash (1 egg beaten with 1 tablespoon water) for brushing on the top crust

Cinnamon-sugar (1 tablespoon raw sugar mixed with ¼ teaspoon ground cinnamon) for sprinkling on top

1. **On baking day,** combine the chopped apples, raisins, walnuts (if using), raw sugar, and cinnamon in a bowl. Toss well and set aside.

2. Grease an 8½×4½-inch nonstick loaf pan. Dust the surface of the refrigerated dough with flour and cut off a 1½-pound (small cantaloupe-size) piece. Dust with more flour and quickly shape it into

a ball by stretching the surface of the dough around to the bottom, rotating the ball a quarter turn as you go.

3. With a rolling pin, roll out the dough until it is a ⅛-inch-thick rectangle. As you roll out the dough, use enough flour to prevent the dough from sticking to the work surface, but not so much as to make it dry.

4. Spread the apple mixture over the rolled-out dough. Roll the dough into a log, starting at the short end. Place the log in the loaf pan and allow the loaf to rest, loosely covered with plastic wrap, for 90 minutes (40 minutes if you're using fresh unrefrigerated dough).

5. **Preheat the oven to 350°F,** with a rack placed in the center of the oven.

6. Just before baking, use a pastry brush to paint the top crust with egg wash, and then sprinkle with the cinnamon-sugar.

7. Slide the loaf into the oven. Bake for 50 to 60 minutes, or until deeply browned and firm. Smaller or larger loaves will require adjustments in resting and baking time.

8. Remove the bread from the pan and allow it to cool before slicing.

100% Whole Wheat Christmas Stollen

Our books are always published in late fall, just in time for holiday baking. Within days of the publication of our first book, we were inundated with requests for *stollen*, a German Christmas specialty rich with butter and eggs, spiced with cardamom, studded with dried and candied fruit, and spiked with just a touch of brandy. Here in Minnesota there is a large German-American population and this festive bread is part of that tradition.

Here is a gorgeous version made with whole grains and marzipan running through the middle. If you find the brandy a bit too festive, then you can replace it with either orange juice or even black tea (see color photo).

Makes enough dough for at least three 1½-pound loaves. The recipe is easily doubled or halved.

Ingredient	Volume (U.S.)	Weight (U.S.)	Weight (Metric)
Whole wheat flour	6 cups	1 pound, 11 ounces	765 grams
Granulated yeast (can decrease to taste, see page 56)	1 tablespoon	0.35 ounce	10 grams
Kosher salt (can increase or decrease to taste, see page 56)	1 tablespoon	0.6 ounce	15 grams
Vital wheat gluten*	¼ cup	1⅜ ounces	40 grams
Cardamom, ground	½ teaspoon		
Lukewarm water	2 cups	1 pound	455 grams
Vegetable oil, olive oil, or melted unsalted butter or coconut oil (see page 28 for options)	½ cup	3¾ ounces	105 grams

*If omitting vital wheat gluten, decrease water to 1½ cups.

Ingredient	Volume (U.S.)	Weight (U.S.)	Weight (Metric)
Honey	½ cup	6 ounces	170 grams
Eggs, large, at room temperature	4	8 ounces	225 grams
Brandy (can substitute orange juice or lukewarm black tea)	¼ cup	2 ounces	55 grams
1½ cups finely chopped dried or candied fruit (raisins, currants, dried pineapple, dried apricots, dried cherries, candied citron, candied lemon peel, or candied orange peel)			
½ cup almond paste or marzipan *per loaf* (can substitute 1 cup slivered almonds) for center of the loaf			
Egg wash (1 egg beaten with 1 tablespoon water) for brushing on the top crust			
Confectioners' sugar for the top of the loaf			

1. **Mixing and storing the dough:** Whisk together the flour, yeast, salt, vital wheat gluten, and cardamom in a 5-quart bowl, or a lidded (not airtight) food container.

2. Combine the liquid ingredients and dried and or candied fruit and mix with the dry ingredients without kneading, using a spoon, a 14-cup food processor (with dough attachment), or a heavy-duty stand mixer (with paddle). You might need to use wet hands to get the last bit of flour to incorporate if you're not using a machine.

3. The dough will be loose, but it will firm up when chilled. *Don't try to use it without chilling* for at least 2 hours.

4. Cover (not airtight), and allow the dough to rest, at room temperature until it rises and collapses (or flattens on top), approximately 2 hours.

5. Refrigerate it in a lidded (not airtight) container and use over the next 5 days. Beyond that, the dough stores well in the freezer for up to 2 weeks in an airtight container. Freeze it in 1½-pound portions. When using frozen dough, thaw it in the refrigerator for 24 hours before use, then allow the usual rest/rise time.

6. **On baking day,** dust the surface of the refrigerated dough with flour and cut off a 1½-pound (small cantaloupe-size) piece of dough. Dust the piece with more flour and quickly shape it into a ball.

7. With a rolling pin, roll out the dough to a ¼-inch-thick oval. As you roll out the dough, use enough flour to prevent the dough from sticking to the work surface, but not so much as to make it dry.

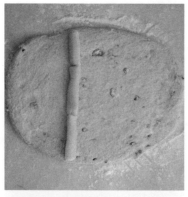

8. Place the marzipan or slivered almonds across the short end of the dough about one-third of the way from the end. Lift and fold the remaining two-thirds of the dough to form an S-shape over the almond filling. The end of the dough will lie near the middle of the top of the loaf. Allow to rest, loosely covered with plastic wrap, on a cookie sheet prepared with parchment paper or a silicone mat, for 90 minutes.

9. **Preheat the oven to 350°F,** with a rack placed in the center of the oven. If you're not using a stone in the oven, a 5-minute preheat is adequate.

10. Just before baking, use a pastry brush to paint the top crust with egg wash.

11. Place the cookie sheet in the oven and bake the stollen for 35 to 40 minutes, or until medium brown and firm.

12. Allow the stollen to cool, then sprinkle it generously with confectioners' sugar.

100% Whole Grain Butterfat- and Yolk-Free Brioche

"We developed this brioche for anyone who is watching their cholesterol but still wants a great treat. We used a butter substitute and eliminated the yolks. This bread is not low-fat or low-calorie, but if eaten in moderation it can be part of a healthy diet. This dough can be used to make pinwheels, strudel, or any other enriched dough recipe."—Zoë

Makes enough dough for at least two 2-pound loaves. The recipe is easily doubled or halved.

Ingredient	Volume (U.S.)	Weight (U.S.)	Weight (Metric)
Whole wheat flour*	7 cups	1 pound, 15½ ounces	895 grams
Granulated yeast (can decrease to taste, see page 56)	1 tablespoon	0.35 ounce	10 grams
Kosher salt (can increase or decrease to taste, see page 56)	1 tablespoon	0.6 ounce	15 grams
Vital wheat gluten*	¼ cup	1⅜ ounces	40 grams
Lukewarm water	2 cups	1 pound	455 grams
Honey	½ cup	6 ounces	170 grams
8 large egg whites, at room temperature			
Zero trans fat, zero hydrogenated oil butter substitute, melted, or other oil (see page 28 for options)	1 cup	7½ ounces	215 grams
Egg white wash (1 egg white beaten with 1 tablespoon water) for brushing on the top crust			

*For whole wheat flours other than Gold Medal or Pillsbury, or for omitting vital wheat gluten, see page 92 for guidelines on adjustment.

1. **Mixing and storing the dough:** Whisk together the flour, yeast, salt, and vital wheat gluten in a 5-quart bowl, or a lidded (not airtight) food container.

2. Combine the liquid ingredients and mix with the dry ingredients without kneading, using a spoon, a 14-cup food processor (with dough attachment), or a heavy-duty stand mixer (with paddle). You might need to use wet hands to get the last bit of flour to incorporate if you're not using a machine.

3. The dough will be loose, but it will firm up when chilled. *Don't try to use it without chilling* for at least 2 hours. You may notice lumps in the dough, but they will disappear in your finished products.

4. Cover (not airtight), and allow the dough to rest at room temperature until it rises and collapses (or flattens on top), approximately 2 hours.

5. Refrigerate it in a lidded (not airtight) container and use over the next 5 days. Beyond that, the dough stores well in the freezer for up to 2 weeks in an airtight container. Freeze in 2-pound portions. When using frozen dough, thaw it in the refrigerator for 24 hours before use, then allow the usual resting time.

6. **On baking day**, grease a brioche pan or an 8½×4½-inch nonstick loaf pan. Dust the surface of the refrigerated dough with flour and cut off a 2-pound (cantaloupe-size) piece of dough. Dust the piece with more flour and quickly shape it into a ball. Place the ball in the prepared pan and allow to rest, loosely covered with plastic wrap, for 1 hour 45 minutes.

7. **Preheat the oven to 350°F,** with a rack placed in the center of the oven.

8. Just before baking, use a pastry brush to paint the top crust with egg white wash.

9. Bake near the center of the oven for 45 to 50 minutes. Brioche will not form a hard, crackling crust. The loaf is done when it is medium brown and firm. Smaller or larger loaves will require adjustments in resting and baking time.

10. Remove the brioche from the pan and allow it to cool on a rack before slicing

Pumpkin Pie Brioche

"In the autumn I bake pies using freshly roasted sugar pumpkins. My kids love the flavors and I love that pumpkin is full of vitamins. It struck me that the same amazing flavors could be used in a sweet and spiced brioche. The pumpkin makes wonderfully moist dough and the bread is so fragrant and tender. It is great with butter and cinnamon-sugar or the cream cheese icing on page 365."—Zoë

Makes enough dough for at least two 2-pound loaves. The recipe is easily doubled or halved.

Ingredient	Volume (U.S.)	Weight (U.S.)	Weight (Metric)
Whole wheat flour	3 cups	13½ ounces	385 grams
All-purpose flour	4½ cups	1 pound, 6½ ounces	640 grams
Granulated yeast (can decrease to taste, see page 56)	1 tablespoon	0.35 ounce	10 grams
Kosher salt (can increase or decrease to taste, see page 56)	1 tablespoon	0.6 ounce	15 grams
Vital wheat gluten*	2 tablespoons	¾ ounce	20 grams
Lukewarm water	2 cups	1 pound	455 grams
Cinnamon, ground	1 teaspoon		
Dried ginger, ground	½ teaspoon		
Nutmeg, ground	½ teaspoon		
Allspice, ground	¼ teaspoon		
Lukewarm water	1¼ cups	10 ounces	285 grams

*If omitting vital wheat gluten, decrease water to 1 cup.

Ingredient	Volume (U.S.)	Weight (U.S.)	Weight (Metric)
Eggs, large, at room temperature	4	8 ounces	225 grams
Honey	½ cup	6 ounces	170 grams
Vegetable oil, olive oil, or melted unsalted butter or coconut oil (see page 28 for options)	¾ cup	5¾ ounces	160 grams
One large pie (or "sugar") pumpkin to yield 1¾ cups pumpkin puree, or use one 15-ounce can pumpkin puree			
Egg wash (1 egg beaten with 1 tablespoon water) for brushing on the top crust			
Raw sugar for sprinkling on top			

1. **If making your own fresh pumpkin puree:** Preheat the oven to 350°F. Split the pumpkin in half, starting at the stem, and place it, cut side down, on a lightly greased cookie sheet or one lined with a silicone mat. Bake for about 45 minutes. The pumpkin should be very soft all the way through when poked with a knife. Cool slightly before scooping out the seeds.

2. Scoop out the roasted flesh of the pumpkin and puree it in the food processor. Set aside 1¾ cups for the dough and use any left over in your favorite pumpkin pie recipe.

3. **Mixing and storing the dough:** Whisk together the flours, yeast, salt, vital wheat gluten, and spices in a 5-quart bowl, or a lidded (not airtight) food container.

4. Combine the liquid ingredients with the pumpkin puree and mix them with the dry ingredients without kneading, using a spoon, a 14-cup food processor (with dough attachment), or a heavy-duty stand mixer (with paddle). You might need to use wet hands to get the last bit of flour to incorporate if you're not using a machine.

5. The dough will be loose, but it will firm up when chilled. *Don't try to use it without chilling* for at least 2 hours. You may notice lumps in the dough, but they will disappear in your finished products.

6. Cover (not airtight), and allow the dough to rest at room temperature until it rises and collapses (or flattens on top), approximately 2 hours.

7. Refrigerate the dough in a lidded (not airtight) container and use over the next 5 days. Beyond that, the dough stores well in the freezer for up to 2 weeks in an airtight container. Freeze it in 2-pound portions. When using frozen dough, thaw it in the refrigerator for 24 hours before use, then allow the usual rest/rise times.

8. **On baking day**, grease a brioche pan or an 8½×4½-inch nonstick loaf pan. Dust the surface of the refrigerated dough with flour and cut off a 2-pound (cantaloupe-size) piece of dough. Dust the piece with more flour and quickly shape it into a ball. Place the ball in the prepared pan and allow to rest, loosely covered with plastic wrap, for 1 hour 45 minutes.

9. **Preheat the oven to 350°F,** with a rack placed in the center of the oven.

10. Just before baking, use a pastry brush to paint the loaf's top with egg wash, and then sprinkle with raw sugar.

11. Bake near the center of the oven for 45 to 50 minutes. Brioche will not form a hard, crackling crust. The loaf is done when it is medium brown and firm. Smaller or larger loaves will require adjustments in resting and baking time.

12. Remove the brioche from the pan and allow it to cool on a rack before slicing.

Indian Spiced Whole Grain Doughnuts

"We are lucky in Minneapolis to have several fabulous farmers' markets. They have a superb variety of locally produced foods, including cardamom-scented whole wheat doughnuts. I was so taken with these little fried treats that I decided to re-create them for you. You will love them with tea, coffee, or a big glass of cold milk (see color photo)."—Zoë

Everyone loves doughnuts, but can they be healthy? Fried doughnuts don't become saturated with oil, so long as you fry them right: So right now you're probably asking, "What are doughnuts doing in a health-conscious book?" But doughnuts don't have to be overly greasy—it's got to do with food's vapor pressure versus the oil's absorptive pressure, or to put it more plainly: If you fry at high temperature (but not so high that it burns), the water inside the doughnut starts turning to steam immediately, and pushes out through pores in the developing doughnut crust. That outward movement prevents inward movement of oil. If you keep the temperature precisely where Zoë recommends, the finished weight of the doughnut will be remarkably close to where you started—it didn't absorb that much oil after all. After weighing a bunch of doughnuts before and after frying, and accounting for up to a 10 percent water loss in finished baked goods, our best estimate is that each doughnut only absorbs between 15 and 45 calories' worth of oil. Use a healthy oil—not lard or hydrogenated shortening—and this will be a reasonable splurge.—Jeff

Makes twelve 3-inch doughnuts

Use any of these refrigerated pre-mixed doughs: Braided Challah with Whole Wheat and Wheat Germ (page 324), Whole Wheat Brioche (page 343), or Pumpkin Pie Brioche (page 354)

1½ pounds (680 grams) (small cantaloupe-size portion) of any pre-mixed dough listed above

½ cup (4 ounces/115 grams) sugar

½ teaspoon ground dried ginger

1 teaspoon ground cinnamon

½ teaspoon ground cardamom

¼ teaspoon ground cloves

Neutral-flavored oil for frying (use a high-smoking-point oil like soybean, canola, peanut, or vegetable blend), enough to fill a medium saucepan 4 inches from the top

Equipment

3-inch and 1-inch biscuit cutters

Deep medium saucepan for frying

Candy thermometer

Slotted spoon

Paper towels

1. **Make the spiced sugar mixture:** Combine the sugar and all the spices in a medium bowl and set aside.

2. Dust the surface of the refrigerated dough with flour and cut off a 1½-pound (small cantaloupe-size) piece. Dust the piece with more flour and quickly shape it into a ball by stretching the surface of the dough around to the bottom, rotating the ball a quarter turn as you go.

3. Roll the dough into a ¼-inch-thick rectangle on a lightly floured surface.

4. Heat the frying oil to 360°F to 370°F, as determined by a candy thermometer.

5. While the oil is heating, use a 3-inch biscuit or round cookie cutter to cut the dough into about 12 circles. Use a 1-inch round biscuit or round cookie cutter to remove the centers of the circles to create the doughnut shape. Reserve the centers to fry as well. Return any scraps to the bucket of dough.

6. Drop the doughnuts in the hot oil 2 or 3 at a time so that they have plenty of room to rise to the surface. Be careful not to overcrowd them or they will not rise nicely.

7. After 1 minute, gently flip the doughnuts over with a slotted spoon and fry for another minute or so until golden brown on both sides.

8. Remove the doughnuts from the oil and place them on paper towels to drain the excess oil. While still warm, dredge them in the bowl of spiced sugar.

9. Repeat with the remaining dough until all the doughnuts are fried. Serve slightly warm.

Pear Tarte Tatin with Whole Wheat Brioche

This is a French tart usually made with a pastry dough, but we discovered that it is excellent made with our whole wheat brioche. It comes out like a wonderful caramelized upside-down fruit pie. It can be served on its own as breakfast or with ice cream for dessert. The whole spices left in the pan as it is cooking and baking impart terrific flavor and look gorgeous. Cooking the pears takes more than 5 minutes, but we promise it is worth the wait (see color photo).

Makes 1 tarte Tatin

Use any of these refrigerated pre-mixed doughs: Braided Challah with Whole
    Wheat and Wheat Germ (page 324), Whole Wheat Brioche (page 343), or
    Pumpkin Pie Brioche (page 354)
½ pound (orange-size portion) of any pre-mixed dough listed above
3 tablespoons unsalted butter, or oil (see page 28 for options)
⅓ cup (3 ounces/85 grams) packed brown sugar
¼ cup (3 ounces/85 grams) honey
1 teaspoon fresh lemon juice
1 cinnamon stick
Two 1-inch round slices fresh ginger

2 whole cardamom pods (optional)
1 star anise (optional)
5 large firm pears, peeled, stemmed, cored, and quartered

1. In a 10-inch cast-iron skillet, melt the butter or oil over medium heat, and then sprinkle the sugar, honey, and lemon juice over it. Drop the cinnamon stick, ginger, and optional cardamom pods and star anise in the middle. Arrange the pears in a circular pattern, cut side up, in the sugar.

2. Cook slowly over low heat until the pears start to absorb the caramel and the juices are bubbling around them, 30 to 40 minutes, depending on the size, ripeness, and firmness of the pears. Spoon the sugar over the pears as they cook. Move the pears around slightly so that they are cooked evenly. If you are using a softer pear, it will go much faster.

3. Once the pears are coloring nicely and the caramel is bubbling, turn off the heat and let them cool while you prepare the dough.

4. **Preheat the oven to 350°F,** with a rack placed in the center of the oven. The baking stone is not essential; if you omit it, the preheat can be as short as 5 minutes.

5. While the pears are cooling, dust the surface of the refrigerated dough with flour and cut off a ½-pound (orange-size) piece. Dust with more flour and quickly shape it into a ball by stretching the surface of the dough around to the bottom, rotating the ball a quarter turn as you go.

6. With a rolling pin, roll out the dough until it is a ⅛-inch-thick circle that fits the pan and extends about 1 inch beyond to make room for any

shrinkage while baking. As you roll out the dough, use enough flour to prevent the dough from sticking to the work surface but not so much as to make it dry.

7. Drape the circle of dough over the pears, and tuck the excess between the pears and the edge of the pan.

8. Bake for 20 to 25 minutes, or until the dough is golden brown. Remove the pan from the oven and allow the tart to cool in the skillet for about 5 minutes. Then carefully invert it onto a serving platter that is large enough that the hot caramel juices don't spill out. Serve warm or cool.

VARIATION: Apple Tarte Tatin

The classic French version of tarte Tatin is made with apples, so we must pay homage to Julia Child, who included an Apple Tarte Tatin in *Mastering the Art of French Cooking*. In Julia's authentic style she called it "La Tarte des Demoiselles Tatin" (Maidens' Tarte Tatin, in honor of the two unmarried sisters who ran the Hotel Tatin in the Loire Valley and were said to have accidentally invented this tart by overcaramelizing apples and then covering up their "mistake" with pastry. It's the easiest variation in our book. Simply swap apples into this recipe and you're done. Bonus: Apples are a little easier to find year-round.

Honey-Caramel Sticky Nut Buns

Just because we want to eat healthier doesn't mean that we want to be austere about it. We need to indulge on occasion, and here is a way to do just that without compromising our resolve to eat better. The caramel is made with honey and the dough is made from whole grains. It may not make you healthier to eat these, but it will certainly improve your mental state. Joy is an important part of wellness and this will bring you large doses of it.

Makes 8 to 12 buns

Use any of these refrigerated pre-mixed doughs: Braided Challah with Whole Wheat and Wheat Germ (page 324), Whole Wheat Brioche (page 343), Pumpkin Pie Brioche (page 354), or Master Recipe (page 79)
1½ pounds (small cantaloupe-size portion) of any pre-mixed dough listed above

The Honey-Caramel Topping and Filling

½ cup (6 ounces/170 grams) honey
½ cup (3¾ ounces/105 grams) packed brown sugar
½ teaspoon salt
½ teaspoon ground cinnamon
¼ teaspoon ground nutmeg
½ cup (4 ounces/1 stick) unsalted butter, softened, or zero trans fat, zero hydrogenated oil margarine, softened
½ teaspoon finely grated orange zest
¾ cup finely chopped nuts (pecans, walnuts, or macadamias are wonderful)
1 cup (6 ounces/170 grams) raisins

1. Mix together all ingredients except the nuts and raisins. Spread half the mixture evenly over the bottom of an 9-inch cake pan. Set aside. Reserve the other half of the mixture for the filling.

2. Dust the surface of the refrigerated dough with flour and cut off a 1½-pound (small cantaloupe-size) piece. Dust with more flour and quickly shape it into a ball by stretching the surface of the dough around to the bottom, rotating the ball a quarter turn as you go.

3. With a rolling pin, roll out the dough until it is a ⅛-inch-thick rectangle. As you roll out the dough, use enough flour to prevent the dough from sticking to the work surface, but not so much as to make it dry.

4. Spread the remaining honey-caramel filling evenly over the rolled-out dough. Sprinkle on the nuts and raisins. Roll the dough into a log, starting at the long end of the dough. Pinch the seam closed.

5. With a very sharp knife or kitchen shears, cut into 8 to 12 equal pieces and arrange over the caramel-covered pan, with the "swirled" edge visible to you. Cover loosely with plastic wrap and allow to rest for about 1 hour.

6. **Preheat the oven to 350°F,** with a rack placed in the center of the oven. If you're not using a stone in the oven, 5 minutes of preheat time is adequate.

7. Bake the buns for about 30 minutes, or until golden brown and well set in center. Run a knife around the edge of the pan to

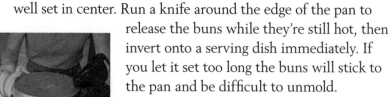

release the buns while they're still hot, then invert onto a serving dish immediately. If you let it set too long the buns will stick to the pan and be difficult to unmold.

8. Serve warm.

Cinnamon Crescent Rolls with Cream Cheese Icing

We've all tasted crescent rolls made from dough that popped out of a tube. Those are modeled on the French *croissant* (which just means "crescent"), the flaky, buttery creation that begs to be dipped into a big cup of café au lait. Neither the popped dough nor the French original are terribly healthy, so we've updated the crescent roll with doughs made from whole grains and healthy oils rather than white flour and butter.

Makes 16 crescent rolls

Use any of these refrigerated pre-mixed doughs: Braided Challah with Whole Wheat and Wheat Germ, (page 324), Whole Wheat Brioche (page 343), Pumpkin Pie Brioche (page 354), Master Recipe (page 79), or Chocolate Espresso Whole Wheat (page 378)

1 pound (455 grams) (grapefruit-size portion) of any pre-mixed dough listed above

½ cup (3¾ ounces/105 grams) packed brown sugar

2 teaspoons ground cinnamon

1 tablespoon neutral-flavored oil or unsalted melted butter.

Egg wash (1 egg beaten with 1 tablespoon water) for brushing on the top crusts

Raw sugar for sprinkling on top

The Honey–Cream Cheese Icing

4 ounces cream cheese, at room temperature (or Neufchâtel cheese)

2 tablespoons unsalted butter, or zero trans fat, zero hydrogenated oil margarine, at room temperature

3 tablespoons honey

½ teaspoon pure vanilla extract

¼ teaspoon finely grated lemon zest (optional)

Pinch of salt

1. Combine the sugar, cinnamon, and oil. Set aside.

2. Prepare 2 cookie sheets with parchment paper or a silicone mat.

3. Dust the surface of the refrigerated dough with flour and cut off a 1-pound (grapefruit-size) piece. Dust with more flour and quickly shape it into a ball by stretching the surface of the dough around to the bottom, rotating the ball a quarter turn as you go.

4. With a rolling pin, roll out the dough until it is a ⅛-inch-thick circle. As you roll out the dough, use enough flour to prevent the dough from sticking to the work surface, but not so much as to make it dry.

5. Spread the cinnamon-sugar mixture evenly over the rolled-out dough. Using a pizza cutter or a sharp knife, cut the dough into 8 equal-size wedges, like a pizza.

6. Starting at the wider end, roll each wedge until the point is tucked securely under the bottom. Bend the ends in slightly to create the crescent shape. Cover them loosely with plastic wrap and allow to rest about 40 minutes.

7. **Preheat the oven to 350°F,** with a rack placed in the center of the oven. If you're not using a stone in the oven, 5 minutes of preheat time is adequate.

8. Use a pastry brush to paint the tops with egg wash, and then sprinkle with the raw sugar. Bake the rolls for 20 to 25 minutes, or until golden brown and well set in the center. Remove the crescents from the oven and let cool on a rack.

9. **Make the Honey–Cream Cheese Icing:** Cream all the ingredients together. Drizzle over the tops of the crescents and serve. Any leftover icing can be refrigerated for a week, or frozen for a month. This is also wonderful slathered on our Carrot Cake Bread (page 368) and Pumpkin Pie Brioche (page 354).

VARIATION: Filling

Before rolling up the crescents you can put a tablespoon of almond paste, preserves, apple filling from the Apple Strudel Bread (page 346), or a 1-ounce piece of chocolate on the triangle of dough.

VARIATION: Savory Rosemary or Herb Crescent Rolls

Mix 3 tablespoons olive oil with ½ teaspoon salt and 2 tablespoons finely chopped fresh rosemary or other herb (halve the amount of herbs if you're using dried). Use that instead of the cinnamon-sugar mixture, and skip the honey cream cheese icing (see color photo).

Carrot Cake Bread

We adore carrot cake, so why not put all that good stuff into a bread? We like ours packed with carrots, coconut, dried fruit, cinnamon, and a touch of brown sugar. It is not only unbelievably tasty, but it is also gorgeous and the carrots are high in vitamin A. Try this bread toasted with the cream cheese icing from the Cinnamon Crescent Rolls (page 365) or just eat a slice with a nice sharp cheddar cheese for a great contrast.

What's up doc? Carrots are loaded with vitamin A and beta-carotene. Beta-carotene is the orange pigment that gives carrots and this bread their vibrant color (the body converts beta-carotene into a number of active forms of vitamin A).

Vitamin A is crucial for normal vision, healthy skin, growth in children, and normal reproductive function in both women and men.

Makes enough dough for at least two 2-pound loaves. The recipe is easily doubled or halved.

Ingredient	Volume (U.S.)	Weight (U.S.)	Weight (Metric)
Whole wheat flour	3 cups	13½ ounces	385 grams
All-purpose flour	3 cups	15 ounces	425 grams
Wheat germ	½ cup	2 ounces	55 grams
Coconut, finely shredded (both sweetened and unsweetened work well)	1 cup	3 ounces	85 grams

Ingredient	Volume (U.S.)	Weight (U.S.)	Weight (Metric)
Cinnamon, ground	2 teaspoons		
Brown sugar, packed	¾ cup	5⅓ ounces	160 grams
Granulated yeast (can decrease to taste, see page 56)	1 tablespoon	0.35 ounce	10 grams
Kosher salt (can increase or decrease to taste, see page 56)	1 tablespoon	0.6 ounce	15 grams
Vital wheat gluten*	¼ cup	1⅜ ounces	40 grams
Lukewarm water	2½ cups	1 pound, 4 ounces	570 grams
Eggs, large, at room temperature	4	8 ounces	225 grams
Carrots, well-packed and finely grated, approximately 4	2 cups	11 ounces	310 grams
Dried fruit (dried pineapple, dried currants, raisins), chopped	½ cup	3 ounces	85 grams
Walnuts, chopped (optional)	½ cup	4 ounces	115 grams
Egg wash (1 egg beaten with 1 tablespoon water) for painting the top crust			
Raw sugar for sprinkling on top crust			

*If omitting vital wheat gluten, decrease water to 2 cups.

1. **Mixing and storing the dough:** Whisk together the flours, wheat germ, coconut, cinnamon, brown sugar, yeast, salt, and vital wheat gluten in a 5-quart bowl, or a lidded (not airtight) food container.

2. Add the water, eggs, carrots, dried fruit, and walnuts (if you're a nut lover) and mix without kneading, using a spoon, a 14-cup food processor (with dough attachment), or a heavy-duty stand mixer (with

paddle). You might need to use wet hands to get the last bit of flour to incorporate if you're not using a machine.

3. Cover (not airtight), and allow the dough to rest at room temperature until it rises and collapses (or flattens on top), approximately 2 hours.

4. The dough can be used immediately after its initial rise, though it is easier to handle when cold. Refrigerate it in a lidded (not airtight) container and use over the next 5 days.

5. **On baking day,** lightly grease an 8½×4½-inch nonstick loaf pan. Dust the surface of the refrigerated dough with flour and cut off a 2-pound (cantaloupe-size) piece. Dust the piece with more flour and quickly shape it into a ball by stretching the surface of the dough around to the bottom, rotating the ball a quarter turn as you go.

6. Elongate the ball into an oval and place it in the loaf pan; your goal is to fill the pan about three-quarters full. Allow the loaf to rest, loosely covered with plastic wrap or an overturned bowl, for 1 hour and 45 minutes (60 minutes if you're using fresh, unrefrigerated dough).

7. **Preheat the oven to 375°F,** with a baking stone placed on the middle rack.

8. Just before baking, use a pastry brush to paint the top crust with egg wash, then sprinkle it with sugar.

9. Slide the loaf directly onto the hot stone or on a rack near the middle of the oven. Bake for 45 to 50 minutes, or until richly browned and firm.

10. Remove the bread from the pan and allow it to cool on a rack before slicing.

Whole Wheat Banana Bread

Let's face it: Despite the healthy attributes of this wonderful fruit, traditional banana bread is packed with sugar and fat. We love it, but it doesn't exactly deserve its healthy reputation. This version has the fabulous taste with just a fraction of the oil, and it's sweetened with honey. Kids will devour it toasted with chunky peanut butter in the morning, and it also makes a killer French toast. This is a great way to use up all of those over-ripe bananas on your counter and get some extra potassium in your diet—bananas are one of the best sources of this essential mineral.

Makes enough dough for at least two 2-pound loaves. The recipe is easily doubled or halved.

Ingredient	Volume (U.S.)	Weight (U.S.)	Weight (Metric)
Whole wheat flour	5 cups	1 pound, 6½ ounces	640 grams
All-purpose flour	3 cups	15 ounces	430 grams
2 teaspoons ground cinnamon			
Granulated yeast (can decrease to taste, see page 56)	1 tablespoon	0.35 ounce	10 grams
Kosher salt (can increase or decrease to taste, see page 56)	1 tablespoon	0.6 ounce	15 grams
Vital wheat gluten*	¼ cup	1⅜ ounces	40 grams
Lukewarm water	1 cup	8 ounces	230 grams

*If omitting vital wheat gluten, decrease water to ½ cup.

(continued)

Ingredient	Volume (U.S.)	Weight (U.S.)	Weight (Metric)
Vegetable oil, olive oil, or melted unsalted butter or coconut oil (see page 28 for options)	½ cup	3¾ ounces	105 grams
Honey	1 cup	12 ounces	340 grams
2 teaspoons pure vanilla extract			
Banana, very ripe, pureed	2½ cups	20 ounces	575 grams
2 cups walnut pieces (optional)			
Egg wash (1 egg beaten with 1 tablespoon water) for brushing on top crust			
Raw sugar for sprinkling on the top of the loaf			

1. **Mixing and storing the dough:** Whisk together the flours, cinnamon, yeast, salt, and vital wheat gluten in a 5-quart bowl, or a lidded (not airtight) food container.

2. Combine the liquid ingredients with the pureed banana and optional walnuts and mix with the dry ingredients without kneading, using a spoon, a 14-cup food processor (with dough attachment), or a heavy-duty stand mixer (with paddle). You might need to use wet hands to get the last bit of flour to incorporate if you're not using a machine.

3. Cover (not airtight), and allow the dough to rest at room temperature until it rises and collapses (or flattens on top), approximately 2 hours.

4. The dough can be used immediately after its initial rise, though it is easier to handle when cold. Refrigerate it in a lidded (not airtight) container and use over the next 7 days.

5. **On baking day,** lightly grease an 8½×4½-inch nonstick loaf pan. Dust the surface of the refrigerated dough with flour and cut off a 2-pound (cantaloupe-size) piece. Dust the piece with more flour and quickly shape it into a ball by stretching the surface of the dough around to the bottom, rotating the ball a quarter turn as you go.

6. Elongate the ball into an oval and place it in the loaf pan; your goal is to fill the pan about three-quarters full. Allow the loaf to rest, loosely covered with plastic wrap, for 1 hour 45 minutes (60 minutes if you're using fresh, unrefrigerated dough).

7. **Preheat the oven to 350°F**, with a baking stone placed on the middle rack.

8. Just before baking, use a pastry brush to paint the top crust with egg wash, then sprinkle it with raw sugar. Place the pan on the stone or on a rack in the center of the oven. Bake the bread for 45 to 50 minutes, or until richly browned and firm.

9. Remove the bread from the pan and allow it to cool on a rack before slicing.

Pistachio Twist

This bread is as pretty as it is tasty, so it is perfect for a special occasion, but easy enough to make any day of the week. The pistachios are full of vitamin E, healthy fats, and antioxidants, so paired with a dark chocolate, you can have a decadent slice and still be eating healthy. We love this rich combination with the Whole Wheat Brioche, but you can make it with several other doughs, including the Pumpkin Pie Brioche, for a fall treat.

Makes one 1½-pound twist

Use any of these refrigerated pre-mixed doughs: Braided Challah with Whole
    Wheat and Wheat Germ (page 324), Whole Wheat Brioche (page 343),
    Pumpkin Pie Brioche (page 354), or any other enriched dough in chapter 10
1½ pounds (small cantaloupe-size portion) of any pre-mixed dough listed above

The Pistachio Filling

½ cup (2½ ounces/65 grams) finely ground pistachios
½ cup finely chopped bittersweet chocolate (about 3½ ounces/100 grams)
¼ cup (2 ounces/55 grams) unsalted butter, melted

Raw sugar for sprinkling on top of the loaf

1. Make the pistachio filling: Combine the pistachios and chocolate in a small bowl. Set aside.

2. Dust the surface of the refrigerated dough and cut off a 1½-pound (small cantaloupe-size) piece of dough. Dust with more flour and quickly shape it into a ball by stretching the surface of the dough around to the bottom, rotating the ball a quarter turn as you go.

3. With a rolling pin, roll out the dough until it is a ⅛-inch-thick rectangle. As you roll out the dough, use enough flour to prevent the dough from sticking to the work surface, but not so much as to make it dry.

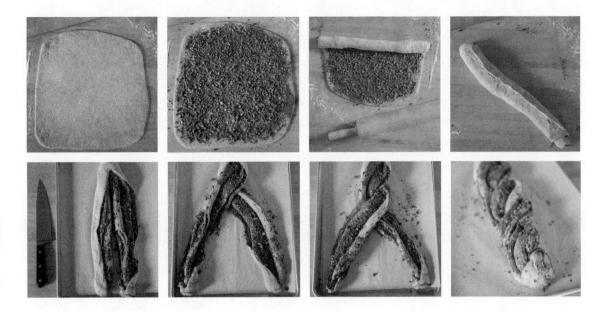

4. Brush 3 tablespoons of the melted butter over the dough. Spread the pistachios and chocolate evenly over the butter. Roll the dough into a log, starting at the long end. Pinch the seam closed.

5. Lay the log on a baking sheet covered with parchment paper or a silicone mat. Starting an inch from the end, carefully cut the dough down the center of the log. Carefully twist the two strands of the log, one strand over the other, keeping the cut side up at all times, so the filling won't fall out. Cover the twisted log loosely with plastic wrap and allow it to rest for about 1 hour.

6. **Preheat the oven to 350°F,** with a rack placed in the center of the oven.

7. Brush the ends of the twist with the remaining 1 tablespoon butter and sprinkle with the raw sugar. Bake for about 30 minutes, or until the ends are golden brown and it is well set in the center.

8. Allow the twist to cool on a rack before slicing

Fruit-Filled Pinwheels

A lovely pastry for a Sunday brunch. This is one of those treats that looks so impressive, but is really very simple to create. We've filled these with a bit of cream cheese and fruit preserves, but we're sure you'll come up with your own creations as well.

Makes 12 pinwheels

Use any of these refrigerated pre-mixed doughs: Braided Challah with Whole Wheat and Wheat Germ (page 324), Whole Wheat Brioche (page 343), Pumpkin Pie Brioche (page 354), or Chocolate Espresso Whole Wheat Bread (page 378)

1½ pounds (small cantaloupe-size portion) of any pre-mixed dough listed above

½ cup cream cheese, at room temperature

1 tablespoon honey

¼ teaspoon finely grated lemon zest

½ cup fruit preserves

Egg wash (1 egg beaten with 1 tablespoon water) for brushing on top crusts

12 raw almonds

Raw sugar for sprinkling on top

1. Combine the cream cheese, honey, and lemon zest in a small bowl. Set aside.

2. Prepare two or three cookie sheets with parchment paper or silicone mats.

3. Dust the surface of the refrigerated dough with flour and cut off a 1½-pound (small cantaloupe-size) piece of dough. Dust with more flour and quickly shape it into a ball by stretching the surface of the dough around to the bottom, rotating the ball a quarter turn as you go.

4. With a rolling pin, roll out the dough into a ⅛-inch-thick, 11×15-inch rectangle. As you roll out the dough, use enough flour to prevent the dough from sticking to the work surface, but not so much as to make it dry.

5. With a pizza cutter, cut the dough into 12 small squares. This is done by making 3 evenly spaced cuts along the length of the dough and then 2 along the short end.

6. Fill the center of each square with 2 teaspoons of the cream cheese filling and then top with 2 teaspoons of the preserves. Cut a slash from the filling to each of the corners of the dough. Brush every other point with egg wash, which will act as a glue. Lift one of the egg-washed points up and to the center, repeat with the rest of the egg-washed points, and press them firmly together over the filling. Cover loosely with plastic wrap and allow to rest about 40 minutes.

7. **Preheat the oven to 350°F,** with a rack placed in the center of the oven.

8. Brush the tops with egg wash, push an almond into the center of each pinwheel, and sprinkle with the raw sugar. Bake for 20 to 25 minutes, or until golden brown and well set in the center.

9. Serve warm or cool.

Chocolate Espresso Whole Wheat Bread

"I was so pleased when the nutritional powers that be deemed dark chocolate and espresso 'good for you' (see sidebar). So in an attempt to make you all a bit healthier and a lot happier, I've come up with Chocolate Espresso Bread. Not too sweet, but packed with flavor."—Zoë

Chocolate may have health benefits: Moderation is the key, because chocolate is high in sugar and fat. But chocolate contains phytochemicals (beneficial plant chemicals). Milk chocolate has less of these phytochemicals than dark chocolate because some of the cocoa is replaced by milk, and white chocolate doesn't have any at all.

Feeling better yet? Well, your coffee contains antioxidants. According to one study, Americans get their highest dose of antioxidants from coffee. It's not yet clear whether that translates into higher body stores of antioxidants, but it's opened up a whole new area of research, not to mention apparently justifying those mocha lattes (careful: sweetened or creamy coffee drinks are a major source of unnecessary calories).

Makes enough dough for at least two 2-pound loaves. The recipe is easily doubled or halved.

Ingredient	Volume (U.S.)	Weight (U.S.)	Weight (Metric)
Whole wheat flour	2 cups	9 ounces	260 grams
All-purpose flour	4 cups	1 pound, 4 ounces	565 grams
Cocoa powder	1 cup	4 ounces	115 grams
Granulated yeast (can decrease to taste, see page 56)	1 tablespoon	0.35 ounce	10 grams
Kosher salt (can increase or decrease to taste, see page 56)	1 tablespoon	0.6 ounce	15 grams
Vital wheat gluten*	¼ cup	1⅜ ounces	40 grams
Brewed espresso or strong coffee	1 cup	8 ounces	225 grams
Lukewarm water	1¼ cups	10 ounces	285 grams
Eggs, large, at room temperature	4	8 ounces	225 grams
Vegetable oil, olive oil, or melted unsalted butter or coconut oil (see page 28 for options)	½ cup	3¾ ounces	105 grams
Honey	¾ cup	9 ounces	255 grams
Bittersweet chocolate, chopped	—	6 ounces	170 grams
Egg wash (1 egg beaten with 1 tablespoon water) for brushing on the top crust			
Raw sugar for sprinkling on top			

*If omitting vital wheat gluten, decrease water to ¾ cup.

1. **Mixing and storing the dough:** Whisk together the flours, cocoa powder, yeast, salt, and vital wheat gluten in a 5-quart bowl, or a lidded (not airtight) food container.

2. Combine the liquid ingredients and the chopped chocolate and mix with the dry ingredients without kneading, using a spoon, a 14-cup food processor (with dough attachment), or a heavy-duty stand mixer (with paddle). You might need to use wet hands to get the last bit of flour to incorporate if you're not using a machine.

3. The dough will be loose, but it will firm up when chilled. *Don't try to use it without chilling at least 2 hours.*

4. Cover (not airtight), and allow the dough to rest at room temperature until it rises and collapses (or flattens on top), approximately 2 hours.

5. Refrigerate it in a lidded (not airtight) container and use over the next 5 days. Beyond that, the dough stores well in the freezer for up to 2 weeks in an airtight container. Freeze it in 2-pound portions. When using frozen dough, thaw it in the refrigerator for 24 hours before use, then allow the usual rest/rise time.

6. **On baking day,** grease an 8½×4½-inch nonstick loaf pan. Dust the surface of the refrigerated dough with flour and cut off a 2-pound (cantaloupe-size) piece. Dust the piece with more flour and quickly shape it into a ball by stretching the surface of the dough around to the bottom, rotating the ball a quarter turn as you go.

7. Elongate the ball into an oval and place it into the loaf pan; your goal is to fill the pan about three-quarters full. Cover loosely with plastic wrap and allow to rest and rise for 1 hour 45 minutes.

8. **Preheat the oven to 350°F,** with a rack placed in the center of the oven.

9. Just before baking, Use a pastry brush to brush the loaf's top crust with egg wash, and then sprinkle with the raw sugar.

10. Bake the bread near the center of the oven for 45 to 50 minutes, or until firm.

11. Remove the bread from the pan and allow it to cool on a rack before slicing.

VARIATION: Muffins

1. **On baking day, grease a muffin pan.** Dust the surface of the refrigerated dough with flour and cut off a 1½-pound (small cantaloupe-size) piece. Dust the piece with more flour and quickly shape it into a smooth ball by stretching the surface of the dough around to the bottom, rotating the ball a quarter turn as you go.

2. **To form the muffins,** divide the ball into 12 roughly equal portions (each about the size of a golf ball). Shape each one into a smooth ball as you did above. Place the balls in the prepared muffin pans. Allow to rest, loosely covered with plastic wrap, for 40 minutes.

3. **Preheat the oven to 350°F,** with a rack placed in the middle of the oven. If you're not using a stone in the oven, a 5-minute preheat is adequate.

4. Just before baking, use a pastry brush to paint the top crust with egg wash, and then sprinkle with the raw sugar. Bake for about 20 minutes, or until the muffins are richly browned and firm.

5. Remove the muffins from the pan and allow to cool on a rack before eating.

Chocolate Tangerine Bars

"Don't tell Zoë, but this recipe was inspired by a prewrapped treat that I was served on an airplane in 1986, when they last served meals in coach. It tasted of delicious chocolate and citrus—the wrapper on the bar said it had tangerine oil in it. Where in the world are you supposed to get tangerine oil? For home use, you get the flavor of tangerine oil by using the zest—it's the colored part of the skin that contains the oil. Usually that's done with a micro zester, but this time, go for the coarse effect of a traditional box grater for a more assertive tangerine flavor. Be sure to avoid getting much of the white pith, which can be bitter. After you get your zest, save the tangerine sections to use as a garnish for the bars—bet you'll never see that at 35,000 feet."—Jeff

Makes about 9 bars

½ pound (orange-size portion) Chocolate Espresso Whole Wheat Bread
     dough (page 378)
2 ounces/60 grams coarsely chopped high-quality bittersweet
     chocolate, preferably Callebaut or the equivalent (or chocolate
     chips)
½ cup (2½ ounces/75 grams) dried cranberries
Zest of 1 tangerine, removed with a coarse grater
Tangerine sections for garnish

1. Grease an 8-inch-square baking pan and set aside.

2. Dust the surface of the refrigerated dough with flour and cut off a
     ½-pound (orange-size) piece of dough.

3. Work the chocolate, dried cranberries, and zest into the dough with
     your fingers. Don't use any flour. Roughly press the mixture into a ball
     with wet hands.

4. Flatten the ball to a thickness of about ¾ inch and press it into the prepared pan. Allow to rest, loosely covered with plastic wrap, for 90 minutes.

5. **Preheat the oven to 350°F,** with a rack placed in the center of the oven. If you're not using a stone in the oven, a 5-minute preheat is adequate.

6. Bake for 20 to 25 minutes, or until firm and set.

7. Cool the pan completely on a rack, cut into squares, and serve garnished with the tangerine sections.

11

NATURALLY FERMENTED SOURDOUGH STARTER (LEVAIN)

∾

Master bread bakers believe that you can elevate breads to greatness by rising dough slowly with *levain* (starter)*:* a bubbly mixture of flour, water, and naturally occurring microbes (wild yeast and bacteria). It takes some time to develop the levain, but once established it can be maintained indefinitely with very little effort, and it can be used in any of our recipes. One word of advice: Don't try this until you're comfortable with our basic recipe in chapter 5. It's definitely more than five minutes of work and takes a little bread-baking experience, but we'll walk you through each step in the process.

∾

A wee bit more science: The microbes come mostly from the flour, not from your local atmosphere, and traditional recipes have probably oversold the supposed regional magic that creates "San Francisco Sourdough," or "Alaska Sourdough." You should be able to make great sourdough in Des Moines, Phoenix, Minneapolis, or New York City.

Making your own new starter from scratch does take at least five days, but if you already have some starter, you can skip ahead to the recipe on page 389, activate your starter, and jump right in. To streamline the sourdough process we don't call for "feeding" the starter as often as is done in traditional recipes. Instead we "dry out" the starter between feedings so you don't have to feed more often than monthly.

You'll use the levain to make full batches of dough that can be stored and used for up to five days—it doesn't rise well beyond that. Your levain will produce a bread of incredible depth, with sourdough characteristics that you can't quite get with packaged yeast. And if you've gotten this far in the book, we think you're ready to try it.

Starting the Levain (Natural Flour-and-Water Yeast Starter)

Ingredients

Whole wheat flour, quantities as below
Water (tap water works fine, you don't need filtered or bottled water as
    specified in many traditional recipes)

1. **Day 1:** In a clean container, mix ½ cup flour (2½ ounces/70 grams) and ½ cup water (4 ounces/115 grams)—it should have the consistency of thick pancake batter. Cover *loosely* and store at room temperature. Dark liquid will collect on top and continue throughout the process—this is normal; it's not mold.

2. **Days 3, 4, 5, and 6—"feeding" the levain:** At about day 3, bubbles will become visible, and the mixture will have a sour aroma that some people describe as

---

Levain has no packaged yeast added to it, but **for a shortcut, add a just a pinch of any granulated yeast** in Step 1. Purists will scoff, but we can't taste packaged yeast in the final product. After a few days, the added yeast will have died off, leaving only wild microbes that were present in the flours (and, to a lesser extent, in the air).

---

pleasantly "barnyardy." Once that happens, mix in ½ cup each of flour and water, then continue storage at room temperature. Within a half-day of feeding, the levain should be bubbling nicely. Transfer to larger containers as needed.

3. **Subsequent days—using the levain:** You can begin to use the levain in baking, after feeding it several times to produce enough for your recipe (that's called "expanding" the starter). Before using, make sure that you've fed it and that it's actively bubbling and puffy. Otherwise keep feeding for additional days, discarding some if you're getting too much. Ultimately, you'll need about 3 cups of activated starter (about 2 pounds) to mix up a full batch of dough.

4. **"Drying out":** Always save some levain after using it in a dough batch to act as the "mother" of the next batch of levain—then refrigerate it after "drying it out," by mixing in enough flour to make it dry and almost (but not quite) crumbly—this preserves the culture and makes it unnecessary to do frequent "feedings." If you ever see mold on stored levain or dough, throw it out and start over (see page 62 for details on recognizing mold versus the typical and normal gray liquid that collects over stored dough or levain).

❧

Are barnyards really "pleasant"? We talk about *levain* having a "pleasant" barnyardy smell, and there's no other way to describe it, even though people who know their barnyards may not agree. Think of this as the sweet smell of hay plus the slight whiff of a farm animal (a recently bathed one). It really and truly should be pleasant smelling. **If at any point in the development of your levain it begins to smell bad, something's gone wrong—but you can fix it.** Just throw out three-quarters of your starter and use what remains to start a new, larger culture with the consistency of thick pancake batter. It will take awhile to develop, but the new culture should get back on the right track.

5. **Monthly feedings—or bringing "dried out" culture back to life ("activate" it):** Starting with 1 cup of dried-out sourdough culture (see step 4), blend in 2 cups water and 2 cups flour, then a little more to bring the mixture to the consistency of thick pancake batter. Cover loosely, then allow to ferment until bubbling and puffy. Expand the starter to make as much as you'll need for your batch, or "dry out" again for storage, discarding any that you don't need.

6. **You can freeze levain or mother culture:** If you don't have time to keep a mother culture alive in the refrigerator, it can be frozen. Traditional books suggest that the culture can't survive for longer than a few months at freezing temperature, but we've thawed and rejuvenated cultures that were frozen for over a year (it can take a number of feedings to wake it up).

❧

Mother culture: Any bit of sourdough that you use to start a new batch is traditionally called the "mother."

100% Whole Grain Levain-Risen Bread

This makes an incredibly flavorful loaf, one that many consider to be the Holy Grail of home bread baking. Just be sure you've mastered the regular yeast-risen Master Recipe (page 79) before you tackle this one. In the ingredients list, we talk about the consistency of the levain, and this will very much affect how much water you need, so be ready to adjust water and flour to match the consistency of your chapter 5 loaves.

And if you're using volume to measure, estimate the volume of activated levain before it collapses with measuring; that's easier said than done unless you store this in a jar or a measuring vessel. Don't seal lids on glass jars, or just use a piece of plastic wrap instead of the threaded lid. Or avoid glass altogether and just use plastic. Otherwise you run the risk of the dreaded exploding glass jar (see page 44).

Makes enough dough for four 1-pound loaves. The recipe is easily doubled or halved.

Ingredient	Volume (U.S.)	Weight (U.S.)	Weight (Metric)
Lukewarm water	1½ cups	12 ounces	340 grams
Kosher salt (can increase or decrease to taste, see page 56)	1 tablespoon	0.6 ounce	15 grams
Activated levain, the consistency of thick pancake batter	3 cups	2 pounds	910 grams
Whole wheat flour*	6 cups	1 pound, 11 ounces	765 grams
Cornmeal or parchment paper for the pizza peel			

*For whole wheat flours other than Gold Medal or Pillsbury, see page 92 for guidelines on adjusting water amount.

❧

Sourdough often produces bread with large, irregular holes. We've found that's difficult to achieve with stored dough that's 100% whole grain.

1. Mix the water and salt in a 5-quart bowl, or a lidded (not airtight) food container, then stir in the levain, using a fork to break it up.

2. Add the flour and mix without kneading, using a spoon, a 14-cup food processor (with dough attachment), or a heavy-duty stand mixer

❧

Using sourdough for flavor instead of leavening—in any of our recipes: If you don't want to go full-bore into the world of sourdough baking, you can use levain as a flavoring agent but allow packaged yeast to act as the leavening agent. Sourdough starter, after it's activated, is 35 to 40% water. Knowing this, you can use it in any recipe in the book calling for yeast. Add about 1½ cups (1 pound/455 grams) of activated sourdough starter to any of our full-batch recipes. Then decrease the water by ¾ cup, and the flour by ¾ cup. Adjust moisture levels and flour as needed. You can also decrease the added commercial yeast well below what we call for in the recipe (see page 56). **Or drop the yeast from any recipe in the book** and use the full dose of starter, adjusting flour and water as needed. One word of advice—sourdough is an assertive flavor and most of our taste testers didn't love it in challah or brioche.

(with paddle). You may need a little extra flour or water to bring the dough to usual consistency, depending on the water content of your levain.

3. Cover (not airtight), and allow the dough to rest at room temperature until it doubles in size. Depending on the condition of your levain and the room temperature, this may be as fast as 2 hours, or it may take as long as 6 to 12 hours. This slow rise will contribute to the taste of authentic levain-risen bread.

4. The dough can be used immediately after the initial rise, though it is easier to handle when cold. Refrigerate it in a lidded (not airtight) container and use over the next 5 days, or freeze for up to 4 weeks.

5. **On baking day,** dust the surface of the refrigerated dough with flour and cut off a 1-pound (grapefruit-size) piece. Dust the piece with more flour and quickly shape it into a ball by stretching the surface of the dough around to the bottom, rotating the ball a quarter turn as you go.

6. Pat the ball into a narrow oval. Allow the loaf to rest, loosely covered with plastic wrap or an overturned bowl, on a pizza peel prepared with cornmeal or lined with parchment paper for 90 minutes (40 minutes if you're using fresh, unrefrigerated dough). Alternatively, you can rest the loaf on a silicone mat or greased cookie sheet without using a pizza peel.

ᘓᘔ

You may need a longer resting time than usual, up to 2 or even 3 hours—the dough should feel relaxed and "jiggly" on the pizza peel.

7. **Thirty minutes before baking time, preheat the oven to 450°F,** with a baking stone placed on the middle rack. Place an empty metal broiler tray on any other rack that won't interfere with the rising bread.

8. Dust with flour and slash the loaf with ½-inch-deep parallel cuts, using a serrated bread knife.

Sometimes the best bread ideas come from classic American literature: In Willa Cather's *My Ántonia*, immigrants from Bohemia (in current-day Czech Republic) make a poor-man's sourdough:

> *"She mixed the dough, we discovered, in an old tin peck-measure that Krajiek had used about the barn. When she took the paste out to bake it, she left smears of dough sticking to the sides of the measure, put the measure on the shelf behind the stove, and let this residue ferment. The next time she made bread, she scraped this sour stuff down into the fresh dough to serve as yeast."*

She's simply using *pâte fermentée* (see page 89) as the leaven. What we can't get over is how the narrator introduces this paragraph:

> *"I remember how horrified we were at the sour, ashy-gray bread she gave her family to eat . . ."*

Not true, to our taste buds. This bread is most definitely not ashy-gray and the sourdough is just what we're going for. But then, this is a matter of taste, and if natural sourdough isn't to your liking, go back to yeast-risen dough.

9. Slide the loaf directly onto the hot stone (or place the silicone mat or cookie sheet on the stone if you used one). Pour 1 cup of hot tap water into the broiler tray, and quickly close the oven door (see page 40 for steam alternatives). Bake for about 30 minutes, or until richly browned and firm. If you used parchment paper, a silicone mat, or a cookie sheet under the loaf, carefully remove it and bake the loaf directly on the stone or an oven rack two-thirds of the way through the baking time. Smaller or larger loaves will require adjustments in resting and baking time.

10. Allow the bread to cool on a rack before slicing.

VARIATION: Short-Cut Levain Loaves from Yeasted Batches

This is just a version of the Lazy Sourdough Shortcut (page 89)—all you need to do is use a lot of dough from your last batch, about 2 pounds of dough (a half-batch), and use that to build a new full batch (halve the ingredients). It may take up to 48 hours for its initial rise. You can keep this up indefinitely (don't use dairy or other perishables in batches you handle this way).

VARIATION: A More Structured Loaf with Vital Wheat Gluten

To create a stronger dough that's closer to the 100% whole wheat loaf in chapter 5 (page 91), whisk ¼ cup of vital wheat gluten into the flour before adding the dry ingredients to the liquids. You'll need to increase the water by about ½ cup.

VARIATION: Levain-Risen Loaf with Some White Flour

You can swap in some white all-purpose flour in this sourdough recipe, using the flour/water guidelines from chapter 5 to adjust moisture (you'll need less water as you swap in white flour). Using white flour may give you more of the open-hole structure that people associate with sourdough bread, and the loaves will be lighter and higher-rising.

APPENDIX

❧

The B Vitamins and Their Function

The B vitamins are crucial to energy metabolism, the chemical reactions that allow the body to use "fuels" like carbohydrates, fats, and proteins to release energy:

- **Thiamine:** Energy metabolism, healthy nervous system/brain function
- **Riboflavin:** Energy metabolism
- **Niacin:** Energy metabolism; prevents pellagra, a serious deficiency disease
- **Biotin:** Energy metabolism
- **Pantothenic acid:** Energy metabolism, prevents fatigue (deficiency causes gastrointestinal distress and nervous system/brain problems)
- **Vitamin B_6:** Crucial for protein metabolism, prevents nervous system/brain disorders
- **Folic acid or folate:** Crucial for DNA and vitamin B_{12} metabolism, prevents spina bifida and other neural tube defects, may prevent heart disease by decreasing blood homocysteine
- **Vitamin B_{12}:** Essential for DNA, RNA, and protein metabolism. Healthy bone, stomach, blood, and nervous system/brain depend on vitamin B_{12}.

Flours: Approximate Protein and Fiber Content per 30-Gram Serving

Flour	Protein (grams)	Fiber (grams)
Whole Wheat Flours		
Whole wheat flour (Gold Medal or Pillsbury)	4	3
White whole wheat flour (King Arthur)	4	3
Rye Flours		
Stone-ground whole grain rye (Hodgson Mill)	3	5
Dark rye flour (Bob's Red Mill)	4	7
Light rye flour (Bob's Red Mill)	2	Less than 1
White Flours		
Unbleached all-purpose (Gold Medal or Pillsbury)	3	Less than 1
Unbleached all-purpose (King Arthur)	4	Less than 1
Miscellaneous Flours		
Bulgur (Bob's Red Mill)	4	5
Corn masa (Maseca)	3	2
Flaxseed meal (Bob's Red Mill)	7	9
Oatmeal (Quaker Oats)	4	3
Spelt flour (Bob's Red Mill)	4	4
Teff flour (Bob's Red Mill)	4	4

Saturated Versus Unsaturated Fat (for Budding Chemists)

Saturated fats have more hydrogen atoms appearing on the carbon chain that makes up a fatty acid molecule. Those kinds of fats are building blocks for so-called "bad" cholesterol.

Fat Content of Common Fat Sources for Baking Based on a 1-Tablespoon (14-gram) Serving

Look for products low in saturated and trans fat, and high in omega-3, polyunsaturated, and monounsaturated fats.

Source	Saturated Fat	Transfat	Polyunsaturated Fat	Monounsaturated Fat	Total Fat
Canola oil	1	0	4 (28% omega-3)	8	14
Olive oil	2	0	1 (12% omega-3)	11	14
Butter	7	0.3	0.4	3	11
Margarine, traditional solid stick (avoid this product)	2.3	2.4	3.8	2.5	11
Margarine, soft tub*	1	0	6	4	11
Vegetable shortening	3	0	6	3	12

*If you want to use margarine, seek out a soft tub product that has zero trans fats and zero hydrogenated oils.

SOURCES FOR BREAD-BAKING PRODUCTS

Bluebird Grain Farms: www.bluebirdgrainfarms.com, 888-232-0331

Bob's Red Mill: www.bobsredmill.com, 800-349-2173

Cooks of Crocus Hill: www.cooksofcrocushill.com, 952-285-1903

Fantes Kitchen Wares Shop, www.fantes.com, 800-443-2683

Hodgson Mill: www.hodgsonmill.com, 800-347-0105

King Arthur Flour: www.kingarthurflour.com/shop/, 800-827-6836

Native Seeds/SEARCH: www.nativeseeds.org, 520-622-5561

Penzeys Spices: www.penzeys.com, 800-741-7787

Tupperware: www.tupperware.com, 800-366-3800

SOURCES CONSULTED

Aggarwal, B. B., and Harikumar, K. B. "Potential Therapeutic Effects of Cucurmin, the Anti-Inflammatory Agent, Against Neurodegenerative, Cardiovascular, Pulmonary, Metabolic, Autoimmune and Neoplastic Diseases." *International Journal of Biochemistry and Cell Biology*. 2009; 41(1): 40–59.

American Diabetes Association. "Standards of Medical Care in Diabetes—2015." *Diabetes Care*. 2015; 38(Suppl 1): S1–S94.

Charles, D. "Fringe No More: 'Ancient Grains' Will Soon Be a Cheerios Variety." National Public Radio, December 8, 2014.

Child, Julia; Bertholle, Louisette; and Beck, Simone. *Mastering the Art of French Cooking*. New York: Alfred A. Knopf, 1961.

Dunaway, Suzanne. *No Need to Knead: Handmade Italian Breads in 90 Minutes*. New York: Hyperion, 1999.

Flax Council of Canada. "Flax, a Healthy Food." Storage recommendations and baking temperatures accessed at http://flaxcouncil.ca/food/nutrition/general-nutrition-information/flax-in-a-vegetarian-diet/cooking-with-flax/.

"Food Chemists Slice Up Healthier Pizza." *Science Daily.* July 1, 2007.

Harding, A., et al. "Plasma Vitamin C Level, Fruit and Vegetable Consumption, and the Risk of New-Onset Diabetes Mellitus." *Archives of Internal Medicine.* 2008; 168(14): 1493–99.

Harvard School of Public Health. "Vegetables and Fruits: Get Plenty Every Day." Accessed at http://www.hsph.harvard.edu/nutritionsource/what-should-you-eat /vegetables-and-fruits/.

Jackson, Tom. *Chilled: How Refrigeration Changed the World and Might Do So Again.* New York: Bloomsbury USA, 2015.

Katcher, H. I. "The Effects of a Whole Grain–Enriched Hypocaloric Diet on Cardiovascular Disease Risk Factors in Men and Women with Metabolic Syndrome." *American Journal of Clinical Nutrition.* 2008 (87)1: 79–90.

Nettleton, J. A., et al. "Incident of Heart Failure Is Associated with Lower Whole-Grain Intake and Greater High-Fat Dairy and Egg Intake in the Atherosclerosis Risk in Communities (ARIC) Study." *Journal of the American Dietetic Association.* 2008; 108: 1881–87.

Newby, P. K., et al. "Intake of Whole Grains, Refined Grains, and Cereal Fiber Measured with 7-D Diet Records and Associations with Risk Factors for Chronic Disease." *American Journal of Clinical Nutrition.* 2007; 86(6): 1745–53.

Pennington, J. A., and Douglass, J. S. *Bowes and Church's Food Values of Portions Commonly Used,* 18th edition. Philadelphia: Lippincott Williams & Wilkins, 2005.

Pillsbury Mills, Inc. Home Service Center. *Bake the No-Knead Way.* Minneapolis: Pillsbury Mills, 1945.

Rolfes, S. R.; Whitney, E. N.; and Pinna, K. *Understanding Normal and Clinical Nutrition,* 8th edition. Belmont, CA: Wadsworth, 2009.

Slavin, J. "Whole Grains and Human Health." *Nutrition Research Reviews.* 2004; 17: 99–110.

Smith, J. S.; Ameri, F.; and Gadzil, P. "Effect of marinades on the Formation of Heterocyclic Amines in Grilled Beef Steaks." *Journal of Food Science.* 2008; 73(6): T100–T105.

U.S. Department of Health and Human Services/U.S. Department of Agriculture. *Dietary Guidelines for Americans, 2015,* http://www.health.gov /dietaryguidelines/2015-scientific-report/.

Xiaole L. Chen, Silver, Hannah R.; Xiong, Ling; Belichenko, Irina; and Johnson, Erica S. Johnson. "Spontaneous Topoisomerase I-Dependent DNA Damage in a *Saccharomyces cerevisiae* SUMO Pathway Mutant." *Genetics.* September 2007; 177(1): 17–30.

INDEX

∽

Visit BreadIn5.com, where you'll find recipes, photos, videos, and instructional material.